Lovewell's Fight

Lovewell's Fight

WAR, DEATH, AND MEMORY IN BORDERLAND NEW ENGLAND

Robert E. Cray

University of Massachusetts Press
Amherst and Boston

ISBN 978-1-62534-107-5 (alk. paper) 106-8 (hardcover)

Designed by Sally Nichols
Set in Adobe Minion Pro
Printed and bound by Maple-Vail, Inc.

Library of Congress Cataloging-in-Publication Data

Cray, Robert E.
 Lovewell's Fight : war, death, and memory in borderland New England / Robert E. Cray.
   pages cm
 Includes bibliographical references and index.
 ISBN 978-1-62534-107-5 (pbk. : alk. paper) — ISBN 978-1-62534-106-8 (hardcover : alk.
 paper) 1. Pigwacket Fight, 1725. 2. Lovewell, John, 1691–1725. I. Title.
 E83.72.C76 2014
 973.25—dc23
                         2014019938

British Library Cataloguing-in-Publication Data
A catalogue record for this book is available from the British Library.

For Cynthia and Pamela Cray

Contents

Acknowledgments

This book came about accidentally. For some reason, probably just for pleasure, I decided to reread a collection of Nathaniel Hawthorne's short stories and came upon "Roger Malvin's Burial." I remembered the story from undergraduate days; what I did not recall was Hawthorne's preface atop the page extolling "Lovell Fight"— his wording— as a well-remembered 1725 battle distinguished by unusual bravery. Nor did I know anything about the 1725 fight or Captain John Lovewell despite my training in early American history. Curiosity gripped me, and thus began the long odyssey to understanding a battle that once resonated among eighteenth- and nineteenth-century New Englanders. Slowly over the last eight years I have acquainted myself with Captain John Lovewell, the Reverend Thomas Symmes, Samuel Penhallow, and other figures of interest. In the process, I have tried to learn something about early American warfare and the moral quandary of men left behind after battle.

The work flagged as other projects invariably intruded; doubts about Lovewell's historical value grew and sometimes assumed nightmarish proportions. Yet it evolved into a rough manuscript sufficient for two anonymous referees to supply kindly, constructive criticisms that enabled the project to go forward. The first-rate editorial staff at the University of Massachusetts Press lent their professional skills as well. I cannot acknowledge the referees by name, but I can thank my acquisitions editor, the ever supportive Clark

Dougan, and the two fine editors, Carol Betsch and Mary Bellino, for their careful shepherding. The same goes for my copy editor, Barbara Folsom, who polished the prose and made it flow. Kate Blackmer, my map drawer, merits praise for a job well done.

Long before the manuscript took book form, individuals generously helped in manifold ways. One friend of long standing, George E. Webb, a former office mate in a university best not named, offered me encouragement and support. Over the years we have exchanged dozens of letters, and inevitably Captain John Lovewell and his men formed part of the discussion. Another friend from the University of Puget Sound, Mary Rose Lamb, a molecular geneticist no less, revealed that the divide between the sciences and the humanities is not as great as some think. Her wise counsel in matters academic has been appreciated. Both individuals have displayed a generosity of spirit in the best traditions of academia.

Closer to home, I benefited from two release time grants from the Faculty Scholarship Program at Montclair State University, courtesy of the Provost's Office, which cut my teaching load by 25 percent over two five-year periods. Dean Marietta Morrissey of the College of Humanities and Social Sciences approved a one-semester sabbatical leave, along with travel money for conferences, and she also came through with funds to assist in the construction of the map, for which I am grateful. Various papers presented at the American Culture/Popular Culture Association Conference and the New England Historical Association conferences provided me with audiences to test ideas for future chapters. I am also indebted to the *Historical Journal of Massachusetts* for publishing an early effort on death and warfare in King Philip's War. What originally had been intended as a manuscript chapter instead became a stand-alone piece; it did provide a few insights for chapter 2, which I have duly footnoted.

Libraries and archives gave assistance from near and far, offering materials and sending documents. Certainly, the Montclair State University interlibrary loan team led by Kevin Prendergast did yeoman work in accepting requests, gathering materials, and keeping the books and microfilms coming. The Fryeburg Historical Society honored request after request without complaint, and my time spent there during a sabbatical semester proved equally worthwhile. Of course, no one can get far without visiting the Fifth Avenue Library in Manhattan, a repository of great value, where early work on the project started, while the Alexander Library at Rutgers University provided a research base closer to home. I should also acknowledge the National Archives in Washington, DC, the Portland Historical Society, the Massachusetts Archives, the Massachusetts Historical Society, the American Antiquarian Society, the New Hampshire Historical Society, and the Bethel Maine Historical Society for their assistance. To all the individuals associated with these institutions I give many thanks.

Some unexpected challenges arose just when the University of Massachusetts Press expressed interest in publishing Lovewell's Fight. My history department colleagues at Montclair State University, unaware of my research efforts, displayed a rich appreciation of irony by encouraging me to finish the previous chair's term. That better candidates existed was known; that my protests failed to budge them goes without saying. Nevertheless, thanks to Susan Goscinski, an administrative assistant of remarkable skill and wisdom, irony did not quite turn to farce or, worse, tragedy while I manned the department's helm—we managed to stay afloat. In addition, Esperanza Brizuela Garcia, a peerless undergraduate adviser, dealt efficiently with students—in particular, freshmen with registration holds. The stalwart Ben Lapp handled fewer students as graduate coordinator, but his wry sense of humor and informative insights kept my professional compass pointed to true north. And, of course, a shout-out should go to Richard Conway, who manned the pumps on several occasions and provided sage advice during a difficult moment. Two former chairs, Leslie Wilson and Mike Whelan, kindly offered guidance anytime squalls threatened. Admittedly, few of my colleagues appreciated (or even recognized) my Humphrey Bogart imitation as Captain Queeg complete with marbles in hand during an early department meeting, but the history department never quite descended to the level of the USS Caine, for which I am grateful.

Then there are those people who touch one's life both professionally and personally. Among the former I count my graduate mentors, Jackson T. Main, Ned C. Landsman, and Wilbur R. Miller, who introduced me to Clio's discipline so many years ago at Stony Brook University. If anything of value comes from this work, it is largely due to them. Any mistakes in it clearly lie at my doorstep.

My family never quite figured out my fascination with Captain John Lovewell, or sometimes did not even recall who I was working upon, as my wife Cindy once politely inquired, although my daughter, Pamela, then age eleven, found one conference paper on scalping and decapitated heads memorable. That we have managed to stay together despite at least two storms of the century, one tornado, innumerable power outages, and seemingly endless home renovations while I tussled with Lovewell and company says something, I suspect. It is to Cindy and Pamela that I dedicate this book.

Lovewell's Fight

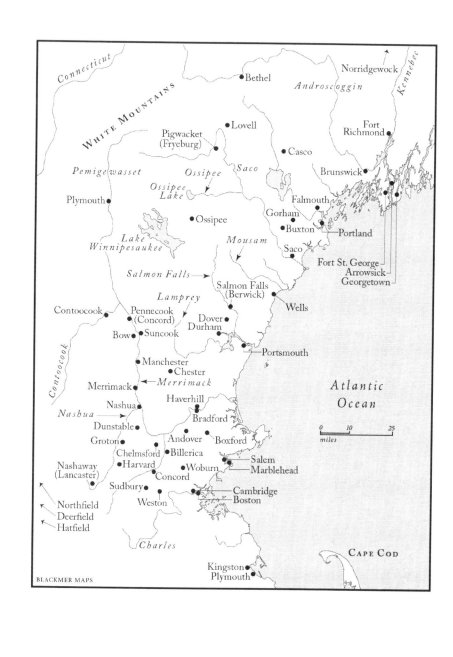

Connecticut

Androscoggin

Norridgewock

Bethel

WHITE MOUNTAINS

Lovell

Fort
Richmond

Pigwacket
(Fryeburg)

Casco

Saco

Brunswick

Pemigewasset

Ossipee

*Ossipee
Lake*

Falmouth

Plymouth

Gorham

Portland

Ossipee

Buxton

*Lake
Winnipesaukee*

Mousam

Saco

Fort St. George
Arrowsick
Georgetown

Salmon Falls

Lamprey

Salmon Falls
(Berwick)

Contoocook

Pennecook
(Concord)

Dover
Durham

Wells

Bow

Suncook

Contoocook

Manchester

Chester

Portsmouth

Merrimack

Merrimack

Nashua

Haverhill

Nashua

Bradford

Dunstable

*Atlantic
Ocean*

Groton

Andover

Boxford

0   10   25
miles

Chelsford

Billerica

Nashaway
(Lancaster)

Harvard

Woburn

Salem
Marblehead

Concord

Sudbury

Cambridge
Boston

Northfield
Deerfield
Hatfield

Weston

Charles

Kennebec

CAPE COD

Kingston
Plymouth

BLACKMER MAPS

Introduction

Captain John Lovewell's 1725 expedition against the Pigwacket
Indians in Maine constitutes an iconic episode in New
England history. Lovewell and his men aimed to surprise their adversaries,
part of the Eastern Abenaki Nation, to acquire scalp bounties and hasten
the end of the Anglo-Abenaki war. Instead, the Abenakis turned the tables,
surprising them at Pigwacket on May 9 in a battle that Francis Parkman
labeled "one of the most obstinate and deadly bush fights in the annals of
New England." Musket balls filled the air for ten hours, interspersed by shouts
and traded insults between the two sides. When the fight ended, Lovewell
and over a third of the thirty-four-man company were dead or dying. Several
others were badly wounded. The Abenakis carefully removed most of their
dead and injured before leaving.[1]

Lovewell's Fight[2] presented its survivors with tough moral choices. Should
they take their wounded with them? What, if anything, could be done for the
dead and dying scattered on the field? If left behind, wounded troopers would
be vulnerable to returning Abenakis, while unburied bodies invited desecration. Both the physically mobile and the injured calmed their anxieties with
hope of assistance from a rear guard stationed some twenty-odd miles away.
Thus men were left behind and bodies unburied, but the departing troopers
split up before reaching the fort to discover the rear guard gone, and with it

any hope of assistance. Remnants of Lovewell's troop straggled on to various settlements. As for the abandoned men, some perished in the woods.[3]

News of the disaster spread rapidly across Massachusetts and New Hampshire. At the start of the fight, one member of Lovewell's company, Benjamin Hassell, had fled and reported his comrades' seeming destruction, prompting the panicky rear guard to flee. Anxious provincial officials sent men to pursue Abenakis, search for survivors, and bury the dead. Hope replaced despair as company members limped home. That Lovewell's men had fought an adversary perhaps twice their number attracted notice; that some had survived the bloody ordeal and disorganized retreat won praise. Massachusetts bestowed pensions on several survivors and assisted widows of the slain. All troopers or their surviving families received land grants. What at first had been considered a tragedy, a bungled venture that resulted in the death of Lovewell, a valued commander, developed into a heroic tale.[4]

Later generations honored John Lovewell and company. The survivors were recognized in poems and ballads commemorating their exploits. At least one such composition ranked among New England's most famous eighteenth-century folk songs. William Henry Longfellow and Nathaniel Hawthorne, both keen students of New England history, found Lovewell's Fight memorable too. The thirteen-year-old Longfellow wrote the "The Battle of Lovewell's Pond," his first poem published in the *Portland Gazette* in 1820, a juvenile bit of bravado that hinted at the career to come. Hawthorne's 1832 short story, "Roger Malvin's Burial," drew upon the battle to craft a moral parable about guilt and broken promises.[5]

Lovewell's Fight belongs to that rare category of military encounters in which defeat transcends an opponent's victory to don the mantle of legend. When early Greeks (and later classicists) trumpeted the battle of Thermopylae in 480 BCE, applauding the Spartan commander Leonidas and his men for defiantly fighting to the death against the more numerous Persians at a strategic pass, they provided a model for others to embrace. Medieval Europeans just as loudly sang the praises of Roland and his 778 CE defeat. Nineteenth-century Americans developed the heroic defeat motif further. The battles of the Alamo in Texas and the Little Big Horn in Montana acquired legendary status although both were clear-cut disasters. No one survived the final Mexican assault on the Alamo in 1836 after Santa Anna ordered the survivors executed; and the Sioux under Sitting Bull and Crazy Horse decimated Custer's command in 1876. Yet, the Alamo turned Davy Crockett, Jim

Bowie, and William Travis into Texas and later national icons. And George Armstrong Custer's brazen assault and resulting death enshrined him and the Seventh Cavalry. In the popular view, such defeated commanders rivaled more victorious leaders as people to be remembered.[6]

Of course, these military reversals had certain characteristics that enabled their wide embrace. Vanquished commanders merited remembrance (rather than scorn) when they lost to a larger adversary; indeed, defiant resistance against lopsided odds made the contest even more memorable; to hold out until the last man was killed supplied an extra dash of heroism. Such courage could be drafted into the service of patriotism and easily grafted onto regional or national narratives. Even better for defeated commanders was a culturally distinct foe, whose alien, if not threatening, customs provided an additional dimension and furnished higher stakes. Greeks disdained Persians; Christian Franks abhorred Muslims. Anglo-Texans and Mexicans possessed far more complex and nuanced relations, often living cheek by jowl in Texas and sharing similar concerns about heavy-handed centralized Mexican authority. Tejanos, people of Mexican ancestry, had died alongside Anglos at the Alamo, reflecting these shared ties and concerns; still, later chroniclers glossed over this fact and simplified the battle as a Mexican versus Anglo affair. The Sioux, on the other hand, were not just fighting Custer at Little Big Horn but American expansion into their lands, opposing the alleged thrust of civilization. In these circumstances, it is easy to see why Americans vilified Mexicans and Sioux as cultural outliers.[7]

Lovewell's Fight more or less contained these basic elements. The Pigwacket encounter, although smaller than the other battles cited, was still an unequal contest, the Abenakis allegedly outnumbering the English two to one. Lovewell's men (minus their captain) fought the war's longest battle, refusing to surrender, and as Nathaniel Hawthorne noted in his preface to "Roger Malvin's Burial": "History and tradition are unusually minute in their memorials of this affair; and the captain of a scouting party of frontier men has acquired as actual a military renown as many a victorious leader of thousands."

The spirited resistance against a culturally distinct foe, the Abenakis, also gave Reformed Christians something to boast about. This battle between Christian Protestants and Catholic-tainted pagans, as Massachusetts clergy saw it, represented a chapter in the contest of the godly against the Antichrist, an essential theme of Dummer's War. Lovewell provided New England with a martyred commander, just as Roland had done for medieval Christians. As the Song of Roland had inspired medieval minstrels, so the Lovewell ballad performed a similar function in eighteenth-century New England.[8]

The first chroniclers noted the long shadow of Lovewell's death as well. While Dummer's War lacked the bloodshed of King Philip's War, or the human drama associated with the Deerfield raid in 1704 during Queen Anne's War, Lovewell's exploits still evoked respect. Thomas Hutchinson, Massachusetts historian and royal governor, praised Abenaki and English combatants as valorous in the manner of classical Romans. Francis Parkman, the Boston Brahmin cum historian, devoted an entire chapter to the battle, "Lovewell's Fight," in his majestic work on the French and Indian wars. The noted nineteenth-century historian George Bancroft boldly announced that "no war parties of the red men ever displayed more address or heroism than the brave John Lovewell and his companions." Herbert Osgood informed readers that the "brave fight" of Lovewell and his men proved the "most heroic episode of the war." Accolades represented standard nineteenth-century fare for Lovewell and company.[9]

Not everyone praised Captain Lovewell and company unreservedly, however. The fact that one trooper, Benjamin Hassell, had deserted the battle consigned him to ignominy—early accounts deliberately omitted Hassell's name as punishment for his cowardice. More privately, Lieutenant Governor Dummer had fumed about the rear guard abandoning their post. Such nineteenth-century social critics as Henry David Thoreau wondered about the forgotten, numerically reduced Abenakis. Who remembered their suffering? That Lovewell and his men had been ambushed while seeking Abenaki scalps sat uneasily with later New Englanders. Was Lovewell more justly extolled as a brave commander or damned as a bounty-hunting profiteer intent on a killing in more than one sense of the word? Compounding the matter was a bit of historical license—when had the incident occurred? Colonials first heard that the date was May 9, but the Reverend Thomas Symmes, author of the first battle narrative, insisted that the action occurred on Saturday, May 8. Perhaps the good minister did not want the Reverend Jonathan Frye to be criticized for scalping an Indian on the Sabbath.[10]

Lovewell's 1725 expedition has nevertheless faded within the more recent scholarly framework of early American Indian–white relations. Contemporary works have enlarged the field beyond narratives of victory and defeat. Instead, Native American fighting tactics and the degree of violence used, the existence of a "middle ground" between indigenous and European empires, and the First People's survival against daunting odds (to cite just a few examples) have created a more complex historical mosaic. Within the literature, John Lovewell generally remains sidelined, occasionally trotted out as an overzealous bounty hunter, while his men have become virtual non-entities, their stories forgotten. But Lovewell was more than a scalp hunter; as a borderland settler in a New England family scarred by violence he attained recognition as a provincial military leader. His two prior scouting sorties had garnered scalps, bounties, and praise. Lovewell's men won payouts from pleased provincial authorities.[11]

Studying Lovewell's Fight also fills the scholarly lacunae on early American warfare by highlighting a downplayed and at times neglected New England battle that was obviously memorable to its contemporaries and their descendants. What the battle, and indeed Dummer's War, lacked in overall size and consequence, bereft as they were of British or French intervention, was compensated for by their perceived importance. To Massachusetts residents, Dummer's War was the culmination of a century-old boundary dispute with the Abenaki Nation. Clerics saw it as a religious battle between Protestants and Catholics—high stakes by their standards. As for Lovewell's Fight, in one instance patriotic praise garbed the retelling in a comparison to the British army. That Lovewell's Fight was the last major Dummer's War engagement supplied added heft. What happened at Pigwacket in 1725 mattered to people. A study of Lovewell and his men shows how early New Englanders fought and remembered the battle. It also reveals the emergence of an alternative, more inclusive reading of the Pigwacket battle, in which different narrated aspects forged an especially enduring memory.[12]

Chapter 1 recounts the Pigwacket battle and elaborates on John Lovewell's earlier expeditions before the fatal encounter. Massachusetts authorities extolled Lovewell as a significant Dummer's War commander. Yet the tactics he favored, which balanced daring with caution, fell apart when the Abenakis ambushed his troop during the fatal third expedition. With Lovewell's death, troopers scurried for cover and turned to new leaders. The particulars of the fight, admittedly derived from chroniclers scripting a heroic saga, can still be teased out in terms of significant and probable occurrences. No battle account can steer clear of bias; editorial coloring may tint not just the survivors' actions but treatment of the dead and wounded too. Still, a general overview of Lovewell's expeditions provides a springboard for the subsequent book chapters.

Chapter 2 traces the evolution of New England borderland fighting starting with King Philip's War. English colonials adopted tactics of "skulking warfare," and Benjamin Church (among others) helped redefine warfare to confront more successfully a fast-moving, indigenous adversary. Scalping, encouraged by provincial bounties, came to distinguish warfare. Hannah Dustin, for instance, emerged as a cause célèbre for escaping her captors and taking their scalps, arriving in Dunstable, John Lovewell's settlement, with her trophies.[13] Dunstable itself weathered attacks while attempting to create a semblance of community life. Not only location but family explained Lovewell's embrace of violence: his grandfather, allegedly one of Cromwell's soldiers, would have been part of an emerging English military tradition. Lovewell's father and mother knew about sudden attacks and testified in a deposition about frontier violence. Indeed, by the time of Queen Anne's War, Dunstable proved a popular springboard for provincial scalping parties. For Lovewell, warfare offered opportunities, with scalps a means to an end, part and parcel of his environment.[14]

Dummer's War may have been fought in the borderland settlements of Massachusetts and New Hampshire, but Bostonians experienced the war's recoil from beyond the battlefield. Reeling from a recent smallpox epidemic, Boston during the 1720s was a city on edge; black arsonists, marauding pirates, and angry borderland Abenakis increased residents' anxiety. Death itself became an issue. Good Christians, and especially good Reformed Christians, died in hope of receiving grace from God. War deaths changed the calculus, occurring violently and unexpectedly, leaving scant time for spiritual reflection. A proper death meant burial in accordance with Puritan cultural norms. Yet, as the Atlantic economy drew Boston into its web, more extravagant funeral rituals evolved, in which eulogies and funereal finery distinguished the fortunate and affluent. By contrast, dead soldiers and ordinary settlers received simple interments—if indeed their bodies could be found. Only modest efforts were made to inter the slain. Nonetheless, though Lovewell's death ranked among the most commemorated of Dummer's War, chapter 3 shows that other deaths also mattered to Bostonians.[15]

Chapter 4 reconstructs the scripting of the fight. As Jill Lepore and others have shown, chroniclers carefully crafted historical narratives to embroider reality in accordance with cultural values. When the Reverend Thomas Symmes and Samuel Penhallow wrote about Lovewell's Fight, they established the master narrative on which all subsequent fight retellings necessarily relied. Symmes's combination sermon/historical preface dramatized the intersection of faith and popular culture. And Penhallow, a prominent New Hampshire official, with the Reverend Benjamin Colman, his editorial sponsor, standing guard, reinforced Symmes's message while quietly revealing certain differences. Both Symmes and Penhallow enshrined Captain John Lovewell and his troop, turning tragedy into a moral victory.[16]

Patriotism and faith could stimulate compassion and sympathy for Lovewell's Fight victims. Survivors and relatives of the slain presented a monetary claim upon the province, revealing that warfare and welfare went hand in hand. Colonial New Englanders were no strangers to this social phenomenon: wartime societies disbursed aid to veterans and their families, and soldiers after King Philip's War also petitioned for assistance. But Dummer's War provided an instance wherein those attached to the Lovewell expedition counted on special recognition beyond the normal compensation—their link to Lovewell, a military martyr, gave them a certain moral cachet that the government felt compelled to honor. And many veterans demanded their due: not only Pigwacket survivors and their families but the hastily departing rear guard wanted payouts. Chapter 5 focuses on a generally neglected aspect of early American public welfare—assistance for veterans.[17]

The passing of Lovewell's generation by the late eighteenth century opened the way for the construction of a more public memorialization. As Alfred F. Young, Michael Kammen, and others have shown, memory was often contested ground on which official and vernacular cultures collided—the former coopting the latter for purposes of nationalism. As chapter 6 reveals, Lovewell became a significant figure in regional folklore, hailed in ballads and poetry, and invariably linked to Fryeburg, Maine, the site of the 1725 battle. While Longfellow, Hawthorne, and Thoreau sounded particular battle themes in their works, Fryeburg employed public celebrations to instill civic pride. A monument eventually marked the battlefield, but interwoven with this narrative was a growing recognition that Native Americans could not be ignored. As the numbers of New England Indians diminished, their value as memorably worthy figures increased.[18]

Thus, the conflict over Lovewell and Pigwackets paralleled the divisions experienced by Americans over the remembrance of the past. Was the battle triumphant or disastrous? Laced with moral certitude or deceitful self-interest? Thus do the intricate strands of memory overlap and introduce contrast into our readings of the past. The expedition of John Lovewell and his men remains a part of the early American experience, and indeed of our present age. Their journey across early New England is about to begin.

CHAPTER 1
Captain John Lovewell's Fatal Expedition

On May 11, 1725, the first men from Captain John Lovewell's expedition into the Pigwacket Indian country of Maine reached Dunstable, Massachusetts, the troop's starting-off point. The Pigwackets had ambushed and decimated the thirty-four-man scouting party. The first source of this intelligence, the company deserter, Benjamin Hassell, had frightened the expedition's Ossipee rear guard into forsaking their comrades. Meanwhile, scattered survivors from the May 9 Pigwacket attack slowly limped home unaided. Nine men including Lovewell had been killed outright at Pigwacket; three more died shortly after the battle's conclusion. Another three injured men, including Lieutenant Josiah Farwell and Jonathan Frye, the company chaplain, perished in the forest.[1]

Lovewell's Fight emerged as the defining event of Dummer's War. No other battle stirred provincial emotions so strongly or created such a lasting impression. Newspapers detailed the conflict and expressed hopes of Captain Lovewell's survival; the *Volunteer's March*, advertised in the *New England Courant* on May 31, 1725, immortalized the attack in popular song; and the Reverend Thomas Symmes of Bradford, Massachusetts, and Samuel Penhallow, a prominent New Hampshire official turned historian, chronicled the fight. Symmes's sermon required two editions to meet popular demand. Despite "the loss of so brave and discreet an officer as Capt. Lovewell," as the *Boston News Letter* solemnly intoned, the troopers had repelled the larger Abenaki force, killed Paugus, a noted chief, and thinned their opponents' ranks. The expedition's dead and abandoned wounded won praise for their actions.[2]

Yet, though New Englanders honored Lovewell and his men, other, harsher realities intruded—the dead and the seriously wounded had been unburied and abandoned. None of the uninjured or walking wounded volunteered to stay with disabled comrades. Instead, the exhausted troopers took off and straggled through the woods, separating into smaller groups to throw off Indian pursuers. Some ventured off alone and forsaken survivors split up. What became known as the Pigwacket fight could just as easily have been labeled the Pigwacket flight, a Pyrrhic victory with decided costs.[3]

Lovewell's Fight tested New England military ideals. As Reformed Christians, New Englanders needed to be steadfast in faith and actions, or, in the Reverend Increase Mather's words, "resolute and undaunted in the way of duty and that because it is . . . duty." There were no exceptions. Cowardice was inexcusable too. Indeed, the Reverend Benjamin Wadsworth at the start of Dummer's War warned that a frightened soldier was "more likely to discourage his partners and fellow soldiers, than to destroy enemies." Hassell's retreat did precisely that—the rear guard had bolted in a panic. Attention to duty and courage under fire was rooted in time-honored military protocols, of course, but the Puritans' descendants perceived battle behavior through the prism of their faith. To fall short dishonored their heritage. Much as nineteenth-century Texans struggled to understand the Alamo, a disaster engraved into their regional identity, New Englanders, and especially Massachusetts residents, had to confront the complexities of Lovewell's Fight.[4]

Dummer's War can easily be described as a *le petit guerre,* a little war, lacking direct intervention by Great Britain or France. The conflict represented a minor, almost invisible sideshow in the larger business of empire when viewed from the perspective of London or Paris. The 1713 Treaty of Utrecht that marked the end of the War of the Spanish Succession had ensured a relatively placid European coexistence for the two nations. To Sir Robert Walpole, Britain's leading political figure, war was a fiscal morass best avoided. As for France, it was still reeling from the War of the Spanish Succession, linked to Spain by family ties, Louis XIV's original goal, but bereft of Hudson Bay and Nova Scotia. New France officials in Quebec found they held limited sway in the French court. After all, Britain and France were allies by 1716, and George I, also the Elector of Hanover, wanted France on board to protect his German holdings against Russian or Prussian attack. Despite suspicion, both Great Britain and France honored the alliance during the 1720s, and squawking colonies would not be permitted to roil the diplomatic calm.[5]

By the early 1720s, however, war clouds loomed threateningly in New France and New England. What appeared small to the courts of Europe seemed large in the New England borderlands, especially among concerned Abenaki Indians. They had fought several wars against New England, assisted by French arms and men; now New England incursions into their land continued and aid was unavailable. Canadian authorities, although eager to thwart New England expansion, refused to commit themselves without French military backing. Instead, French missionaries such as Father Sebastian Rale offered spiritual and moral support, insisting that English soldiers leave the disputed territory. When Massachusetts troops failed to seize Rale from his mission in 1722, putting a price on his head, the war clouds darkened. Angry Abenakis swooped down and kidnapped English settlers. New Englanders killed sleeping Abenaki in the spring of 1722. The storm officially erupted in late July with Governor Samuel Shute's declaration against the Abenakis, but the turbulence had been building beforehand.[6]

John Lovewell came to embody the soldierly ideal of Dummer's War, at least in terms of his outsized public persona. Lovewell had commanded two previous expeditions, returning with scalps, a prisoner, and armaments. Chroniclers heaped praise upon him. Samuel Penhallow, who knew about borderland fighting from his son John, a soldier, described Lovewell "as well acquainted with hunting the Woods." The Reverend Thomas Symmes added that "Some of them / the Lovewell troop / were well acquainted with the Woods and with the customs and lurking places of the enemy." Familiarity with the "fatigues of long marches, both in winter and summer," testified to their mettle and to Lovewell's leadership. Both Penhallow and Symmes had talked to Lovewell expedition men. By the early 1800s, John Farmer and Jacob B. Moore, two New Hampshire chroniclers, credited Lovewell with having killed seven Indians in New Hampshire before beginning his scalp-hunting ventures atop "the foot of what is now called Lovewell's mountain." The naming of a mountain after Lovewell underscores his iconic status.[7]

Lovewell organized his first scouting expedition in the autumn of 1724, aided by fellow Dunstable residents Lieutenant Josiah Farwell and Ensign

Jonathan Robbins. Robbins offered tangible experience, being a veteran of a 1723 December expedition along the banks of the Merrimac and Contoocook Rivers. Farwell was the lone survivor of an Abenaki ambush. Nevertheless, Lovewell's rank of captain suggests a measure of popular and official recognition beyond that which Robbins or Farwell enjoyed. Like Benjamin Church in King Philip's War, a man whose scouting forays redefined English fighting tactics, Lovewell intended to fight Indian style; economics and patriotism figured for Lovewell and company too—the one-hundred-pound Massachusetts bounty for Abenaki scalps ranked among the highest offered. Killing became a business enterprise and recruits would-be profiteers. Yet the grisly business of stalking Indians for scalping demanded that greed be buttressed by wood lore, and chancing upon Abenakis often required trekking into regions removed from Anglo-American settlements and assistance. In other words, experience helped.[8]

Lovewell's first two expeditions set forth in late autumn and midwinter. Weather conditions remained impossible to predict for eighteenth-century scouts aside from general seasonal changes, and almanac editors offered little more than predictions on monthly conditions spiced by displays of bravado and attempted wit. Nathan Bowen claimed that his 1724 Boston almanac "may without sensible error (Tides Excepted) serve at all adjacent places from New Foundland to Carolina," a remarkable boast. For the November and December months during Lovewell's first expedition, Bowen predicted snow turning to rain between the twenty-first and twenty-second of November, with the twenty-ninth and thirtieth featuring snow "or something as bad." Early December, Bowen noted, should see wind "with some snow or I don't know," followed by the "Alteration of weather." A rival almanac by Nathaniel Whittenmore, a Lexington, Massachusetts, surveyor, opined that rain, snow, and stormy weather were in the offing, with warm rain on December 4. Whatever almanacs predicted, scouting parties knew they could expect volatile weather—they were just uncertain when bad weather might erupt.[9]

In northern Massachusetts along the New Hampshire border, Lovewell had seen his share of cold, windy winter weather. So, apparently, did potential recruits—only thirty men volunteered instead of the forty to fifty individuals Lovewell, Farwell, and Robbins had expected. Perhaps potential recruits knew about previously unsuccessful scouting ventures launched from Dunstable. Or, just as likely, the thirty signed up because a recent provincial law specified that Dunstable needed to equip that number of men with snowshoes. Officers would drill the snowshoe men "by running or marching on the snow that they may be expert in the use thereof." To get an additional thirty men would be difficult for other reasons: nearby Lancaster residents had refused to volunteer in spring of 1724, afraid their defenseless village would suffer attack. Other towns might have harbored the same concern. Lovewell remained unfazed, and Lieutenant Farwell drew 487 pounds of bread from the provincial stores on November 26, 1724.[10]

The path ahead was due north-northeast from Dunstable. One chronicler claimed Lovewell took a well-known route by way of Ossipee Lake. Woodland trails provided bearings, along with rivers and streams. Nevertheless, Puritans instinctively perceived unsettled forested terrain (by English standards, that is,) as "howling wilderness." Scouting parties left behind farms, meetinghouses, and mills, bidding adieu to the bridges and fences that physically marked boundaries. Forest had only natural boundaries of woods, valleys, and hills, while Indian fields and dwellings contrasted sharply with New Englanders' tracts and structures. Corn was common to both Indians and English, but the Abenakis' conically shaped bark wigwams supported by poles bore scant resemblance to the cut planks or unfinished logs of New England dwellings. Mission settlements with Roman Catholic chapels featuring altar and cross were anathema to Reformed Christian churchgoers. Even the woods changed farther north: the familiar oak slowly yielded to more dominant beech, maple, spruce, and fir.[11]

No journal of Lovewell's first expedition survives to detail the campaign. If it had, the terrain would have been minimally described or unmentioned. Instead, entries about the mileage covered, weather, and troop conditions would have been prevalent. The troop marched for over three weeks. Frederic Kidder, a nineteenth-century chronicler, asserted the men were close to exhaustion and supplies dangerously low. The company's bread ration, if based on a daily consumption of one pound per man, would have been half gone. Samuel Penhallow offered a different assessment: the original manuscript of his *History of the Wars of New England with the Eastern Indian,* before edited for publication, praised the troopers' speedy march. They traveled light "having little or nothing with them at their setting out but bisquit and salt." Additional food came from killing "bears and other . . . which they had in plenty."

On December 19, about forty-four miles above Winnepissock Pond, Lovewell's men sighted a Native wigwam occupied by a man and a boy: the former they quickly shot and scalped—the unburied body they purposely left as a message to any Abenakis passing by. What Peter Silver has referred to as the "Anti-Indian sublime," a cultural dynamic that powered white attitudes against Indians and often employed dead bodies as symbolic messengers, was partially in evidence here. Instead of scalped European bodies used by whites to stir outrage against Indians, as Silver has revealed for 1750s Pennsylvania, the scalped Abenaki corpse left to rot above ground would signal New Englanders' work and disdain for their foe if any subsequent Natives should chance upon the site. The captured boy became a trophy of war.[12]

One slain Abenaki and one prisoner taken without the loss of a single scout constituted success in the troops' definition. More significant to them was the large amount of powder and shot as well as smoked beef discovered in the camp; it hinted that many more Abenakis were on their way. Despite what Penhallow had said earlier about the men's hunting skills, he also admitted that the trek had weakened them—translation, they refused to stay in the camp to set a trap for any potentially bigger returning adversary. Besides, Lovewell's men could expect to receive one hundred and fifty pounds for the dead Indian and his son. And they had already left a calling card, the scalped corpse, for the Abenakis to view. Why risk their lives further? They returned through Dover, New Hampshire, a town attacked by Abenakis earlier in the war.[13] In Boston, a delighted Lieutenant Governor Dummer added fifty pounds to the one hundred and fifty required by law. As the *Boston News Letter* noted, the additional money was due to "good service" and for "further encouragement."[14]

Bostonian Samuel Sewall, an inveterate diarist and chief justice, neglected to record the event. When the missionary Father Sebastian Rale was killed and scalped along with dozens of Abenakis in Norridgewock in 1724, Sewall duly noted the news: Rale symbolized New Englanders' fear of Catholic infiltration among Native Americans, and momentous events typically piqued Sewall's interest. Yet, reward and publicity notwithstanding, killing one Abenaki and capturing another represented a small event to a war-weary Boston. Another Boston diarist, Jeremiah Bumstead, never mentioned Lovewell's exploits either. Official Massachusetts delight at Lovewell's success did not extend very far among Boston's citizenry.[15]

Borderland settlements reacted differently. Inhabitants familiar with Abenaki raids eagerly assembled scouting companies in hope of duplicating Lovewell's feat, and further enticed by Dummer's bonus offer. Enthusiasm notwithstanding, the resulting scalp-hunting parties never found Abenaki tracks. One company only managed to uncovered empty wigwams. Crestfallen scouts battled weather and presumably picked up blisters and sore feet instead of the hoped-for rewards. Their lack of success, according to Penhallow, was because the Abenakis had regrouped away from their usual haunts, the result of the Norridgewock raid by the English in the summer of 1724 that had scattered the Abenakis.[16]

Lovewell wasted little time in organizing another scouting venture, his "noble spirit" in the words of Samuel Penhallow, spurring him on again. Nearby Groton men and once shy Lancaster residents descended on Dunstable by January 27, 1725, joined by Haverhill and Billerica recruits the following day. Dunstable residents filled out the troop. The total number may have exceeded ninety people, although chroniclers fixed it at eighty-seven. Lovewell's enhanced reputation drew more volunteers this time. That the expedition occurred in the dead of winter encouraged men to join as well: outdoor farm activities had tailed off. Winter also remained the preferred season for catching the Abenakis off guard. Lovewell's new command was almost as large as the English assault party against Mystic Fort in the Pequot War of 1637. Still, as Nathaniel Whittenmore noted in his 1725 Almanac, January was a treacherous month to travel: "Now with many warm clothes preserve thy skin / A New Year and cold is entered in." February proved little better for campaigners: "cold winds do from the North west blow / the wind is finely cloath'd in Snow." Lovewell and his oversized company embarked on January 30.[17]

A surviving scout journal records the troop's progress. Equally important, Lovewell's marching distances, tactics, and overall leadership can be examined. The men trekked north by northeast, crossing the frozen Merrimac River on the first day without mishap. The second day Lovewell marched five miles up to Nantecuck, unwilling to push the men too hard. Many were farmers first, scouts or scalp hunters second. Then, in early February, the men logged ten, fifteen, and twelve miles in three successive days. At the Lower Pond below the Winnepesecocket River, scouting parties broke off from the main troop to search for signs of Natives. On February 7, an injured man hurt "very bad" with an axe went home accompanied by a six-man detachment. A snowstorm the next day forced the troop to hunker down.[18]

So far, little of consequence had occurred. Scouts did indeed injure themselves while Native Americans went unsighted. However, the emerging picture suggests that Lovewell favored prudence over recklessness, resting his men and tending the wounded. Lovewell also sent small groups of men ahead to reconnoiter. Detached men performed double duty: they traveled light and stealthily, trusting to concealment to locate their quarry. Upon returning, they set out again with the main troop, doing the fatiguing but necessary work that defined such expeditions.[19]

The following days saw more excitement. Near Cusumpe Pond, on February 11 detached scouts reported smoke; others thought they heard guns. Subsequent probes the next two days found no Indians, and again Lovewell refused to hurl his entire troop against an undiscovered adversary, being more interested in identifying the target first. Meanwhile, Lovewell decided to release thirty men from service; either the troop had been too lightly provisioned or Lovewell had expected the campaign to be completed at this point. Unprepared scouting parties had occasionally returned home, starving and sick. Lovewell's selection criteria would be useful to know: Did the captain retain the hardiest, most skillful men? Or were community ties and personal links to troopers more important? Jeremy Belknap, an eighteenth-century New Hampshire historian, claimed that Lovewell resorted to a lottery. If so, Lovewell's authority had certain limits—he could not order volunteers off, expecting them to sacrifice potential scalp money; this was a business venture garbed in military gear.[20]

Coincidentally, conditions soon improved. A moose shot the next day temporarily relieved supply concerns and provided a welcome relief from salt pork and bread. Then, on February 16, the troop spotted an Indian track. Lovewell assigned forty or so troopers to follow the prints, while sixteen men stayed behind to guard the packs. The men returned empty-handed and hungry. However, on February 20, the troop discovered a recently occupied wigwam, fresh tracks, and rising smoke in the distance—the Abenakis had relocated their camp.[21]

Lovewell bided his time, planning a nighttime sortie to maximize surprise. Here his authority over the men went unquestioned. A premature musket shot would have alerted the Indians before the trap was sprung; loud tramping in the woods or snapped branches might do the same. If snow was on the ground, footprints would be muffled, but any fire was out of the question—too much risk of the Indians seeing a light or smelling smoke. Then there were the dogs that accompanied the troop. A reference to them excised from the published edition of Penhallow's work appeared in the manuscript version. Their handlers would need to keep them quiet. At 2:00 a.m., Lovewell struck. One part of the troop fired instantly. The other held their powder before firing into the surprised victims. Accounts differ as to a few particulars: one report claims that Lovewell personally killed two Indians; another suggests that a company dog pinned down an Abenaki before he was slain. Other accounts indicate that French Mohawks were numbered among the slain.

Whatever their identity, ten Natives were killed and scalped on February 21, with Lovewell's men escaping injury. As before in the first expedition, albeit on a much bloodier, graphic scale, the ten scalped individuals would alert any venturing Abenakis about war's consequences. The men rested from their slaughter and hatchet work. On February 22, the departure day, the cautious Lovewell positioned a scout on the "Back Tracks" to guard against attack. Lovewell drove his men hard, once covering thirty miles in a single day, before halting two days afterward—his men had pulled up lame. The troop arrived in Boston by sloop on March 9.[22]

Accolades once more were showered upon Lovewell. The troop had endured long marches, withstood a snowstorm, and secured a sizable haul of scalps. One nineteenth-century historian, Justin Winsor, claimed that Dover, New Hampshire, residents supplied an ovation. Striding into Boston, Lovewell's force grandly advertised their success, with scalps positioned on hoops for all to see. In Boston, Jeremiah Bumstead acknowledged the "10 Indian scallps brought in." This counted as news. Samuel Sewall wrote to the Reverend Timothy Woodbridge on February 26, 1725, apparently alerted to Lovewell's earlier success, that the captain had killed ten Indians in stormy weather and "Took ten guns, twenty pair of snow shoes, and some beaver." The extra snowshoes suggest that the Natives sought captives for ransom. Lovewell swore to his account before Lieutenant Governor Dummer, drawing one thousand pounds from the treasury, with the sold muskets yielding an additional seventy pounds.[23]

Lovewell's success became imprinted on the popular memory. That he had dispatched the Indians in a night raid without a single casualty became fodder for tale telling. Long afterward, Lovewell's deed prompted reminiscences: Jeremy Belknap noted in the 1790s that the "elderly people, at this distance of time," referred to the encounter "with an air of exultation." New Englanders had many battles to recall, with recent Revolutionary battles such as Lexington, Concord, and Bunker Hill instilling patriotic pride in the citizens of the early republic. However, hoary elders had a tale or two of their own to relate from a bygone age, and, as Belknap acknowledged, "it was a capital exploit."[24]

Lovewell's second expedition suggests remarkable luck, decided expertise, or more likely some combination of the two. He erred on the side of caution: when a man injured himself, he provided an escort; when provisions ran short, he sent men home. Lovewell's nighttime attack capped by his men's safe return with plenty of plunder underscored his overall exploits. Perhaps his forced march back pushed men beyond their endurance, but his company had returned intact. What New Englander could fault such an effort?

Lovewell's campaign laurels left him little to prove. Yet, he soon organized a third expedition intent on venturing forth once more in search of Abenaki scalps. Why was he so determined to move so soon? Samuel Penhallow described Lovewell as "still animated with an uncommon zeal." John Farmer and Jacob B. Moore claimed he was "inured to danger"; and Samuel Green, a nineteenth-century town historian, thought Lovewell "ambitious to distinguish himself."[25] Additional scalp bounties may have also been tempting—more money could always come in handy. Perhaps, too, Lovewell's thoughts had turned to Jeremiah Moulton and Johnson Harmon, the Norridgewock attackers who had slain Sebastian Rale and produced twenty-seven scalps for payment in 1724. Lovewell's scalp victims were fewer and lacked anyone of note. Moreover, Moulton and Harmon had surprised an entire village; Lovewell had destroyed small encampments. And therein rests an intriguing bit of speculation that might explain Lovewell's third expedition—was the captain hungry for promotion? Johnson Harmon had gained a colonelcy for his effort. Lovewell was still a captain. A more impressive feat of arms might secure higher rank, and the Pigwacket Indian village by the Upper Saco River, a major seasonal encampment, provided a tempting means to that end. Then there was Paugus, whose "name inspired terror on the frontier settlements," a Native American bogeyman feared by New Englanders. His slaying could rival that of Rale in the popular mind. Might such considerations possibly have swayed a military man allegedly inured to danger to set forth once more?[26]

As a branch of the eastern Abenakis, the Pigwackets intermingled among their Penacook, Amasekonti, and Norridgewock relations. Their village, identified by innumerable English spellings meaning the "cleared place," was located sixty miles inland along the Saco River, a one-acre site protected by a palisade of logs. Major Hilton's unsuccessful 1703 winter raid there had discovered one hundred empty wigwams. Not surprisingly, except perhaps to Hilton and his troop, the Pigwackets typically hunted in winter for moose, deer, and caribou; they returned to Pigwacket to await spring planting before going down the Saco River to fish by the coast. Whether any Pigwackets were there after the 1724 Norridgewock attack by Jeremiah Moulton and Johnson Harmon remained to be seen. Nor could Paugus's movements be ascertained. In effect, Lovewell gambled that a deeper interior probe might yield substantial results.[27]

As always, the elements came into play. An April departure as Lovewell planned marked spring's arrival on the calendar but not necessarily so in the field. People recalled the "great snow" in February and March of 1717, in which eight-foot drifts had accumulated and forced people to descend from chamber windows. Snow could stay on the ground for weeks. One account claimed that a giant snowstorm had erupted in April that year. Moreover, winter still gripped northern New England in April 1725: while trekking north of Dunstable in early April, Colonel Eleazer Tyng encountered rain and snow that forced him to halt. The same weather thwarted Lovewell. In his last official communication, he remarked, "I should have marched sooner if the weather had not prevented me."[28]

Recruits from Dunstable, Woburn, Concord, Groton, Haverhill, Weston, Nutfield, Andover, and Billerica joined Lovewell's scouting party. The forty-six volunteers included one Native American, Toby, and the young Reverend Jonathan Frye as chaplain. None of the men except for Farwell and Robbins had served under Lovewell before. Indeed, although John Grenier claimed the volunteers were Bostonians, these men were actually rural villagers drawn to the party by Lovewell's record of success. For some, scalp hunting resembled a family affair, as seen by David and Eleazer Melvin, half-brothers separated by over a dozen years, or the Johnson cousins Noah, Josiah, and Ichabod, clustered within four years of one another. Others followed their neighbors and enlisted. Most men were in their twenties, over 60 percent of the total, with the rest in their thirties, leaving forty-year-old Thomas Richardson the group's oldest member.[29]

One recruit did stand out from the mix—Seth Wyman. The thirty-nine-year-old Wyman had firsthand experience leading scouting expeditions; indeed, he had commanded a scout in 1707, located a large Indian encampment, and had to watch his troop unravel without firing a shot after the Abenakis had been sighted. Despite impassioned appeals from Wyman and his sergeant, the men broke and ran upon hearing the Indian numbers. A subsequent court martial cleared Wyman, but his days as a commander were apparently over. Still, he ranked above the sergeants and ordinary scouts in the troop and was answerable in the line of command to only Lovewell and his two lieutenants. Someone recognized his command experience sufficiently to grant him that rank. Later events would reveal Wyman's mettle.[30]

Before departing, Lovewell received a warning. Tradition claims that a neighbor urged him to beware of lurking Abenakis. Twice, Lovewell had escaped detection; twice, he had caught Abenakis off guard—the only scout to register such success in late 1724 and early 1725. Would good fortune favor him again? Lovewell angrily dismissed his neighbor's warnings, snorting "That he did not care for them" and bending a small nearby elm into a bow to emphasize that "he would treat the Indians in the same way." Such cockiness, if not downright arrogance, seems uncharacteristic of the cautious captain, especially as the account was derived from folklore. Still, a recent mishap reported in the newspaper gives the tale some foundation: before embarking, a certain Flag from Woburn, a volunteer, had presented a gun to his brother, saying, "Now brother suppose I were an Indian." Neither man knew the musket was charged. Flag's brother promptly killed him with a ball through the neck. It was an inauspicious start for a captain whose men had always returned safely.[31]

The company marched north by northeast from Dunstable, the early way familiar enough to Lovewell from his woodland rambles. By mid-April, winter's grip slowly eased in northern New England. Certainly, the weather would be warmer than during Lovewell's February jaunt. But unexpected mishaps occurred that, while hardly disastrous, were nonetheless annoying, such as the Indian Toby's illness, which compelled him to return to Dunstable. Toby might have been useful for reconnaissance or for choosing routes to Pigwacket. At Contoocook, William Cummings of Dunstable dropped out due to an old injury and was sent home with a kinsman. At Ossipee, as the troop began closing in on Pigwacket, Benjamin Kidder of Nutfield became too ill to proceed, so Lovewell halted the troop and constructed a stockade, leaving Kidder and the expedition's doctor behind with a sergeant and seven men to keep guard.[32]

Looking after the wounded and preparing a fortification if danger threatened—this was the sensible Lovewell thinking, not the blustering man threatening to bend Indians into a bow. The fort's outline, still visible many years later, showed that considerable quantities of earth had been removed in digging cellars; its location adjoined a river providing a ready source of water. The rear guard could hold out until Lovewell's return; most of the troops' provisions were in their keeping; Lovewell intended to travel lightly for the final push to Pigwacket.[33]

Pigwacket stood roughly forty miles away from the stockade according to Symmes, although later chroniclers placed the distance at twenty-two miles. As the troop drew closer, they feared being "dog'd by the enemy." Fear was an understandable emotion. Threats of attack often led settlers to petition for military protection; at other times settlers fled homesteads, afraid of attack.

Now these settlers/soldiers were away from home with only a small rear guard for assistance, and their nerves started to fray. Clerics safely ensconced in a meetinghouse pulpit would have stressed Christian resolve and performance of duty. Yet such words were hard to remember in the woods. Apparently, Jonathan Frye had neither pulpit nor words to calm them; at least no account of his speaking survives. Lovewell, Farwell, and Robbins, old hands at scouting expeditions, might have reassured the men. Seth Wyman would have been wise to stay quiet—he knew firsthand how easily soldiers became unmanned. Even so, whatever was said or unsaid, these troops were new to Lovewell and their ranks had been depleted by sickness and redeployment. They were also nearing a major Indian encampment. Sentries reported hearing Indians by the camp on Friday evening. Daybreak revealed tracks from Indians pushing canoes into the water.[34]

The actual chronology of events now becomes cloudy. On Saturday (or Sunday?) the men went to prayers, heard a gun, and saw an Indian by Saco Pond. Different accounts argue for May 8 and others suggest May 9 for the sighting. In any event, Lovewell called the men together. The Abenakis, Lovewell believed, had been alerted, the lone Native was a possible decoy, and withdrawal might be advisable. Surprisingly, the men rallied their spirits, hopes buoyed by a potential target and perhaps the fact that they greatly outnumbered the lone Pigwacket who had been sighted. The Reverend Symmes described the troop responding with a defiant no to Lovewell's warning: "we came out to meet the Enemy, we have all along Pray'd God we might find 'em, and we had rather trust Providence with our lives yea Dy for our country then try to return without seeing them, if we may, and be called Cowards for our pains." Lovewell ordered packs removed for the advance.[35]

Lovewell's decision would later draw fire. Neither Symmes nor Penhallow had questioned his plan to leave the packs unguarded. Yet, if Lovewell thought there were Indians near, he normally advanced with the entire troop, packs and all, or left men to guard them. In 1768, when the Reverend Paul Coffin toured the area, he mused in his journal that "leaving packs with none to guard them, seems hardly prudent." More damningly, Lovewell had broken one of the cardinal ranger rules, according to John Grenier, that of "measured audacity." In other words, gauge your ability to strike unexpectedly. But these men wanted a scalp and Lovewell expeditions had never failed to produce results. Why should this time be any different?[36]

After advancing between a mile and a half and two miles, Ensign Seth

Wyman spotted an approaching figure and signaled the men to lower themselves. Wyman killed the passing Pigwacket, but not before the Indian had wounded Lovewell in the belly with beaver shot and injured Samuel Whiting. These facts were to become pivotal. Although Lovewell's injury proved serious, he "made little complaint" and continued walking. He should have ordered the men to be on their guard—an exchange of gunfire close to Pigwacket and discovered Abenaki tracks would seem to have dictated caution. Instead, the Reverend Frye and another man scalped the fallen Indian.[37]

If Lovewell's injury was clouding his judgment, another experienced officer, Farwell or Robbins, should have stepped up. Then again, Lovewell was walking, and no one ventured a cautionary opinion at the right moment. As it was, the troop blundered into an ambush. Two Indians parties (double the size of Lovewell's troop when combined) had chanced upon the packs, counted them, and quietly waited. Paugus, the intended prey, commanded one of the groups. The Abenakis attacked in ranks three and four deep at both the front and rear of Lovewell's troop in a pine grove between a brook and a pond with a few trees and bushes offering cover. The English ran to meet the Abenakis. The two groups exchanged three or four rounds while several yards apart. For a moment, the English appeared to repel the Indians: Penhallow claimed that victory favored Lovewell's men; Symmes noted that the troops had pushed the Abenakis back several rods. But the Indians' shots proved more telling. Lovewell's initial wound either overcame him or else subsequent shots killed him. Indeed, the Indians killed or injured several expedition leaders: Ensign Harwood died at the first attack, while Lieutenants Farwell and Robbins were both seriously hurt. Only Wyman among the officers escaped injury. Someone signaled a retreat. Back the battered troopers went, leaving dead comrades in the field. The pond behind them prevented an Indian encirclement while a ridge in front offered cover.[38]

Amid the English advance and retreat, Benjamin Hassell ran off. Lovewell's cousin Hassell had remained by his commander's side when he fell while the other men had clung close to the trees. After "seeing such a great number of Indians," as Colonel Eleazer Tyng later reported, Hassell "thought it best to return to some men they had left with a sick man at a fort." Perhaps, too, in Hassell's mind the retreat had signaled a decisive turn in events. The Indians appeared too numerous to resist; several officers were down; and his comrades were pulling back. Or possibly Hassell had simply become separated from the troop. The *Boston News Letter* reported that the Abenakis "were even mixed

among them." Gaps opened as men drove forward and fell backwards, sometimes filled by advancing Abenakis. Whether or not Hassell acted appropriately would supply no end of judgments. More damningly, however, Hassell's
tale of disaster after rushing back to the Ossipee rear guard set them fleeing
for Dunstable, any hopes of rescue quickly forgotten.[39]

The battle minus Hassell settled into a stationary fight, with men firing from
covered positions. No massed assaults were made by either side. Pigwackets
screamed and whooped, "Yelling and howling like wolves, barking like Dogs,
and making all sorts of Hideous noises" to throw fear into their opponents.
The English responded by "Shouting and Huzzahing." Even so, the Indians, as
Symmes remarked, "got the Ground where our Dead lay," an unstated implica-
tion hinting at scalping and dismemberment. The Indians also held up ropes,
offering the English quarter. The English defiantly promised gun muzzles for
their assailants.[40]

For ten hours the fighting continued. At one point the Indians stopped
shooting to hold a conference, striking the ground loud enough to excite
Ensign Seth Wyman's curiosity. With his superiors dead or seriously wounded,
Wyman took charge. Wyman's leadership at the front of the expedition before
the battle—signaling the men to cover themselves—showed his readiness to
assume responsibility. Now he crept close to the noise, shot the chief powwow dead, and broke up the assembly while safely returning to his men.
Indeed, Wyman, according to Eleazer Davis, one of the lucky survivors whom
Penhallow personally questioned, "behaved himself with great prudence and
courage by animating the men and telling them 'that the day would yet be
their own, if their spirits did not flag.'" The men loaded and discharged their
muskets, some shooting between twenty and thirty musket balls.[41]

The ability to rally and encourage men defines a good commander. Unlike
the 1707 fiasco, in which Wyman's authority had crumbled as men broke and
ran off, this time his words roused the men to hold their ground; his badly
needed reassurance steadied them, surrounded as they were on all sides, with
a pond at their backs. The fact that Wyman had returned safely from spying
and shooting at the Pigwackets gave his words added authority, confirming
his command persona. Even so, Solomon Kies had other ideas—he crawled
to Wyman confessing "He was a Dead Man," wounded by several shots. Kies
doubted he would survive long and asked Wyman, "if it be possible, I'll get out
of the way of the Indians, that they mayn't get my Scalp." As Kies approached
the pond, he spied an abandoned canoe, climbed in, and drifted down the

Saco River safe and undetected. The Reverend Symmes labeled this a miraculous providence. On the other hand, Penhallow wondered why Kies's action had remained unmentioned until Symmes's pamphlet appeared. Quite possibly Kies had simply slipped away without consulting Wyman.[42]

Others held their own in battle. The injured Jonathan Frye allegedly prayed aloud and asked God to safeguard the troop. The *Boston News Letter* later asserted that Frye had killed five men and "fought with undaunted courage and scalped one of the Indians in the heat of the engagement." Another unnamed man cited in a report made by Colonel Tyng to Lieutenant Governor Dummer behaved "courageously to the last," applauded by his comrades. Who was this man? It was not Wyman, who went on to receive a captain's commission and silver-hilted sword—he arrived in Dunstable after the letter carried by the unnamed hero had been sent. Possibly Tyng was describing Edward Lingfield, later promoted to ensign. On the other hand, Jacob Fulham "distinguish'd himself with much bravery," in Penhallow's words, by killing one of the first Indians and then a second just as his adversary's musket slew him.[43]

Individual heroics aside, the battle raged from late morning to near sunset in a most uncharacteristic manner for borderland fighting. Encounters between New Englanders and Natives, often reliant on ambush and sudden charges, seldom lasted an entire day. This engagement between New Englanders and Abenakis—the longest battle waged in Dummer's War—proved the exception. There were no flanking or frontal assaults with massed volleys after the initial encounter; instead, men shot independently behind cover, loading and reloading, hoping to pick off an adversary. Their bullets in the trees evidenced the encounter's magnitude, and people decades later would find the balls.[44]

The Abenakis were the first to break off the fight. With the death of Paugus, they needed to take stock. That more Indians were dying or injured turned the battle into a bloody standoff. Whether they were out of ammunition or too few to continue, the Abenakis left the field at sunset carrying their dead according to custom.[45]

Darkness concealed the retreating Indians before Lovewell's men stirred. Exhaustion and fear of lurking Pigwackets kept them from venturing beyond the protective ridge. Near midnight, hours after the last shot, the troop collected itself. Whether Josiah Farwell or Jonathan Robbins, the ranking officers, or the energetic Wyman took charge is unstated. Rank may have been meaningless in any event; the survivors first needed to count their casualties. Nine men lay dead: John Lovewell headed the list, followed by Ensign John Harwood from

Dunstable. Ichabod Johnson from Woburn, Josiah Davis and Sergeant Jacob Fullam of Weston, John Jefts and Jonathan Kitteredge of Billerica, and Daniel Woods and Thomas Woods, cousins from Groton, rounded out the fatalities. Jacob Farrah of Concord and Robert Usher of Dunstable were expiring rapidly. A badly wounded Lieutenant Robbins, recognizing the extent of his injuries, asked for a charged gun to hold, remarking, "The Indians will come in the Morning to Scalp me, and I'll kill one more of 'em if I can." No one could begrudge that request. The men's next decision would be far more difficult.[46]

No one considered removing or concealing the seriously wounded. Physically hoisting and carrying them on the arms and shoulders of the roughly nine healthy individuals was impossible. No one wished to stay behind to defend Robbins and the others either—their fear of returning Indians was too great, the odds too daunting. Besides, Robbins had more or less sanctioned the troops' departure; the other two men were unable to speak. As for burial, no rocks or covering shielded the deceased, and no narrative even hints that the dead were handled or repositioned. What undoubtedly influenced the men's actions was the Ossipee rear guard: they could make for the fort and send the detached troopers back to search for survivors and bury the dead.

The troop's behavior contrasted strongly with Lovewell's normal leadership. He had pointedly tended the injured and ill, releasing them from duty and usually sending them back with a companion or a group of men. Only Indian Toby had walked home alone. When men became too lame, he had stopped the march. But Lovewell's leadership lessons worked poorly here. A decimated troop bloodied from an extended battle and lacking provisions was focused upon individual survival. Those who knew Lovewell best, Farwell and Robbins, favored abandonment. Robbins accepted death with a musket alongside him, but Farwell's reasoning was more complicated. As the lone survivor of a 1724 Indian ambush in which clever concealment had saved him, Farwell drew from his experience and sought to put distance between his battered men and the battle site; it was a form of mobile concealment, and preferable to waiting for any returning Abenakis.[47]

Planned intentions and physical injuries complicated Josiah Farwell's decision as the troop moved out. Seriously wounded, he slowed the troop's pace, and a mile and a half later the men halted to consider their dilemma. Farwell, Jonathan Frye, Eleazer Davis, and Josiah Jones were too hurt to keep pace. Hampering the troop as they did would delay the presumed assistance from Ossipee. A discussion followed. None of the arguments or comments have survived, except for Farwell and his three comrades bestowing their "free consent," in the Reverend Symmes's words, to be left behind. The men hoped "to come back with Fresh Hands to relieve them." But no one wished to stay with the four wounded men until then—those who faltered had to shift for themselves. Ensign Wyman assumed command of the depleted, battered troop by virtue of his rank and battlefield exploits.[48]

Wyman faced a different challenge than before. Urging men to remain calm and hold their position while firing upon an enemy had been comparatively easy. Except for Kies, the men understood the consequences of bolting from the pond. Now the exhausted and hungry troopers worried about pursuing Indians. The walking wounded who were still with the troops would be understandably concerned about keeping up with their comrades lest they suffer the fate of Farwell and the others. An early nineteenth-century account claimed the soldiers had heard a shot from Robbins's two muskets the next day, followed by a third from a foe, evidence that "his sanguinary purpose had probably been accomplished." Already edgy, the men halted again. This time they divided into three separate companies in order to cover their tracks better; in other words, fewer men made less of a trail. None of the chronicles claimed that Wyman had ordered this plan; it may have been a collective decision, or else men in the ranks decided on their own path and companions. Three Indians did pursue one of the detachments, and a frightened Elias Barrow "strayed from the rest" over the Ossipee River, never to be seen again.[49]

Barrow's abrupt departure (and which group he broke off from) prompts speculation as to whether anyone was exercising authority. Wyman may not have been able to keep the men together. He was uncomfortably familiar with this scenario from his 1707 command in which fear of an enemy had caused men to panic despite their superiors' entreaties. Nor could the men—in whatever group they were—convince Barrow to stay. Such fragmentation after battle, at least in early Anglo-American history, has rarely been examined aside from isolated episodes of individuals trying to regroup after fighting. Cabeza de Vaca's sixteenth-century account of a disaster-ridden Spanish expedition along the Gulf of Mexico constitutes a classic exception. Three hundred would-be conquistadors suffered sickness, starvation, desertion, and disintegration after coming ashore on Florida in the spring of 1528. By 1529, only fourteen of the men were left in coastal Texas. Earlier, Cabeza de Vaca had argued against efforts to divide the troop, three times insisting that they stay together, but when the healthy became too weak to help the sick, he relented.

When Cabeza de Vaca himself was near death, abandoned by his comrades in Texas, he accepted their reasoning. Cabeza de Vaca survived for eight years among Native Americans before reaching Spanish-held territory. Lovewell's men found group unity equally challenging while stumbling a much shorter distance through the woods.[50]

At some point two of the three groups linked up and reunited at or near the Ossipee fort. Eleven men from Lovewell's ill-fated expedition had made it through the woods and were surprised to find Ossipee vacant—they could not have known that Hassell had preceded them. Any hope of aiding their abandoned comrades would have to wait. Meanwhile, food left by the hurriedly departing rear guard restored their strength, and a missing companion, Solomon Kies, joined their number. No one openly branded Kies a coward; it was Hassell who would have to bear that stigma. Besides, Kies could point to his wounds, and the men at Ossipee might have been wondering about their companions left behind with what now proved to be empty promises. No one volunteered to rejoin them.[51]

The twelve men had time to assess their situation. With full stomachs and Indians for the moment eluded, they could have waited in reasonable safety for Wyman's arrival with the remaining men, but they opted to push on. Perhaps they had too little powder and shot; or maybe they thought a speedy departure the best recourse for saving forsaken companions. Who could predict when a relief expedition would find them? As for Wyman, his arrival was uncertain. Who could say the Abenakis had not waylaid him? Whatever thoughts they entertained, the group pushed on to Dunstable without incident on May 13.[52]

Seth Wyman and his erstwhile command arrived in the settlement two days later. Wyman was down to four men. Whether deliberately or accidentally, Wyman bypassed Fort Ossipee. Just possibly Wyman's group included more injured men, hence slowing his return. Lovewell troopers, we know, were reluctant to keep pace with anyone who faltered but quick to offer promises to return. They had left Farwell, Frye, Davis, and Jones with such assurances, so why not Wyman and his companions? Wyman's group did face great hardship in their meandering trek back to Dunstable—at one point Wyman told Symmes they went without bread from Saturday morning to Wednesday—until they caught and roasted two mouse squirrels; later some partridges and other small game sustained them. Consequently, according to Wyman, they "scarce felt at all Hunger bitten."[53]

Lieutenant Farwell's ragged, injured command of four men, on the other hand, had little to sustain them except hope. And that commodity grew even scarcer as the hours and days multiplied. Eleazer Davis's account of events to Samuel Penhallow balanced feelings of loyalty with self-survival. At first, the four men stayed at or near where the troop had parted company, hopeful that the rear guard would show. Then they began hobbling toward the fort. The four men no longer relied, it seems, on comrades' assurances, as Davis and Jones led the faltering Farwell and Frye. Command structure, if indeed it ever existed, began falling apart: Jones "steered another way," to use Davis's polite phrasing, preferring to take his chances alone in the woods. Farwell could not order him to stay; nor could Davis prevent Jones, a fellow Concord resident, from departing. Community ties and military rank dissolved when men were few and exposed in the woods to possible attackers. Now Davis had two seriously injured companions to shepherd.[54]

The three men continued toward the fort, hampered by injuries and hunger. Frye succumbed first: his mortified wounds evidenced his worsening condition; three days after Jones left, Frye implored his comrades to leave him behind, instructing Davis to tell his father "that he was not afraid to dy." (However, this may have been a literary salve for Frye's family courtesy of the Reverend Symmes; Penhallow never cited these remarks.) The two men agreed to Frye's request. Shortly thereafter, Farwell began to falter. Reduced to a diet of roots and water, Farwell steadily weakened as worms passed through his wounds. After eleven days Davis caught and boiled a fish—but Farwell was too far gone to chew. Now Davis faced a difficult moral choice: he could stay and await Farwell's death, possibly compromising his own survival; or he could leave his companion while he himself was still strong enough to travel. Davis opted for the latter course. No words of farewell were recorded, but Davis was reduced to a "melancholy desolate state" according to Samuel Penhallow.[55]

Davis somehow found the Ossipee fort, along with the provisions left behind for any late-arriving survivors. That it took Davis so long to reach it may reflect uncertain directions or his slow rate of travel. Indeed, either or both reasons may explain why Davis ended up in Berwick, one of the northernmost settlements in New England, instead of Dunstable. From there he was sent to Portsmouth, New Hampshire, where a "skillful Surgeon" tended his belly wound and blown-away thumb. In Portsmouth, Penhallow constructed his version of Lovewell's Fight from Davis's account.[56]

Josiah Jones might have wished he stayed with his comrades; at least with

Davis he would have gained the fort and provisions. If later accounts are true, Jones suffered even greater deprivations. One contemporary newspaper account simply noted that Jones had been shot above the hip. John Farmer and J. B. Moore, in their *Collections, Topographical, Historical, and Biographical,* recorded that Jones had undergone a "fatiguing ramble" across the forest, "almost dead from loss of blood, the putrefaction of his wounds, and the want of food." Unidentified forest vegetation later supplemented with cranberries sustained Jones. May cranberries in northern New England seem highly suspect or else reflect a bit of poetic license. Whatever Jones ate, it soon passed out of his wounds before he arrived in Saco, Maine, where one Dr. Allen nursed him back to health.[57]

It was the first set of returnees, the absconding Ossipee rear guard egged on by Hassell's tale, who spurred Massachusetts authorities to action. The panicky rear guard's account forwarded to Lieutenant Governor William Dummer painted a grim picture: in Hassell's words, "non Returned but I to ye teen men and we and no more are yet Come to Dunstable." Hassell held out faint hope for any survivors. Sergeant Nathaniel Woods, commander of the Ossipee Fort, bemoaned the rear guard's quick departure and refusal to search for survivors. Lieutenant Governor Dummer boiled over with indignation, for the men had "so cowardly deserted their commander & Fellow Soldiers in their Danger." Reformed Christian clerics who had warned about the dangers of cowardice could have seen their prophecies come true. Cowardly soldiers had indeed unmanned companions and compromised campaigns, leaving men to die who might have been saved.[58]

Samuel Sewall heard Tyng's accounts on May 13 in council, "which made us fear that Capt. Lovewell was slain by the Indians near Peguntkick, and many of his men on the Lord's Day, May 9." Three days later, Theodore Atkinson, a provincial commissioner returning from Quebec, learned the news in Marlborough, Massachusetts, "of the misfortune of Cap Lovell & Company being Dislodged." Newspapers added to the details. By May 20 the *Boston News Letter* claimed that between twenty and thirty Indians had been slain. The next issue, based largely upon Wyman's testimony and "others," asserted that just twenty of the eighty Indians had survived. Such estimates were precisely that—estimates based on uncertain evidence grounded on possibly wishful thinking, as the Abenakis had left no bodies above ground to count. Whether twenty Indians could transport or bury sixty dead and wounded companions is a stretch. Newspapers also dashed hopeful rumors. For a time, stories of

Lovewell's survival circulated, until the *New England Courant* labeled them "groundless" on May 31.[59]

Massachusetts and New Hampshire authorities combined efforts to hunt the Abenakis, locate Lovewell company survivors, and bury the fallen. Colonel Eleazer Tyng went from Dunstable, ordered to impress men if none from Captain John White's company enlisted. Lieutenant Governor Dummer instructed Tyng to "make the best search you can when you come into the ground where the action happened for the dead and wounded that none may perish for want of our care."[60]

A New Hampshire rescue party never reached Pigwacket. Upon arriving at the deserted Ossipee fort, the men found a note from the survivors that unnerved them. Worse, they suspected that Indians lurked nearby. They quickly left for home. Others were too frightened to go farther as well: Hassell, the deserter, refused to return to Pigwacket, claiming illness, although fear may explain his decision. Lieutenant Governor Wentworth of New Hampshire felt compelled to defend the men's action in a report to Dummer. He emphasized that the troop had found the fort shut, observed several Indians in the vicinity, and heard dogs barking, prompting them to leave, "least they meet with the same fate as Capt. Lovewell did." They were, Wentworth insisted, "stout men." Tyng's troop located and interred the bodies found at Pigwacket without help from the New Hampshire men.[61]

At this juncture, the details of sepulture become murky. Were the bodies left scattered where they had originally fallen? Or had company survivors arranged them for later burial? No account of their disposition survives. Had the Indians scalped Lovewell and his men during the battle or returned later to do the deed? John Grenier insisted that the Abenakis scalped Lovewell and mutilated his body after a small group of them broke off from pursuit of the survivors. Other secondary sources relying on Abenaki oral traditions asserted the bodies went untouched. However, whether scalped or not, a week in the forest would hasten bodily decay, while open wounds invited parasites. Flies would circle around the wounds and gaping mouths of the dead; and the shattered bones and tissues, punctured by musket balls, invited birds and beasts to peck at the flesh. Tyng's men could not hunt Indians and transport the dead at the same time, so they dug a mass grave without stone or monument for the final resting place.[62]

Tyng's men did notice some recently dug ground, began excavating, and found the remains of Paugus, "a vile and bloody wretch" in Penhallow's phrase, discernible by his body markings, buried alongside two deceased comrades. At least that provided something tangible to report to the Massachusetts authorities. Abenakis typically buried the dead on an elevated place facing east, the body covered in red ochre with grave goods placed alongside it. But this hastily dug grave appeared bare, and why Paugus and only two others had been interred may indicate that there were fewer Indian fatalities than New Englanders believed.[63]

The search for more bodies did not go far beyond the battle site. The Reverend Jonathan Frye's body went missing; predators and the elements had the final earthly claim upon him. Nevertheless, Captain Jeremiah Moulton led a subsequent expedition to Pigwacket in early June. They found the graves dug by Tyng, and proceeding down the Ossaby River, chanced upon a corpse believed to be "Captain Lovewell's Lieutenant." A later nineteenth-century account by John B. Hill, relying on the stories of his grandfather, Colonel Ebenezer Bancroft, embroidered the account to state that Farwell had bent down a sapling and tied a handkerchief on top of it to signal rescuers. Farwell's friends later discovered and buried the remains.[64]

The war against the eastern Abenakis sputtered out after the Pigwacket encounter. Already battered by the Norridgewock catastrophe, the Abenakis had lost the ability to control events. The French refused to help their erstwhile allies, and without a steady supply of muskets and gunpowder the Abenakis were militarily compromised. Newspaper reports seldom listed killed and wounded settlers anymore; instead, stories focused on the approach of war's end. Governor William Dummer announced on May 26 that "we have lost some brave men, we have through the favor of God, destroyed most of the Savages." He asked the General Court to consider ending the impressment of soldiers—bounties or premiums sufficed to encourage recruits. Not all news was good. The newly promoted Captain Seth Wyman died leading a scout party in late summer of 1725, felled by dysentery instead of the Abenaki Indians. Another scout, Captain John White, who had marched in Lovewell's second expedition, suffered the same fate. Still, Dummer informed the general assembly that generous payments for volunteers had prompted "hardy and brave men" to enlist, forcing the Indians into negotiations.[65]

For eastern New England, Dummer's War ended in 1726. That summer and in the summer of 1727, conferences held in Falmouth, Maine, hammered out the particular details of the peace. The western Abenakis under Gray Lock followed suit in 1727. Death had visited Abenakis and English violently and unexpectedly. Scalping and bodily dismemberment had figured in the fighting. Nor could either side quickly forget what had occurred. Surviving Abenakis saw incoming settlers slowly pushing into their lands. New Englanders, in turn, remembered the war dead and wounded, with many recalling that Lovewell more than Dummer embodied the Anglo-Abenaki conflict, often naming the conflict after him.[66]

In 1732, the Reverend Oliver Peabody added a fitting codicil to the war when delivering a sermon before the Honorable Artillery Company of Boston. An august body typically recruited from men of parts and affluence, the company sponsored an annual sermon for the new membership. Such homilies fortified the spirit and reminded men of their responsibilities. For Peabody, the years of peace following Dummer's War necessitated a warning. It was not a future unforeseen enemy that worried him as much as his fellow New Englanders. In his words, Massachusetts needed "valiant and accomplished soldiers," as the present generation paled in comparison to their predecessors. The time for beating swords into plowshares had yet to dawn; instead, the sons of the fathers required a renewed martial spirit to properly defend Massachusetts.[67]

Peabody carefully explained how to achieve this goal. Security demanded courageous provincial defenders who embodied a martial spirit: "to our enemies, this would curb their pride and damp their spirits, and the terror of our arms might force them to be at peace with us." In other words, deterrence was the best defense. And the best deterrence came innately from military character, of which Peabody listed a prime example: "we have seen something of this by the happy consequences of the valiant and heroic exploits of our brave Captain LOVEWELL, and his worthy company, whose death we still lament whose memory is precious, and ought to be immortal." The new generation needed to emulate Lovewell and "travel in the woods and swamp, in which there is a great art, and know the hills, mountains, and rivers." Survival, Peabody acknowledged, was never guaranteed, but valor should never be forgotten: "some mighty and valiant soldiers* have fallen gloriously fighting for us in the fields of the woods." Lest anyone wonder whom Peabody meant, the asterisk in the published sermon identified "expert and valiant Capt. Lovewell, Robbins, Frye, Harwood, Fulham, and several others." These were the kind of men the sons of Massachusetts should aspire to become.[68]

Lovewell's men, however, were hardly the first to become enshrined in New England's military annals. Others before them had fought Indians, lost comrades, won victories, and suffered defeats. Earlier generations had established a military tradition of borderland fighting that provided Lovewell and others with a blueprint to follow and revise. Questions of how to fight the war, employing traditional or New World tactics, entered into military strategy. War against the living also turned into a war against the dead. Collecting scalps and body parts became military custom, as did questions about how to care for the wounded and properly inter the dead. In Dunstable, Lovewell's hometown, war taught lessons that would underscore his desire to fight.

CHAPTER 2

War and Survival in Dunstable, Massachusetts, 1673–1725

Timothy Dwight, president of Yale, delighted in countryside rambles that enabled him to visit towns and villages, taking the measure of residents. Almost anything was fair game for the opinionated cleric, with past events and present realities providing ample scope for commentary. Thus, upon entering Dunstable, New Hampshire, in the early nineteenth century, Dwight observed that the ferryman who guided him across the Merrimack River "seemed very much like a stranger to the world in which we live." If his observation was true, the boatman might not have known that early Dunstable had been home to the "celebrated John Lovewell," whose exploits, Dwight recalled, were the "theme of frequent conversations when I was a boy." But no one in Dunstable cared to talk about Lovewell or indeed much of anything for that matter—the village inn had offered Dwight nothing to eat, leaving him reliant on the town clergyman for supper and "polite conversation."[1]

The town that Dwight visited no longer resembled John Lovewell's settlement. Time and circumstance had altered the town's character: guards mounted for protection against Indian attack were a faded memory; the borderlands had expanded far northwards to include other communities; and the Abenakis, once feared, had been greatly reduced in size after the French and

Indian wars. Instead, Dunstable was a mature community, part of which had split off to become Nashua, New Hampshire, by the time of Dwight's visit. The scalping bounties that had propelled men into the borderlands were gone. Yet, if Dwight could have traversed time as easily as space, he would have observed a struggling settlement coping with warfare in the late seventeenth and early eighteenth centuries. Back then, sorties by Native Americans left settlers fleeing to garrison houses for protection while some residents abandoned the settlement entirely. Some Dunstable inhabitants lost their lives in raids; still others avenged themselves by launching raids against Indians. When John Lovewell began his campaigns, he was following in the footsteps of his predecessors and neighbors, a man of his time and very much a Dunstable man.[2]

Little separated Dunstable at first glance from other second-generation New England borderland towns. There was the obligatory Congregational church, led by a Harvard-educated divine, plus an assortment of settlers and speculators. Some were well-to-do and others less so; all hoped to find better opportunities. But, unlike earlier Massachusetts coastal communities, the beneficiaries of massive Indian depopulation, the interior community of Dunstable abutted Native American communities. In peace, the two cultures coexisted and traded; in war, violence and bloodshed upended commercial relationships. For John Lovewell and other Dunstable residents, killings furnished an enduring, not easily forgotten, part of their town's heritage.[3]

The Abenaki Nation was the dominant Native American group in northern New England. A mixture of hunting and farming, their life also involved trade with other Indians and wary interactions with the first Europeans. Visits by Giovanni da Verrazzano and Jacques Cartier led to exchanges and kidnappings as Europeans sought guides and interpreters. During King Philip's War, some Abenakis tried to remain apart from the fighting; tribes such as the Androscoggin and Saco were compelled to take sides, while the Kennebec and Penobscot chose neutrality or exile. Whatever the response, the Abenakis dominated the landscape.[4]

Just to the west and north of Dunstable, the Nashaways, Pennacooks, Wamesits, and other Indian nations resided along freshwater rivers that cut across northern Massachusetts and southern New Hampshire. Corn and freshwater fish dominated the Indians' indigenous economies; moreover, their position gave them access to the fur-bearing animals so highly prized by Europeans. Trade between the two cultures subsequently increased. In time, Native Americans would discover that the advantages of commercial exchange—European metal goods, blankets, alcohol, and sometimes guns in return for pelts—were overbalanced by heavy costs and increasing economic dependency. Arriving English settlers also reshaped the landscape: the newcomers surveyed tracts, cut trees, and planted crops, and their livestock intruded upon Indian cornfields.[5]

Disputes between the two cultures turned ugly. Different conceptions of fair price and market costs collided during exchanges between English and Indians. Disagreements and sometime bald-faced cheating occurred. One notable episode involved John Cromwell, a trader, whose Merrimac River trucking house drew Indian visitors. There was haggling over furs and goods, and the price based on the pelt's weight apparently came into contention—Cromwell repeatedly used his foot as a pound weight on the trading scale, and he had to beat a hasty retreat before angry Indians destroyed his house, leaving a stash of coins to be discovered by a later generation.[6]

The Pennacooks who were located along present-day Concord and Manchester, New Hampshire, interacted most with early Dunstable settlers. They also exerted a degree of authority among smaller Indian bands such as the Wamesits and Agawam. Yet disease had thinned the Pennacooks' ranks by the sixteenth century, and conflict with the Mohawks, their mortal enemies to the west, jeopardized their security. By the 1650s, the Pennacooks numbered approximately 2,500, far below the 12,000 or more they once had been; by the time of King Philip's War, they mustered only 1,250. Passaconaway, a leading Pennacook sachem, warned his people that retaliation against white settlers would be costly—the English would never go away. Instead, he urged peaceful coexistence, petitioning the Massachusetts government in the 1640s to place the Pennacooks under its jurisdiction.[7]

Wannalancet, Passaconaway's son, followed his father's advice after gaining tribal leadership in 1662. When the noted Puritan missionary John Eliot preached to him, Wannalancet replied that his days had been passed in an old canoe but now "I yield myself up to your advice to enter into a new canoe and do engage to pray to God." Whether truly converted or merely out of politeness, Wannalancet did attend Sabbath services at Wamesit, a Christian Indian community, accepting the Puritan faith in the 1670s. In coming years Dunstable settlers and Wannalancet saw their friendship tested. While Wannalancet sought to preserve his people's continuing existence, during wartime his tactics aroused settlers' suspicions. Pennacooks alienated by Wannalancet's conversion preferred new leadership and different survival tactics. The specter of war would materialize and try the relationships built between settlers and Indians.[8]

For Dunstable settlers, the story of their existence as a legally established town in the Abenaki realm dated from 1673. Until 1741, when a divisional line placed most of the town in New Hampshire, Dunstable remained attached to the Bay Colony. Neither a "Peaceable Kingdom" nor a "Christian Utopian Closed Corporate Community," it was a roughhewed settlement driven by speculation.[9] Despite a few possible earlier settlers, it was only after 1673 that such men as the Reverend Thomas Weld, Joseph Hassell, John Cummings, and the first John Lovewells, the grandfather and father of the future ranger, appeared. Jonathan Tyng also numbered among the early petitioners, receiving a tract of land in 1673 beyond "the Merrimac River by the Chelmsford," accompanied by his father, Edward, a respected Boston merchant and brewer. Most of the town proprietors (twenty-one) were nonresidents who resided in Boston, Salem, and Marblehead, so Dunstable represented an investment opportunity for them. However, fourteen proprietors including the Hassells and the Tyngs took up tracts in the town.[10]

Dunstable residents obviously wished to keep their investments fully in view. Not for them the speculation and land dealings from afar. As such, these individuals could chart the town's development more closely, steer local politics, and keep an eye on their holdings. They could also become the town fathers. Staying in Boston or Salem would have meant competing with other more affluent families; in Dunstable, some of these men might become the proverbial big fish in a small pond, overshadowing less-well-to-do neighbors. Resident proprietors such as Jonathan Tyng emerged as town leaders, serving as selectmen, treasurers, and town moderators. Less affluent men took turns as fence viewers and constables; still others might patrol the town's borders during wartime. For many, perhaps even most Dunstable residents, gaining a "competency" for their offspring by working the land and passing something down to them outweighed political service.[11]

Economic dreams took a backseat to survival when King Philip's War ravished New England in 1675. The Wampanoag Indians led by Metacom, or Philip to the English, vented their long simmering outrage against Puritan authority, joined by the Narragansetts, Nipmucs, and other Native nations. New Englanders fled settlements, their houses, crops, and livestock destroyed.

Casualties mounted and hopes dimmed as settlers frantically tried to regroup against an adversary that held the upper hand. In response, Captain Benjamin Church and others adopted a more mobile form of warfare that employed stealth and mobility while utilizing Native American allies to fight alongside them. New modes of fighting took time to catch on, and not all soldiers performed as expected. Church, for instance, found himself imploring and threatening the men under his command: on one occasion, he literally "stormed and stamped" at retreating troops to hold their ground so that their wounded comrades could be secured, but only two soldiers heeded the call; the rest simply fled, deeming discretion the better part of valor.[12]

What Benjamin Church encountered was not unusual. In most instances Massachusetts settlers were civilians trying to behave as soldiers; notions of self-preservation caused men to bolt at unexpected moments even if wounded comrades were left behind to struggle alone or in small groups. Ministers inveighed against men who abandoned comrades, living and dead, insisting that soldiers succor the wounded and provide the fallen safe burial lest predators or Indians tear apart their corpses. But in battle's aftermath, the wounded and the dead received short shift. Benjamin Church left a graphic account of a Pyrrhic victory over the Narragansetts in 1675, the Great Swamp Fight, in which the English torched the Native village against Church's wishes instead of using it as a field hospital. Many of the English dead were left behind, and some of the wounded died during the cold, blustery evening retreat. To Church, the memory remained vivid over forty years later when his account went to press.[13]

Other chroniclers celebrated the return of men believed dead from Indian attack. When the Reverend William Hubbard chronicled King Philip's War, he went beyond identifying battles to note the men who, in his mind, miraculously survived as people symbolically risen from the dead. But the means by which people survived sometimes involved their making hard choices. Witness Jonathan Wells, a soldier wounded in 1676, who had heard his commander, Captain William Turner, say, "it is better to lose some than all," and then leave the rear guard that Wells was in to deal with the Indians alone. A small surviving detachment next left Wells behind with another wounded man, John Jones. Jones declared that his wounds were mortal, at least in Wells's account, and the two agreed to separate to search for a path. Wells was happy to have separated from Jones, "lest he should be a clog or hindrance to him." That the sixteen-year-old Wells should voice such sentiments was revealing. Apparently it was every man for himself. When Wells made it back to Hatfield, Massachusetts, on the Sabbath after dodging Indians and gnawing horse bones to survive, he was greeted as "one having risen from the dead."[14]

Interring the dead was almost as important as securing the wounded in wartime. As we have seen at the Great Swamp Fight courtesy of Benjamin Church, bodies were left behind; ironically enough, friendly Indians later buried them. Yet what the Reverend William Hubbard labeled the "last office of love," interment, was part and parcel of Puritan religious tradition and not to be disregarded lightly. The Reverend Cotton Mather spared few words about unburied bodies left in fields as a result of Indian violence: he described such corpses as "weltering in their own blood." When an Indian assault forced soldiers to abandon the dead, Mather proclaimed that the men had left comrades behind "as meat for the fowls of heaven and their flesh unto the beast of the earth."[15]

New Englanders did try to bury their war dead when possible. The task was just difficult to perform with any degree of reverence or extended compassion because time was often short and circumstances challenging. The aforementioned Jonathan Wells, after separating from his wounded companion, discovered a human head unearthed by animals; this time Wells paused long enough to search for the original grave, in which he "laid the head by the body" and covered it with wood. Major Robert Treat commanded a relief expedition that interred the bodies of Captain Richard Beer and his men, slain by Indians in September 1675. However, the dismembered bodies received "hasty funeral rites," although Beers merited a grave separate from his men; rank had privileges even in death. Still, it was better than the action of an earlier June expedition that, upon discovering the bodies of dismembered settlers arrayed on poles, threw the limbs and scalps into a river—no time for ceremony or interment was wasted by these men intent on pursuing a band of Indians. Treat held to much the same philosophy: after burying Beers and company, he evacuated the survivors of an Indian attack in a nearby village, leaving the slain residents exposed above ground. One nineteenth-century chronicler explained, "As they had been dead five days, and may have been in an advanced state of decomposition, there is some excuse for neglecting the rite of sepulture." The Reverend Solomon Stoddard simply remarked, "they left the bodies unburied."[16]

Injured and dead soldiers and civilians provided the dramatic fallout from King Philip's War. Over fifty towns suffered attack, with a dozen settlements destroyed and perhaps twenty-five hundred New Englanders dead. Estimates of Native casualties indicate that as many as eight thousand eventually died from fighting or starvation. Bodies littered fields and streams, while torched structures and blackened fields offered mute testimony to the horror unveiled. Some English settlers simply gave up and moved to other communities. Native American nations suffered irreparable losses. As for Dunstable, it prepared for assault though spared fighting's worse excesses.[17]

New England's bloodiest war unnerved both Indians and Dunstable settlers. News of rampaging Wampanoags and Narragansetts prompted friendly Indians nearby the town to consider options: several Native laborers working for Jonathan Tyng left their employer; the sachem Wannalancet and his followers took to the woods, reaching Canada before wary townsfolk urged them to return. Wannalancet forewarned settlers about a possible attack. When a minister thanked God for the town's escaping destruction, Wannalancet supposedly rose up in the meeting to remark "Me next." He knew his value to the settlers. A group of fifty to sixty local Christian Indians were less fortunate: provincial authorities ordered them to reside near Jonathan Tyng. Their value as domestics and laborers kept them close to their employers. Nevertheless, those Indian Puritans garnered more suspicion than acceptance, and Charles J. Fox, a nineteenth-century town chronicler, considered them ill-used.[18]

Other Dunstable settlers missed these events. Many inhabitants fled to Boston and Concord, balancing concerns for property and personal safety, and even Jonathan Tyng sent his family away. Tyng, accustomed "to managing people and things," had created a garrison for defense and was the superintendent of the "friendly Indians." Dunstable survived the war intact but depopulated. Captain Samuel Moseley, a former privateer, oversaw the town's defense, and his troop—an assortment of pirates, servants, and sailors—effectively deterred any attack. Meanwhile Tyng footed the bill for the soldiers, procuring fresh meat from Boston as an out-of-pocket expense. No one felt like hunting for game. Eventually Massachusetts compensated Tyng, but until then he (and the remaining settlers) adjusted to life in an armed camp. With peace, residents trickled back until by 1680 approximately 180 people inhabited the town.[19]

Dunstable functioned administratively despite a scattered populace. The first town meeting, held in Woburn, Massachusetts, on November 28, 1677, elected only one resident selectman out of the five chosen, Jonathan Tyng. Nonresident proprietors from Boston, Marblehead, and Salem preferred meetings closer to their homes, avoiding Dunstable until 1711.[20] Even so, John Cummings, who arrived around 1680, soon provided a core of stability as the oft-elected town clerk. Captain Thomas Brattle, Captain Elisha Hutchinson, and Jonathan Tyng numbered among the early selectmen. By the 1680s, the "hog constable" fined owners of errant swine while other town officials assessed and collected taxes. Some of this revenue went to construct roads— Dunstable linked itself to Groton, or more accurately, the two towns' respective meetinghouses. Bridges provided passage over waterways. But even with peace, mounted border guards continued their patrols.[21]

Finding a minister also occupied the town's attention. Lay persons could ponder the scriptures at home, but the Lord's Supper during Sacrament Sunday properly required a clergyman to officiate. The aforementioned Thomas Weld, Harvard class of 1671, arrived in Dunstable on May 1, 1679, the recipient of a house, thirty acres, and a 600-acre share in the town commons. By 1681, the town sweetened the deal for their minister by adding a firewood allotment. Weld's marriage that year to Elizabeth Wilson, granddaughter of Edward Tyng, Jonathan's father, linked him to the local elite. By 1682, the town began building a larger meetinghouse for Weld.[22]

The new meetinghouse, completed in 1684, became Weld's office. Later generations of ministers such as Weld, according to David Hall, may have been less inspiring than those Puritan stalwarts who fled England in the 1630s to carve out a "City upon a Hill," but they continued to enjoy considerable authority and respect nonetheless. Parson Weld could scan the congregation from his pulpit, recognize his two church deacons, John Cummings and John Blanchard, and observe the orderly workings of the Reformed Christian faith. Profane behavior drew frowns and penalties: one errant individual, John Atherton, who wet his hat to use as a buffer in a shoe during the Sabbath, paid a forty shilling fine for "flagrant wickedness." He deliberately absented himself from church for the next three months and earned a public whipping. Other Sabbath-day offenders, according to a later minister, suffered incarceration in a cage located next to the meetinghouse. As for the village dogs, a common wintertime presence in some meetinghouses, there was Samuel Gold, the dog whipper, meting out punishment. A tithing man stared down unruly boys, and a widow lady swept the church clean.[23]

Weld could also see Jonathan Tyng, John Cummings Sr., John Blanchard, Cornelius Waldo, Samuel Warner, Obediah Perry, and Samuel French, who comprised the first seven male church members. These congregational pillars set the tone for the parish. How they behaved drew notice. Not surprisingly, these men had subscribed to a covenant announcing: "We avouch the Lord our God and ourselves to be His people in the truth and simplicity of our spirit." As godly men and Christians, they also "promised to walk with our brethren with all watchfulness and tenderness, avoiding jealousy, suspicion, backbiting, censuring, provocation, secret rising of spirit against them."[24]

Watchfulness was an appropriate word to apply to Dunstable and its Indian neighbors. English and Native Americans coexisted cautiously. The Pennacook community had been split over Wannalancet's accommodationist policy, prompting many Indians to follow Kancagamus, a more aggressive leader. Dwelling north of the town, these Pennacooks feared Mohawk attacks from New York, and despite petitioning Massachusetts for assistance, they decided to retreat farther east and north, arousing New Englanders' suspicions. Avoiding "jealousy, suspicion . . . and secret rising of spirit against them," as stated in the church covenant, did not apply to Indians, especially non-believers. Still, Kancagamus signed a peace treaty with New Hampshire and Massachusetts in 1685 establishing protocols to prevent warfare. Wannalancet, meanwhile, had sold his land on the Merrimack to Jonathan Tyng in 1686, content to fade peacefully away.[25]

King William's War in 1689 plunged Dunstable and indeed all of New England into disarray. The war entailed large sea-based operations requiring professional troops and Royal Navy vessels. An attack upon Port Royal, the center of French Acadia, led to its capture in 1690, while an assault on Quebec that year ended in failure. For many New Englanders, the far distant campaigns against a Catholic Canadian adversary still exposed borderland settlements to French and Indian attacks. New England could never garrison the permeable boundaries that separated English towns from French allied Indian communities. In Dunstable, Wannalancet lived under Jonathan Tyng's supervision after suspicious Massachusetts authorities had jailed him, but Kancagamus rose up against Dover, New Hampshire, attacking and killing Richard Waldron, a much hated Indian trader. The Pennacooks remained divided: some, unable to forestall the attack themselves, had warned New England authorities of the pending assault against Waldron.[26]

In response, Massachusetts borrowed a page from King Philip's War and turned once more to Colonel Benjamin Church. The old frontier scout had definite ideas about warfare, requesting experienced soldiers, English and Indian, to be used as raiders. The colony ordered Church to "pursue, fight, take, kill or destroy the said enemies," while punishing "Drunkenness, swear-ing, cursing or such other sins, as do provoke the anger of God" among his own men. Church never located Kancagamus, but he managed to capture his wife and children, kill his sister, and destroy the Indian corn supply. Church then repelled a subsequent Indian attack, sending Kancagamus an ultimatum to surrender if he wished to see his family again. A recalcitrant Kancagamus capitulated in late 1690, blamed the French for deceiving him, and acknowl-edged a desire for peace. Church led subsequent expeditions against other Indian nations, relying upon stealth and mobility. In time, his mantle would pass to others, and ranger companies employing stealth and mobility would multiply.[27]

King William's War directly affected Dunstable. Friendly Indians had warned of an attack, sending settlers scurrying to the nearest fortified house. Companies of scouts continued to watch the borders. Yet, despite warnings and precautions, settlers in scattered homesteads were caught unaware. The Hassells—Joseph, his wife Anne, their son Benjamin, and a visiting female acquaintance—were among the first town fatalities in September 2, 1691. That the Hassells ranked among the leading families added to the tragedy. Death was no respecter of class in wartime. A note penned in the book of town records, most likely by the Reverend Weld, tersely announced that the family had been "slain by our Indian enemies." Several weeks later Obediah Perry and Christopher Temple met the same fate. Attackers could move at will and escape capture. Such assaults dramatically drove home life's fragility on wartime borderlands.[28]

That was enough for many Dunstable residents—it was time to leave town lest they become the settlement's next fatalities. A wave of terror gripped towns-folk, "punctuated by Indian war-whoops." A 1694 provincial law prohibited settlers from leaving communities under forfeiture of property, but Dunstable residents left anyway. Despite a fortified parsonage house, the Reverend Weld chose to relocate his family to Boston by 1695. Besides, Dunstable's garrison houses only protected residents who reached them in time; none could pre-vent crops, livestock, and domiciles from destruction. Town fathers grimly noted that "near two thirds of the inhabitants have removed themselves with their ratable estates out of town." The thirty town families in 1680 numbered twenty-five by 1701 after several years of peace. Provincial representation suf-fered as well, as the town stopped sending a representative to the General Assembly by 1693, a practice that was continued until 1733.[29]

Other wartime episodes offered a shred of hope to the beleaguered residents. Unlike Schenectady, New York, where a 1690 raid killed close to sixty people and torched many of the buildings, Dunstable had escaped widespread damage. And compared to Salem, Massachusetts, where Indian fears and refugees fed the infamous witchcraft scare of 1692, Dunstable remained religiously unified. The Reverend Weld returned in the late 1690s, the recipient of a provincial stipend from Boston authorities after he had satisfactorily explained the reasons for his departure. But perhaps most remarkable, and certainly talked about, was the unexpected visit of Hannah Dunston to Dunstable in 1697, a woman as famous in her own right as John Lovewell.[30]

A woman who bested males in combat was a rarity. An Englishwoman who took on Indian captors was rarer still. Yet Hannah Dunston not only escaped her Native captives, she scalped ten Indians before leading two other English prisoners to safety. Her account not only thrilled New Englanders but provided scalping with a certain cachet as well as added publicity. Scalping had been a New World practice. Native Americans normally decapitated heads of their enemies; taking just a portion of the head, the scalp, provided similar proof and was much easier to transport for both Indians and English interested in collecting bounties for their handiwork. During the Pequot War of 1637, Connecticut offered a reward for enemy heads; by 1675, head skins fetching thirty shillings apiece had become the norm. Massachusetts joined the scalping bandwagon in 1689: soldiers received eight pounds per scalp plus whatever booty they could find. Settlers looking to even scores or gain extra money had added incentives to go on the offensive, turning war into a financial enterprise.[31]

Enter Hannah Dunston. The recently pregnant mother had been abducted from Haverhill, Massachusetts, and her child killed on the march to Canada. Weeks passed and miles mounted. A dozen Native Americans guarded Hannah, Mary Neff, a nurse, and a young English boy, but there were only two adult males among the captors, with three adult females and seven children rounding out the numbers. After traveling a hundred and fifty miles, Dunston hatched a plan to escape. She also wished to avenge her slain child. One night she quietly stole a hatchet from a sleeping adult male and calmly proceeded to scalp everyone—men, women, and children. Only an older woman and a child awoke in time to escape the stealthy attack. Dunston then attached the scalps to her belt and guided Neff and the boy to safety. Little wonder she would be described as the most "famous woman in New England."[32]

Hannah Dunston's actions transcended Puritan notions of gender. That is, if women were considered the "weaker vessels" in Puritan minds, Dunston certainly gave the lie to that image, having outdone male scalp hunters in a decidedly tight situation. That she avoided recapture and returned with scalps in hand and companions safely in tow was equally remarkable; even experienced scouts would have found the elements and the terrain daunting, not to mention the fear of lurking Indians. As for provisions, Dunston must have used her captors' supplies. They may not have been sufficient, as a nineteenth-century source touted Dunston's safe return, "notwithstanding the dangers from the enemy and from famine in traveling through woods and across mountains and rivers." A grateful Massachusetts government awarded her twenty-five pounds. Neff and the English boy split another twenty-five. In fact, upon hearing the news the governor of Maryland offered an additional reward. Boston's leading citizens paid court to Dunston, and the Reverend Cotton Mather published an account of the episode.[33]

Stories of Dunston's exploits rippled across New England. The sheer sensationalism of the tale—a woman taking scalps and marching through the woods—furnished a compelling story line. Moreover, Dunstable residents claimed that Dunston had reached their settlement first. This is difficult to verify. Contemporary sources provide no information on this story; it may simply be a case of folklore linking together two of the best-known scalp hunters, Dunston and Lovewell. If it is true, however, the six-year-old Lovewell could have viewed the scalps and the woman carrying them. He certainly would have heard stories about Dunston's exploits, giving him something to ponder when the opportunity came to him to go venturing after Abenaki scalps.[34]

Peace in 1697 did not immediately restore the normal rhythms of life. The shock of recent events undoubtedly lingered, as wartime damages far eclipsed those of King Philip's War. Several selectmen, including William Tyng, Jonathan Tyng's son, petitioned the Massachusetts government in 1701, bewailing their town's pitiful state. Too few people had returned to Dunstable, they declared, and many who had were in "low circumstances," beset by failing grain crops that necessitated buying "bread corn out of town." Many nonresident proprietors were dispersed (some as far away as England), creating a leadership void. The recently glazed meetinghouse went unmentioned, but the selectmen could not support a clergyman. Massachusetts agreed to supply funds. Yet the Reverend Weld, the intended beneficiary, died in 1702, leaving Dunstable with the need to search anew for a spiritual leader with its meager

fiscal resources. Prospective candidates for the pulpit might well deem borderland Dunstable unattractive.[35]

Queen Anne's War jolted Dunstable further. The War of the Spanish
Secession, as it was called in Europe, saw the usual array of European nations
and their American colonies lined up to fight. In Dunstable, defensive considerations outweighed the search for a new minister by 1703. Events were seemingly repeating themselves—the Indians and the French attacked towns, killed
settlers, took captives, and burned buildings. New Englanders struggled to
respond. Dunstable should have been prepared. The memory of King William's
War was fresh enough and garrison houses stood sentinel as before, with men
such as William Tyng, Joseph Hassell, and others manning them. Precautions
notwithstanding, in 1703 an Indian war party surprised Robert Parris and his
family, killing the couple and their oldest daughter. The two younger daughters
safely hid in a cellar hogshead, but another wartime funeral took place.[36]

This time enraged Dunstable residents responded differently. Encouraged
by a government bounty that promised forty pounds for every male Indian
scalp (a tidy sum equivalent to a country minister's annual salary), Captain
William Tyng organized an early ranger party. Mobile hunting parties for-
malized what Benjamin Church had previously done. Only in this case vengeance and economics mattered as much as patriotism. Indeed, borderland
Dunstable's location was an apt staging ground, and William Tyng provided
the appropriate social imprimatur. News of Colonel John March's two expeditions to Pigwacket may have been additional factors: the first, in September,
turned up empty-handed; the second, in October, netted squaws, children,
and one old man. Captain William Tyng led his "snowshoe men" in December
and January of 1703 and 1704. No journal survives to detail the men's daily
treks and overall travails, but snowshoes meant "less difficulty in traveling."
That the company scalped five Indians resulted in a two-hundred-pound payout and Tyng's eventual promotion to major.[37]

What Tyng, March, and others did was to create a new kind of mobile
warfare based on subcontracting. Instead of relying on militia or impressing
local inhabitants, Massachusetts authorities employed scalping bounties as
an economical means of raising troopers to fight a particularly nasty type of
war. The patriotic could earn a tidy sum if successful; the greedy could appear
patriotic—after all, they had performed a wartime service. Enlistments ran
the length of the scout. Tyng had certainly done his part, but raids launched
from Dunstable may have put the town in the Indians' sights.

In 1706, Dunstable witnessed its bloodiest year of fighting: ten settlers died in assorted raids, which one chronicler attributed to Indian revenge for Tyng's campaign. One of the costliest occurred when Captain John Pearson of Rowley lodged his squad of men in Nathaniel Blanchard's house in July 1706. Armed men in the house should have guaranteed protection, except for the fact that Pearson neglected to post a guard. When Blanchard and his wife went out to milk the cow (another version suggests that they saw sheep placed by the Indians in the corn), the Indians killed John and kidnapped his wife. Entering the house, the assailants were surprised to see sleeping troopers yet recovered sufficiently to kill several of them and wound five others. Jacob Guletia, another Dunstable settler, was killed in his home at or near the same time.[38]

Nor did this end the bloodshed. Native Americans attacked John Cummings's residence, killing his wife, while he, with a broken arm, escaped to a swamp under cover of darkness. Cummings eventually reached Farwell's blockhouse. Three families in one month had suffered assault, with recently arrived soldiers offering no guarantee of protection. Any Abenaki payback for Tyng's earlier raid had been collected.[39]

Other tragedies followed in Dunstable. If Native Americans wished to settle scores, their elimination of Joseph English, Dunstable's foremost Indian ally in July 1706, was a capstone achievement. English, as his name suggests, had cast his lot with the colonists. That did not sit well with fellow Indians. They got their chance at English when he accompanied Lieutenant John Butterfield and his wife through the woods. A group of Natives captured Mrs. Butterfield while her husband escaped as other Indians caught English, intending to torture him. In response, English taunted his captors into shooting him, avoiding the lingering demise they had planned for him. Even so, Queen Anne's War had claimed another Dunstable casualty, and this a Native American who had sided with the townsfolk.[40]

No tombstone marked Joe English's grave, if indeed his body was ever found. Still, there were occasions when people recovered their dead killed in warfare for proper burial. The Deerfield raid of 1704 is a case in point. A large French and Indian raiding party carried off dozens of settlers, among them the Reverend John William and several family members. His wife was killed on the march north. Nonetheless, Williams derived comfort from the fact that neighbors had located the body and provided a "Christian burial" in Deerfield, far better than the alternative of being "left for meat to the fowls of the air and beasts of the earth."[41]

Dunstable residents knew how to render sepulture properly during wartime when circumstances allowed. In 1704, James Blanchard, a leading citizen, received the customary winding sheet and coffin at the cost of one pound, eight shillings. But even the poor could expect such niceties. What gave Blanchard's send-off a certain style were the funeral gloves at one pound, one shilling, which provided an additional touch of status, indicating that even rural Dunstable was no stranger to funereal fashions.[42]

New England scouting parties thought more about leaving the bodies of Indians they had dispatched above ground as a message to any passersby. The degree of success such troops experienced remains difficult to gauge: historians are divided on whether American ranger companies weakened Indian resistance effectively. That these companies destroyed Native villages and crops while killing relatively few Indians became the pattern. As always, foul-ups occurred. In 1707 western New England, Captain Stoddard led a dozen Deerfield settlers following French and Indian tracks, then managed to mistakenly kill a white woman. Two years later Captain Benjamin Wright and company acquired two scalps on the way to Lake Champlain. Afterwards, they collided with a party of French and Indians holding English captives: frightened troopers dropped their packs and ran when inconclusive fighting threw them into a state of confusion; one scout was lost and presumed dead. Yet the Massachusetts House of Representatives praised Wright, being sold on scalping parties as an effective war tactic.[43]

What happened to scout commanders was as important as what occurred among their men. Success and failure were relative to the prize sought and the price paid. And Dunstable found itself paying unexpected costs yet again involving Major William Tyng. As battalion commander, Tyng held sway over local defense, keeping men trained for war and providing leadership. Injured between Groton and Lancaster, Tyng went to recuperate in Concord, Massachusetts, leaving the town deprived of its foremost defender. Tyng's death in 1710 added another name to the town's list of casualties.[44]

Queen Anne's War left Dunstable settlers emotionally shaken. The choice before them carried risks and consequences: should they stay and be on guard or relocate entirely to build a new home? Many chose the latter course. By 1711, only eleven families remained—too few to support a minister, if indeed one could be found—and the town bemoaned the "calamities of the several Indian rebellions and depredations," which had "reduced in our estate, and lessened in our numbers . . . so that we are not capable wholly to support the ministry of the Gospel." Dunstable's ministers found this out for themselves: after two years' service, the Reverend Ames Cheever declined the offer of the position; the Reverend Samuel Hunt complained about going unpaid for over half a year. The Reverend Samuel Parris, the minister during Salem's infamous witchcraft scare, assumed the pulpit by 1708 before leaving several years later for Sudbury, Massachusetts. Whatever Dunstable's covenant said about Christian behavior, church members must have been growing impatient if not angry about not being able to keep ministers long in their pulpit. Not until 1720 would the Reverend Nathaniel Prentice take on that responsibility for a lengthy sojourn.[45]

What can be said about Dunstable? Among the farmhouses stood the ever-present garrison houses—silent structures reminding its inhabitants of the unsettled state of borderland life. They had been inadequate in 1706 to stop stealthy attacks that claimed the lives of several townsfolk. People seeking the consolations of faith often had to look within themselves or consult their family Bible—ministers seemed to be running from the pulpit too. As one chronicler observed: "Thus fear and suffering had been the condition of the settlement for many years. Fear and desolation reigned everywhere. Compelled to dwell in garrisons, and to labor at the constant peril of life, how could the settlers thrive?"[46] How indeed could they prosper when neighbors departed or died, ministers stayed but briefly, and peace appeared tenuous and short-lived? To characterize Dunstable as a community on edge might seem to be an overstatement—other communities suffered more heavily from Indians raids and depopulation—but townsfolk had plenty of reasons to wonder about their life.

The Lovewells lived amid this uncertainty. They noticed settlers' departures, watched clergy come and go, and knew about fatal Indians attacks. That some Lovewells remained in Dunstable indicates a degree of stubbornness—they were part of that small group still hanging on in 1711. But they resided in the shadows of other families. The Tyng family dominated the town and the region; people turned to them first for political and military leadership. People mourned their demise: when Jonathan Tyng died in 1724, for instance, his death drew a "great number of persons of distinction from other towns" to his Woburn, Massachusetts, burial. The nearest thing to local gentry, the Tyng family seemingly knew how to get things done, whether it meant defending the town or leading assaults against the Abenakis. Accordingly, Eleazer Tyng donned the family mantle by becoming a justice of the peace in 1721 and a colonel in 1722, his lineage a springboard to office and rank. People were comfortable with a Tyng at the helm. Still, Eleazer fell short of the family standards despite his offices and "never achieved his father's honors." The first Tyng in Dunstable had preserved the struggling settlement and helped lead the settlers. His son William Tyng had commanded snowshoe men in an early scalping party. Eleazer Tyng relied on the family name more than his past achievements for recognition. Could the Lovewells hope to attain recognition in their stead?[47]

The Lovewells possessed more modest antecedents than the Tyngs, Cummingses, or Hassells, who dominated affairs in Dunstable. Respectability proved to be within their reach, but prominence required something more. Only a few could truly stand out. None of the Lovewells assumed a leadership position in the church; their political participation, although more substantial, did not overshadow that of other middling citizens called to public service. Yet, at times, the Lovewells desired notice and positioned themselves more advantageously.

John Lovewell's fame as an Indian fighter induced chroniclers and genealogists alike to graft limbs upon his family tree. If some elements had a basis in fact—Lovewell did have fighting forebearers—other aspects reveal suspect social embroidery designed to embellish the family lineage. The Lovewells had missed the first great wave of Puritan migration in the 1630s. While thousands arrived to the "City upon a Hill," motivated by a mix of economic, religious, and family considerations, the Lovewells stayed in England; neither Charles I nor the English Civil War drove them off. Consequently, John Lovewell's grandfather, also named John, had missed an opportunity to fight in the Pequot War in 1637. Chroniclers nevertheless argued that John Lovewell, the Indian fighter, came from heroic English stock.[48]

In the 1640s, king and Parliament unfurled their respective standards to mark the English Civil War. The swirl and confusion of fighting featured musketeers, pikemen, and cavalry. Artillery also hewed down soldiers in battle. The Thirty Years' War had been longer and bloodier, devastating large swaths of Europe, but the English Civil War uprooted certain regions with a destructive force as great as that experienced in the Continent. Years of fighting laid waste to the landscape. If Londoners sat smugly behind their defenses, seemingly removed from battlefield violence, other English citizens felt the war's fury directly, whether perpetrated by Cavaliers or Roundheads. And John Lovewell, the grandfather of Captain Lovewell, was just old enough to recall that war.[49]

Tradition relates that the first John Lovewell served under Oliver Cromwell; if this is true, he must have learned something about military discipline, for Cromwell had revolutionized seventeenth-century English fighting with his New Model Army. Cromwell's campaign against the Irish displayed a mix of aggression and savagery that cowed the populace into submission. Yet stories about John Lovewell put him as an ensign under Cromwell in 1653, several years after the Civil War's end, with Ireland already put to the sword. The British Isles were relatively peaceful. Perhaps soldiering meant that John Lovewell manned a garrison, following commands and mastering drill; it did not necessarily mean going into battle.[50]

Further confusing the issue is the fact that John Lovewell and his son, the father of Captain John Lovewell, shared the same name. More than one account claims that the John Lovewell who served under Cromwell lived to a ripe old age of one hundred and ten or one hundred and twenty in the eighteenth century. This Lovewell was commonly depicted as a devout churchgoer and spry centenarian who chased errant youths from his orchard, cane in hand. Some poetic license as well as shabby research and identical names gave this myth a foundation in town histories.[51]

More recent accounts have corrected these mistakes. John Lovewell, the family's New England founder, arrived in Boston sometime during the 1650s, worked as a tanner, married Elizabeth Sylvester in 1658, and had a son, John Lovewell, in 1660, the vigorous, noncentenarian cane-wielding father of John the scalp hunter. He may have lived into his nineties, but he did not reach the century mark.[52]

In Massachusetts, the first John Lovewell started out in Boston, the destination of most overseas arrivals. If the immigrant Lovewell found the Puritan seaport unappealing, he wisely relocated and acquired land in Rehoboth and Lynn. He may have put his military training to use: during King Philip's War one of the Lovewells, either the father or grandfather of Captain Lovewell, saw service in the Great Swamp Fight and was fortunate to survive that Pyrrhic victory without lasting injuries. The first Lovewell moved to the borderlands of Dunstable after 1682, the date of the first land allotment. Various people awarded two hundred, three hundred, or even more acreage appeared, but no Lovewells were on the list. Indeed, only two troopers, John and Daniel Waldo, "by the order of the selectman," actually resided in the town to be. Nevertheless, Lovewell impressed the inhabitants enough to be chosen a selectman in 1689. But age conditioned Lovewell senior to be cautious—the fear of Indian attacks during King William's War prompted him, his wife, a son, Joseph, and his three married daughter to relocate to Sudbury, Massachusetts, leaving John Lovewell II to continue the family name there.[53]

The younger Lovewell presumably received a share of the estate after his father relocated. Indian threats did not scare him off. If life in Dunstable meant fortified houses and stationed troops, then Lovewell would make the necessary adjustments. The younger Lovewell had married Anna Hassell in 1688, member of an extensive clan active in town affairs. Dunstable agreed with John II: one chronicler intoned that John II "was industrious, honest, and respected and frequently was elected to office." Like the Cummingses, Tyngs, Hassells, and others, in 1699 John II dutifully paid his wood rate for the minister. Starting out as a surveyor of the highways in 1688, Lovewell served as a hog constable, fence viewer, and field driver over the next three decades, and was perceived as "industrious, honest, and respected." In 1693 he became a selectman. In 1718 Lovewell was part of a five-man committee selected to pour over the town books to determine the original proprietor grants and ensure that settlers received just allotments. This was a delicate matter—no one liked to be called out for land grabbing. This also appears to have been Lovewell's last political service.[54]

John II did distinguish himself economically. The former selectman had developed the confidence to diversify. In September 2, 1718, he and the future Captain Lovewell received government permission to dam Salmon Brook to construct a sawmill.[55] Such ventures required capital, skill, labor, and location; few farmers contemplated undertaking such enterprises. Indeed, sawmill ownership meant importing fine-edged steel from England, hiring masons for millstones, and constructing a dam for the sluice. Too much or too little water would halt operations during droughts, freshets, and freezes. However, a well-run mill would produce a hundred board feet of plank an hour, more efficient than two men sawing logs in a pit. Humming saw blades meant business, and the Lovewells felt confident enough to take this gamble. No one worried about sawdust fouling rivers or streams—resources seem inexhaustible—and with luck Lovewell's mill would rank John II above typically middling farmers.[56]

John Lovewell II also built a store. Both the sawmill and the store represented investments as well as hazards: stockpiles of wood and sawdust provided combustible materials, while guns and gunpowder might attract warring Native Americans more interested in theft than payment. Yet, Lovewell's establishments survived Indian threats to Dunstable, perhaps because of "his kindness to them," as one chronicler observed. Did Lovewell trade with Indians? One account appears to indicate as much. Whatever the truth, John II occupied an economic niche in Dunstable that propelled him into the broad middling ranks of the community.[57]

The Lovewells did recognize the precarious nature of early Dunstable life. In their old age on March 16, 1744, John and Anna Lovewell filed an affidavit, classified by one town historian as the first town history. The deposition was a highly personal memory portrait, and what they remembered was telling. Instead of painting a picture of growth and harmony, their ownership of sawmill and store, John and Anna bemoaned neighbors lost to Indian attacks. Twenty-five residents had been killed over the years—modest numbers compared to hard-pressed Deerfield, Massachusetts, of course, yet memorable enough to the Lovewells. The Lovewells talked about their home and listed neighbors and family lost. Anna cited her father, mother, and brother slain in a "surprise attack." Two weeks later her aunts' husbands, Obediah Perry and Christopher Temple, lost their lives by the Nashua River. The Temple Rock by the river later served as a de facto memorial and memory site. The Lovewells mentioned the Dunstable garrison houses too. With seven garrison houses and thirteen families in 1711, crowding was rarely an issue, but since some of the Hassells, Perrys, and Temples had never reached these sanctuaries, it obviously proved an issue for the Lovewells.[58]

The Lovewells' deposition, given in a court lawsuit in the Supreme Court of Judicate for New Hampshire, came about because of a legal action between Joseph Kidder and the Proprietors of Londonderry. More important, the deposition opens a window into John Lovewell's early life. He had seen the town grow and scatter. What his parents related, John had heard or observed. In wartime, violent death often befell the unfortunate or unprepared, as weak borders separated the living from the dead—or in this instance, the settler exposed in the field from the neighbor in the garrison house. Lovewell family stories were constructed around such tales emphasizing the fragility of life.[59]

John Lovewell witnessed some of this. Born in 1691, the year his maternal grandparents were slain, John III spent his early boyhood in a struggling community whose inhabitants often decamped when Indian trouble arose. The call to arms and the retreat to the garrison house were parts of this life. Lovewell was not alone: besides his parents there was a sister Hannah, born in 1698, and brothers Zaccheus and Jonathan, born in 1701 and 1713 respectively, who rounded out the brood surviving to adulthood. Yet, the gap in years suggests that other siblings had died young. No Abenaki could be blamed for that; it was simply something that occurred in some families more unlucky than others. As the oldest son, Lovewell could foresee a future beyond farmwork, courtesy of his father's mill and store. Accounts and ledger figures would occupy young John if he chose to follow his father's path. Even so, the timber cut in the family mill came from the nearby woods; so did furs exchanged for store goods. Perhaps this explains why young Lovewell was an "eager and successful hunter"—he wanted to see the source of the products. Prowling the woods in Queen Anne's War and guarding the borders with the town's mounted patrol were expected activities for young Dunstable males. Dunstable residents, familiar with the exploits of Hannah Dunston and William Tyng, knew about scalping, and John was certainly no exception. After all, if the legends were true, Hannah Dunston had stopped by the Lovewell household.[60]

Family responsibilities superseded the call of the forest. Lovewell had agreed to help his father with the sawmill in 1718, and his marriage to Hannah, a woman of uncertain background—no genealogist has determined her surname—quickly produced two children. Lovewell also had a two-hundred-acre tract to farm. Perhaps he preferred that activity to the family business.[61] With peace in 1713, John Lovewell, and indeed the rest of Dunstable residents, could concentrate upon their livelihoods. The local Indian population had diminished. John the Indian received a seven-shillings coffin in 1719 courtesy of a benevolent benefactor, but any mourners went without funeral gloves to his interment. The church, meanwhile, prospered under the Reverend Nathaniel Prentice, and Lieutenant Henry Farwell and Joseph Blanchard erected family pews. If positioned close to the Reverend Prentice, a "man of wit and good sermons," they received good value for their money, able to see and be seen.[62]

Yet peace, however welcome, could hardly obscure Massachusetts's tangled relationship with the Abenaki Nation. Nor could Dunstable residents rest easy. Three wars with the Abenakis had resulted in raids and scalping. Who was to say they might not occur again? After 1713, the Abenakis hedged their bets, trading with both the French and the English, while Father Sebastian Rale continued his missionary work among the Abenakis. But the Abenakis did not need Rale to warn them to be suspicious of English trading activities in Maine—they could see their effects for themselves. Tensions simmered in 1721 after the Massachusetts government placed a price on Father Rale's head. Near present-day Vermont the Western Abenakis, led by the charismatic Gray Lock, resented encroaching English settlements. A scenario for war was developing. It was only a question of when and how Dunstable would be drawn into the approaching conflict.[63]

Dummer's War in 1722 ended hope of continuing peace in Massachusetts, and especially in borderland communities such as Dunstable. Attacks by Abenaki war parties compelled New Englanders to again call upon scouting parties to invade the Indian backcountry. The sporadic hit-and-run nature of these raids, English and Indian, would draw Dunstable more directly into the fray.[64]

In Dunstable, life seemingly continued as before minus one singular wartime exception—this time the town refused to panic as its residents held their ground. Nor did they flee to the nearest garrison houses. Perhaps those structures had outlived their usefulness. In Queen Anne's War, for instance, the dreaded year of fatalities in 1706 had occurred among people in or by their homes. Not everyone could make it to these sanctuaries in time, and if Indians attacked stealthily, who would spread the word among the settlers to go to the buildings? Venturing into the woods, residents knew, was to court danger unless individuals went armed and in numbers, and perhaps the same was true for garrison houses unless the alarm had been rung well in advance.

Yet the fighting drew men to Dunstable. The town's location by the New Hampshire border had turned the community into a jumping-off point for scouting parties; it was also near well-worn trails to Abenaki interior villages. In September 1722 Captain John Cagon led forty-eight men intent on securing scalps. His approach from Dunstable took him northward up the Merrimac River before veering along other rivers, reliant upon smaller scouting parties to check for signs of Indians. Terrain hampered Cagon's troop, who never discovered Abenaki tracks. Ironically, the scouts did locate tracks of New Englanders, indicating that others had gone in pursuit of the same goal. As Cagon concluded in his journal, "we passed down said river to Dunstable again and which tedious march through gods goodness to us we accomplished in seventeen days—but twenty days from our habitations."[65]

A more telling episode brought Dummer's War directly to Dunstable's border in September 1724. Two men, Nathan Cross and Thomas Blanchard, decided to extract turpentine north of the river, a seemingly mundane task. Naval stores provided added revenue for farmers, and numerous sap-running trees dotted the New Hampshire and Massachusetts borderlands. But this was wartime and two men alone might run the risk of attack. Perhaps Cross and Blanchard were overconfident; or maybe sap tapping trumped personal security. In any event, raiding Indians seized Cross and Blanchard, but not before one of them had scribbled a message without his captors' seeing. When the two men did not return, concerned Dunstable residents knew where to look for them, spotted the turpentine seeping from the hoopless barrels, and deduced their neighbors' plight from "certain marks on the trees made from coal mixed with grease." Ten settlers set off in hot pursuit. The Abenakis, however, ambushed and killed most of the would-be rescuers along the banks of the Merrimack River. At the column's rear, Josiah Farwell escaped detection by hiding in a thicket. Another injured survivor may have also reached town before dying. An exhausted Farwell led townsfolk to the site to retrieve the dead.[66]

Somber townsfolk collected the remains. Leaving the corpses in the wood to be ravaged by birds and animals was unthinkable. Had not Cotton Mather made the consequences of that clear in his late seventeenth-century diatribe? Discovering eight bodies, the townsfolk ensured that they were "decently interred in one capacious grave." Interestingly enough, family members did not distinguish among the survivors, suggesting the corpses had been mutilated. The *Boston News Letter* reported that the slain men had been "carefully gathered together," given individual coffins, and "decently inter'd . . . being much lamented not only by near Relations, but also by the numerous Assembly attending the Funeral." In time, one of the men, Thomas Lund, merited a monument, an inscription on which read: "This man with seven more that lies in / this grave was slew all in a day by the Indians." The tragedies of 1706 seemed to be repeating themselves.[67]

It was at this juncture that John Lovewell entered the picture. As an experienced woodsman, Lovewell offered sorely needed expertise; he also had a personal stake in this matter—Josiah Farwell was husband to his sister Hannah. Some of the slain rescue party may have been leading citizens, but they were amateurs in woodland fighting. In contrast, tradition held that Lovewell was "inured to danger" and the slayer of seven Indians north of town in an earlier escapade. That he had not been among the original party indicates how quickly the men had dashed off. Like William Tyng, the snowshoe scout in 1704, Dunstable residents wanted revenge, and the recently commissioned Captain John Lovewell, assisted by his brother-in-law Lieutenant Farwell and Ensign Jonathan Robbins, seemed the ideal man for the task.[68]

The three men drafted a petition to the provincial government. They asked for expenses, five shillings a day, "in case they killed any enemy Indians and possessed their scalps, they will employ in Indian hunting one whole year and if they do not within that time kill any, they are content to be allowed nothing for their wages time and trouble." It was a curious choice of words. These men knew about the hundred-pound bounty for Indian scalps, at one point asking the government to give them "over and above their wages" for any scalps. But they insisted upon expenses if they did not kill any Abenakis. Perhaps they were being cautious. A twenty-man detachment—smaller than the norm—would have cost five pounds a day, or roughly 150 pounds for a month in the field. By November, the General Court responded with a counteroffer—the men would receive two shillings, five pence a day "for the time they are actually out in service," verified by "exact journals or accounts at the time they [are] out in the woods and where they go, as well as the time they may be at home." No expense padding would be tolerated; nor could the expedition number above fifty individuals. The one-hundred-pound scalp bounty would take care of any financial needs.[69]

Other factors influenced Lovewell's decision. Massachusetts towns sent expeditions lured by the prospect of bounties to hunt Indians. They represented a chance for young men to supplement income from farmwork and perhaps gain a measure of social recognition by a feat of arms. For instance, John Lovewell came from a moderately situated family with agricultural and commercial holdings. Yet he had little political standing, being respected more for woodland knowledge than government leadership. On the other hand, Captain Lovewell was now a man with a provincial title. This set him upon his odyssey as an officially sanctioned and recognized Indian hunter, providing a seal of official approval not otherwise forthcoming. Like Dunstable men before him, Lovewell was going to war to hunt for scalps.

Dunstable had grown from a fragile settlement into an established borderland community over the course of the late seventeenth and early eighteenth centuries. The village's location in northern Massachusetts, overwhelming to some early settlers, including Lovewell's grandfather, meant that they departed for safer terrain when violence threatened. Despite Indian raiding, Dunstable residents hunkered down in garrison houses; and some who left it returned home when peace reappeared. That any sort of institutional life developed was impressive. Resident town selectmen slowly took over from nonresidents; the church managed despite an uncertain supply of ministers.

The region's leading family, the Tyngs, provided a certain social tone: they had supplied early leadership, built fortified homes, stayed put while others fled, and led early scalping expeditions. The Tyngs were still esteemed in the 1720s—their wealth and status assured that—but the villagers now chose men closer to them such as John Lovewell to go after Abenakis. In their neighbors' minds the Tyngs had moved on.

For John Lovewell, the war between the Abenakis and Massachusetts would provide a testing ground. Whatever the truth or fabrication of the tales that circulated about his youthful exploits, tales that multiplied after his 1725 expedition, the fact that townsfolk desired him to be their captain remains instructive. John Lovewell was deemed to have leadership qualities. The scope of these talents would reveal itself in 1724 and 1725.

CHAPTER 3
Deaths and Burials in Dummer's War, 1722–1725

On July 25, 1722, Samuel Shute, the Royal Governor of Massa-chusetts, proclaimed the province at war with the eastern Abenakis. The long-simmering tensions over territorial claims and Indian hostages had finally boiled over. Attempts to reconcile these differences in 1721 had failed, resulting in provocative English actions and Abenaki retal-iation. Accordingly, Shute condemned the Indian nation, branding them "Robbers, Traitors, and Enemies to his Majesty King George." For several years Massachusetts, New Hampshire, and the Abenaki Nation exchanged raids and counterraids. With the arrival of peace in 1726, the eastern Abenakis' threat to Maine and New Hampshire was contained; Shute was in England, a political casualty, victim of the unusually fierce battle he waged with the Massachusetts assembly; and Captain John Lovewell emerged as New England's newest mar-tyred hero, his 1725 death trumpeted in verse and song.[1] Yet, Lovewell, the fallen captain, was hardly the only notable or remembered casualty to emerge from the war. His death, although detailed in newspapers and sermons, shared space alongside other fatalities giving New Englanders pause. Those slain before Lovewell warranted a niche in the popular memory too. No final tabulation of deaths apparently exists, but William Williamson, a nineteenth-century historian, claimed that Maine alone suffered two hundred people dead, mortally wounded, or seized—modest figures compared to King Philip's War yet very real to the victims' families and friends. The mode of death added poignancy as well. Military men recognized the risks involved in their calling— they guarded settlements, scouted woods, or assailed Abenaki villages—but civilians caught off-guard in fields or homes sometimes did not. Nighttime proved especially dangerous to such folk. In fact, the Massachusetts government advised borderland settlers in 1722 to be prepared against "their barbarous, murdering adversaries, who seldom or never appear or face any in the day time but in the silentest time of the night."[2]

Once people died, the wartime dynamic changed. Rescuing the dead from defilement, securing the remains, and properly burying them became major responsibilities. Interments redefined war deaths by bestowing upon the fallen the final office of respect, in keeping with New England faith and practice. Typically, Spartan affairs near or at battle sites afforded a measure of emotional closure, protecting bodies from predators and the elements. Slain Abenakis inspired different usage. Listed as approximate numbers in reports and newspapers, dead Abenakis were usually left where they had been slain, with many of them scalped for good measure. Military expeditions into Abenaki territory could not inter enemy remains—the threat of counterattack loomed menacingly; besides, sepulture's denial marked an additional, final triumph over a foe, a victor's calling card bloodily imprinted upon the landscape.[3]

Dummer's War interments constituted a political as well as cultural dynamic. That the dead should be buried was expected. If and how the wartime dead would be buried proved more difficult, reflecting the distance from the fighting. While soldiers and borderland civilians tried to retrieve and safeguard the bodies of fallen neighbors and comrades, Boston residents (secured from Abenaki assaults) could indulge in more traditional burial practices. Indeed, officials, clerics, and citizens orchestrated interments along class lines while mindful of propriety and funeral extravagance. Newspapers detailed and commented upon noteworthy interments. Yet even Boston residents saw war's shadow occasionally descend: citizens still focused on battlefield fatalities too tragic to ignore. The mode of death in battle or the person slain might evoke sympathy or outrage. Then Bostonians confronted the perceived enemies from within: arsonists, for instance, whose action set off alarms; or pirates from outside who threatened the seaport's commerce. Both, if caught, might grace Boston's gallows. Bostonians' obsequies emerged within the context of graveyard ceremonies, circulated warnings, public executions, and funeral tributes. Before Captain John Lovewell secured his niche as a military martyr, other individuals received public attention as part and parcel of Dummer's War deaths.[4]

Dummer's War represented a small-scale affair in the larger realm of imperial rivalries, dwarfed by the recently ended War of the Spanish Succession in 1713. Europe had entered a moderately quiet period. France, Great Britain, and their respective allies acted to minimize continental violence. What British Imperial historians have labeled the Age of Salutary Neglect meant more or less precisely that: the center of empire in London would legislate; the colonists would overlook inconvenient statutes. Aggressive colonists rarely feared, or heeded, European restrictions anyway. For Massachusetts, with land claims extending into present-day Maine, the eastern Abenaki Nation's subordination remained crucial to furthering trade, encouraging settlement, and preserving peace. The French in Canada, intent on retaining connections with the Abenakis, disapproved. The Abenakis wanted to preserve their autonomy. European calm could not hide the very real tensions in this northeastern corner of the New World.[5]

Massachusetts's involvement with the Abenakis dated from the seventeenth century. Three prior wars had been followed by treaties and agreements. As settlers ventured into the eastern territories, the Abenakis had to balance the lure of trade goods against the price of the newcomers' demands. Particular personalities added to the uncertain relationship. Governor Samuel Shute had insisted on Abenaki acknowledgment of George I's sovereignty; Father Sebastian Rale, a Jesuit missionary living in Norridgewock, a major Abenaki settlement, wished to maintain France as the paramount presence among his charges. In this contest, Shute proved to be outmatched: he was a governor battling a defiant assembly; Rale was a respected, well-established preacher. Even so, the Abenakis, intent on preserving their autonomy, refused to be bullied. Shute's 1722 declaration of war resolved any uncertainty over the character of eastern Abenaki and Massachusetts relations.[6]

Boundary issues paved the pathway to war. According to the 1713 Treaty of Utrecht, Great Britain assumed ownership of French Acadia, now Nova Scotia; less clear was who owned the parts of Maine, notably the area around the St. George River, which belonged to Britain. Governor Shute corresponded with his French counterpart, Governor Vaudreuil, denouncing French influence over the Abenakis; Vaudreuil insisted that the English steer clear of the St.

George River lest Native hostilities result. After Shute's departure for England, Lieutenant Governor Dummer vainly continued to press these points and roundly condemned Father Sebastian Rale's meddling with the Abenakis.[7]

Rale remained a pivotal figure of the war. What New Englanders labeled Dummer's or Lovewell's War was referred to among the French Canadians as Rale's War. While Lovewell came to define English courage and martyrdom, Rale garnered similar accolades among Native Americans and French Canadian Catholics. A missionary priest killed by Protestants could be seen by them as a martyr to his faith. New Englanders thought otherwise. Francis Parkman described Rale as possessing a "strong, enduring frame, and a keen vehement, caustic spirit." By contrast, Cotton Mather usually subjected Rale to a barrage of anti-Catholic abuse. The opinionated Mather also perceived him as the instigator of Abenaki strikes against English settlements. A more nuanced view reveals Rale to have been a conscientious Jesuit whose mastery of Abenaki language and custom over long years of service had won his charges' trust. In fact, it might even be argued that Rale had not only converted the Abenakis but had to a degree been converted by them.[8]

New England officials had recognized Rale's importance long before Dummer's War became a reality or Captain John Lovewell attained prominence. The various Anglo-Abenaki wars had made officials sensitive to perceived threats on their borders. Massachusetts razed Rale's early chapel in 1705, part of the destruction resulting from Queen Anne's War, in hope of derailing the missionary's work. This only inspired Rale to rebuild a more lavish structure. With peace, the English changed tactics, dispatching the Reverend Joseph Baxter to the region in 1717. Ideally, they thought, Abenakis converted to Reformed Christianity would counter Rale's influence. Baxter learned little of the Abenaki language, a strategic mistake in the quest for converts, and resorted to distributing trinkets to Native children. In fact, Baxter avoided Rale's Norridgewock mission and any nearby villages where the Jesuit might preach. Nonetheless, Rale left nothing to chance, threatening to leave the mission if any Abenakis accepted conversion from Baxter. He followed this up with a pledge to excommunicate the apostates.[9]

Rale and Baxter clashed more directly in print. Baxter had scornfully denied the validity of Catholic sacraments, icons, and rituals before the Abenakis, prompting Rale, in what James Axtell has called a "master stroke," to take up his pen. As a former professor of rhetoric and Greek, Rale wielded a quill as sharp as any sword, skewering Baxter with a one-hundred-page Latin response, then dismissing Baxter's defiant curt reply as bad Latin. In fact, a follow-up letter from Rale pointedly targeted Baxter's grammatical shortcomings. That Rale employed a classical Latin and Baxter a more contemporary Latin style may explain the stylistic dispute. When Governor Shute wrote Rale that Baxter was a missionary, not a Latin scholar, it underscored New Englanders' frustration in the battle for Abenaki souls. By 1719, after Baxter's departure, a still resolute Cotton Mather insisted to the Reverend James Woodside, a Scots-Irish minister in New England, that the Abenakis needed conversion, and that "you need not be shy of encountering the poor priest / Rale / that poisons them." Illness prevented Woodside from accepting the challenge.[10]

Other contacts between Rale and New Englanders proved more amicable. A troublesome shoulder injury sent the Jesuit to the Reverend Hugh Adams of Arrowsic, a talented physician, in 1716. For several days Adams tended Rale, refusing compensation. Adams believed that Rale could preserve the peace. What Rale thought about his doctor remains unknown—he never mentioned the episode in his correspondence—but Samuel Sewall, a prominent Boston official and dutiful diary writer, also extended an olive branch to the Jesuit. After negotiations in 1721 between Massachusetts and the Abenakis, Sewall sent Rale a book of religious meditations. He customarily offered books as gifts to friends, so his gesture represented a cultural overture designed to encourage communication. The gift also went unrecorded by Rale. Nonetheless, such efforts do testify to the perceived political stature Rale had among the Abenakis that made him too significant for Massachusetts to ignore.[11]

A series of provocative incidents set the Abenakis and the English on a course toward war. Rale and the Abenakis deposited a letter at an English fort in 1721 demanding that Massachusetts settlers leave. Massachusetts responded with a one-hundred-pound bounty for Rale's capture. Rale narrowly escaped a one-hundred-man force sent to capture him in Norridgewock in January 1722, but Colonel Thomas Westbrook, the expedition's leader, discovered Rale's papers, proof to Massachusetts officials that French officials were behind Indian aggression. Enraged Abenakis kidnapped several Maine families in June, burnt a New England sloop, and assaulted the Massachusetts fort at St. George River.[12]

Abenaki attacks left some Massachusetts residents more thoughtful than vengeful. Indian hating, a perennial cultural staple in the colonial borderlands, displayed a more complex dynamic in early eighteenth-century Massachusetts. There were, for instance, the captive New Englanders, whose possible recovery overshadowed any declaration of war: What would happen to them if fighting broke out? Some Massachusetts legislators blamed the Indian violence on crafty, corrupt merchants using alcohol-fueled exchanges to fleece the Natives. Should the Abenakis be condemned when the blame lay with others? Simple Indian hating would not have permitted such questions.

People also noted the cost of warfare, if declared, and the government's failure to provide enough trading houses as stipulated in Indian treaties. Opponents countered that the Indians, if so abused, should have approached the government first, as stated by treaty. The Abenakis' failure to do so, these critics argued, necessitated a declaration of war. An Abenaki attack on Brunswick, Maine, in the summer of 1722 that destroyed the settlement put an end to any debate. What was most likely Abenaki retaliation for the Norridgewock raid impelled Governor Shute to declare war.[13]

Governor Shute's rocky relationship with the Assembly undermined military planning. The legislature jealously guarded its prerogatives, concerned about executive encroachment. As Thomas Hutchinson remarked, "Foreign wars often delivered Greece and Rome from their intestine broils and animosities but this war furnished a new subject for confusion." The appointment of military commanders produced an administrative stalemate between governor and legislature. Until Shute's departure from Massachusetts in late December 1722, permitting the less controversial Lieutenant Governor William Dummer to take charge, political combat proved as heated, if less deadly, than the violence-torn Massachusetts borderlands.[14]

To add to the troubles, the western Abenakis rose up against Massachusetts. Growing Indian concerns over English incursions—in particular the settling of territory—had finally exploded. Not surprisingly, shaky trade relations between the English and Indians spurred the violent outbreak; Grey Lock, a prominent sachem, led the uprising. Less bloody than the eastern conflict, the western Abenakis compelled the Bay Colony to wage a two-front war. Neighboring Connecticut refused assistance, more concerned with defending its borders than sending troops into eastern Abenaki territory. Only French neutrality limited Grey Lock's assault. The English relied on blockhouses before resorting to scouting parties against the western Abenakis. Despite the eastern Abenakis' capitulation in 1726, the western Abenakis would continue fighting until 1727.[15]

In response, Massachusetts tightened its security. Governor Shute prohibited friendly Indians from entering settlements without written government permission; they were further forbidden to harbor hostile Native Americans. Local villagers sent suspicious Indians to Boston for interrogation. Six Indians picked up in Dunstable, Lovewell's hometown, appeared in the Bay Colony capital on July 23, 1722, to be examined; two days later fifteen Indians arrived from Nashaway. Eager for allies, Massachusetts approached the Mohawk Nation, an important Iroquois Confederation member, in search of aid. The Iroquois Confederation stayed officially neutral, unwilling to provoke the French in Canada, despite repeated pressure from Massachusetts. It did permit individual Mohawks to fight alongside New Englanders, however. Now the issue was persuading those individual Mohawks to take up arms.[16]

Boston knew how to woo visiting Indians when necessary. Whatever individual borderland settlers felt about Abenaki raiders, Boston officials recognized that waging war involved more than just recruiting scalp-hunting settlers. What scouts such as Lovewell and others did Native allies could also do, and perhaps do better. Consequently, the attempt to gain Indian support, underscored by gifts and entertainment, was part and parcel of colonial diplomatic protocol. Once, when a group of French Mohawks arrived in Boston, city fathers boarded them for nineteen days, paying for food, drink, and tobacco while footing the bill for broken chairs, tables, mugs, and utensils—out-of-hand entertainment costs were simply absorbed. In September 1723, visiting Indian chiefs witnessed a demonstration of New England firepower, in which a specially designed musket shot eleven balls in two minutes. At Castle William, the seaport's defensive bastion, the Council and House of Representatives set off the fortress guns for the Indian visitors. The HMS *Seahorse* delivered a broadside for good measure, joined by several merchant ships. The festivities climaxed on Boston Commons, where an open-air feast drew thousands of residents, highlighted by Indian music and dancing. Even though the payoff proved modest—only six of the visiting Mohawks volunteered to fight the Abenakis—Bostonians had elaborately showcased their good intentions.[17]

Some Indian visits to Boston presented unexpected challenges. When an Indian chief suddenly died, provincial authorities spared few efforts. According to the *New England Courant*, the unnamed Mohawk was "magnificently interred" in October 1722, his coffin decorated with a drawn sword and the pall supported by six militia captains. Councilors, town justices, and other local worthies, including Colonel Penn Townsend and Judge Samuel Sewall, two of Boston's leading citizens, were numbered among the mourners.

Four other Mohawks followed the procession to the South burying ground. The somber spectacle, appropriate to what a prominent official might expect, dramatized the authorities' efforts to court friendly Native Americans. That so few Indians were present was not at issue—both the living and dead had been honored, and news of the burial ceremony might impress potential Native allies.[18]

Bostonians and death were well-worn acquaintances despite the city's distance from the battlefield. Newspaper accounts reiterating the horrific slayings normally reported more mundane urban deaths. Homicides were few and suicides rare, but deaths from illness, injury, accident, or natural causes were commonplace. If anything, Boston residents accepted life's uncertainties and recognized their responsibilities as Reformed Christians toward the deceased. Even sermons about the dead were published. That Puritan saints had died in the Lord did not prevent people from honoring their departure, for the deceased had once walked among the living as family and neighbors. As Cotton Mather reminded Bostonians in 1713, "We sojourn in a dying world; and the dead in all parts of the civil world, have their obsequies from the living." Respect was due them.[19] The aforementioned Mohawk funeral reported by the *New England Courant* shows the political aspects of death and burial during Dummer's War. The war that came to be associated with the slaying of Captain John Lovewell nevertheless witnessed other notable deaths, especially those with elaborately staged funerals. Newspapers not only informed readers of events but offered critical, provocative essays. News constituted a commodity capable of different presentations, and even such seemingly commonplace occurrences as death could be scrutinized in terms of interments. Boston boasted three newspapers, one of which the *Boston News Letter* founded in 1704, that dutifully reported ship arrivals, government proclamations, foreign events, and local happenings. The *Boston Gazette* challenged the *News Letter*'s monopoly in 1719, offering readers a more stylistic lead-faced news type. The *New England Courant,* edited by James Franklin, Benjamin Franklin's older brother, went beyond typeface to introduce belles lettres to Bostonians in 1721. The *Courant*'s sharply aimed essays often irritated Boston's political and religious elite. In fact, pointed essays and journalistic sallies would eventually land James Franklin in jail. One of the milder assaults concerned funerals. That the *Courant* had described a Mohawk chief's funeral would hardly disturb Boston's governing elite. But a September 1722 *Courant* article denouncing funeral orations for wealthy citizens that "flatter the deceased" rather than "instruct and admonish the living" more accurately reflected the paper's edgy tone. Because the Mohawk chief had received no oration his funeral was justifiable; white Bostonians whose money enabled them "to embalm their memory" were fitter subjects for criticism in wartime Boston.[20]

Still, it was the *Boston Gazette,* not the *Courant,* which first graphically alerted the public to borderland fatalities by commenting upon Moses Eaton's death. This incident provides a kind of social primer for understanding the New England response to Dummer's War deaths prior to John Lovewell's 1725 slaying. What the *Gazette* did was highlight the state of Eaton's corpse, distinct from the normal name, date, and location that such fatalities typically rated, providing a wartime lesson in sepulture's costs and benefits that emphasized an "anti-Indian sublime" designed to rally people against the Abenakis. At first, not everyone had blamed the Abenakis, fingering immoral traders or inadequate trade goods as the culprits. The manner of Eaton's death served to redirect blame to the Abenakis by reminding readers of the type of warfare Indians waged.[21]

Moses Eaton's death ended his relative obscurity and gave him a temporary celebrity. Either the son or brother of Samuel Eaton of Brunswick, Maine, Moses claimed ancestry among the town's early settlers, in particular one Captain Joseph Eaton, a militia captain and trapper.[22] When Captain Johnson Harmon, an emerging war hero, retaliated against the Abenaki attackers of Fort St. George in 1722, slaying eighteen or twenty of them, he discovered a grisly Indian war trophy, according to the *Gazette:* "they found the hand of a white man laid upon a stump and the body to which it had belonged hard by, which the Indians had most barbarously murdered, by cutting his tongue out and cutting off his noise and private parts besides having giving him innumerable stab wounds all over his body." Later accounts asserted that Eaton's arms and legs had been sliced off as well. Under English law, death followed by dismemberment was the usual punishment for traitors and state enemies. Here, an otherwise unknown settler, his carved body parts resembling those of a slaughtered animal, revealed to *Gazette* readers in graphic fashion war's bloody consequences. The scattered limbs and members added to the indignity. To the Indians, on the other hand, bodily desecration and the exchange of body parts represented a time-honored tradition according to which wartime foes not adopted into tribes could be dismembered. For the English, the death narratives of Eaton's scattered corpse presaged the arrival of a grisly mode of warfare—not necessarily different from that of King Philip's War several generations before, but one that settlers and wartime critics would have to muster courage to face.[23]

What happened to Eaton's remains was also crucial. Would they be left where they were scattered, or buried? Captain Johnson Harmon ordered the body parts to be gathered, determined to save the corpse from further depredation. The current battle site covered with recently slain Indians was an inappropriate burial site—returning Abenakis could easily discover the upturned earth—and time was pressing. Fear of pursuing Abenakis probably influenced Harmon's decision. Collecting and carrying the remains without a coffin must have been ghoulish business. In Brunswick, where Eaton was interred, funeral rituals typically included a coffin and pall, with eight men to accompany the corpse, "four carrying it until tired and they being relieved by the other four." Whatever the mode of interment, Eaton had at last received a proper burial.[24]

Eaton's retrieval was not without cost, however. An unnamed soldier, "notwithstanding his [Harmon's] care," went missing in the melee following the Abenakis' pursuit. That Harmon had procured and kept Eaton's corpse was praiseworthy; however, that the lost soldier was probably dead and impossible to find only reaffirmed the costs of sepulture in the eyes of Boston's wartime readers. Eaton's retrieval may not have caused the soldier's disappearance—retreats could fragment and become disorganized. Still, pausing to collect body parts did delay the troops' departure and drew the Abenakis closer.[25]

The attack and the rapid disengagement received attention in verse. As a poetic fragment of the assault noted, in what one chronicler described as "doggerel rhyme," New Englanders fired two volleys at the sleeping Abenakis before hastily departing. Fear of alerting other nearby Abenakis prompted the strategy: "And, with haste, we made away / For fear the Indians would surround us / And we should not get away. / Some did say that we did kill thirty / Others say we did kill more. / The number to us is uncertain. / I believe we hardly killed a score." Eaton's scattered remains went unrecorded, but their retrieval—which presumably took longer than the firing of the two rounds—displayed Captain Harmon's sense of responsibility toward the dead.[26]

Moses Eaton's death found a place in the public memory that, while decidedly more modest than remembrance of Lovewell's demise, nonetheless had made an impression. At least among Boston's newspaper readers, it suggested that bodies should be recovered and buried despite the risks involved; it also inspired poetry that if not set to song could still be recited. What might have become a quickly forgotten episode continued to resonate privately among

Massachusetts settlers. James Cochran, an eighteen-year-old captive of the Abenakis, identified Eaton's murderer in 1725. One of Cochran's Abenaki captors had boasted about the slaying, adding Eaton's name to those of an Englishman and a black man he had previously killed at Black Point. If he expected the news to frighten Cochran, the stratagem failed. At nightfall, while his two captors slept, Cochran "nockt them bouth in the head and took of their sculps," according to John Gyles, the reporting officer. Cochran received a two-hundred-pound bounty and promotion to sergeant. Eaton's name, although escaping newspaper coverage, had remained sufficiently well known for Cochran, Gyles, and a boastful Indian to recall.[27]

Graphic death accounts such as Eaton's reemphasized classic thinking regarding the treatment of the dead. As in King Philip's War, New Englanders expected burials to follow death as a matter of course; in reality, abandonment often occurred. Newspapers added to the "rhetoric of fear," intensifying the incipient Indian menace by describing the mutilated corpses and settlers' subsequent outrage. In this case, one Indian's boasting, along with the incentive of a scalping bounty, had inspired Cochran to act.[28]

Other Dummer's War dismemberments merited less graphic detail. On May 20, 1723, the *Courant* reported an attack in Salmon Falls in which eight Native raiders killed two cattle-tending residents. Afterward, however, the assailants "barbarously cut and mangled them with their hatchets." The only thing missing in the report was a precise description of the sliced body parts. Aaron Rawling and his daughter spiritedly defended themselves at Lamprey River in 1723, only to pay a high price for their defiance. Furious Indians scalped Rawling and decapitated his daughter—that was something easily visualized by readers. The other family members were taken captive. At Casco, Maine, Indians cut the head off an unnamed woman in late summer 1723, arranging it in a pottage pot alongside her slain nursing infant. Yet none of these descriptions proved comparable in impact to that of Eaton's scattered limbs. His death during the war's initial stages had underscored Governor Shute's stern declaration of war and alerted soldiers and civilians to the challenges ahead.[29]

Beyond the pulpit, death's aftermath could be more directly observed when passing by the Old North burying ground atop Copp's Hill and the Old South burying ground—two of the earliest Boston cemeteries. The King's Chapel burial ground was home to the city's smaller Anglican population. Sparsely inscribed tombstones of green-covered stone or slate dotted grave sites; some were decorated with representations of death. Family burial vaults contrasted with the more numerous simple plots. Nevertheless, interments, regardless of class, had to follow certain protocols: by 1701 Boston prohibited Sabbath burials unless approved by two selectmen, and it outlawed Sunday funeral services because disorderly children and servants loitered in the streets after the worship service. Growing funereal extravagance increasingly drew scrutiny. By 1721, costly mourning scarves had become customary, taxing middle-class finances and prompting a General Court ban.[30]

That the ban was imposed while a smallpox epidemic was wreaking havoc may have been more than coincidence. Almost one in twelve residents perished from the pestilence in 1721. Why were funeral scarves used when death seemingly stalked victims and left the living fearful of contagion? It may have been an attempt to preserve some degree of normalcy in a chaotic time. With Boston's populace seemingly besieged, the crisis exposed deeply rooted political divisions over inoculations against the pox. Giving people a small portion of the pox as a preventive measure proved too radical for some Bostonians. Nevertheless, Cotton Mather championed the procedure, whereas the *New England Courant* derided the practice. The corpses piled up, and business slowed to a standstill by spring. In terms of funeral practices, however, the picture was mixed. Samuel Sewall observed that Mrs. Frances Webb, a smallpox victim, had the first funeral to forgo scarves in September. Even so, Colonel Samuel Checkley distributed rings and scarves in October after his wife's smallpox death. That he violated the law against scarves apparently never disturbed Sewall. An African American funeral that took place the same day for one Mrs. Checkley probably dispensed with scarves altogether— African Americans had limited economic resources and little inclination to imitate white funeral customs. However, a later December funeral for a white individual during the waning of the smallpox epidemic featured only mourning gloves and rings, observing the law while preserving time-honored death usages.[31]

Although the smallpox outbreak subsided by 1722, drought was the next threat to the province. Dry weather withered crops and reduced yields, while pastures produced less fodder for livestock. No deaths could be directly tied to the drought, but both farmers and town dwellers suffered. Certainly, destructive weather conditions contributed to the sense of crisis: What should Bostonians do? As the Reverend Benjamin Wadsworth warned in August 1722, God's anger toward them, evidenced by disease, drought, and warfare, had been made manifest. God's enemies would assail his people, forcing them to resist and destroy the foe. Still, Wadsworth chided Bostonians, "We are a professing but a very degenerate people," and "True Piety," as he labeled his discourse, was "the best policy in war." Other ministers issued similar moral warnings.[32]

The Reverend Wadsworth's admonition cast in Puritan boilerplate still left Bostonians unprepared for the events of the following year. Bay settlement residents inured to epidemic, war, and drought witnessed a rash of suspicious fires in the spring of 1723. Fire represented an immediate tangible danger. It was also a vivid memory to seaport inhabitants. Many could undoubtedly recall the conflagration of October 2, 1711, that had spread across Corn Hill, King and Queen Streets, and much of Pudding Lane. Close to one hundred people lost their homes in the inferno, and both the Old Meeting House and the Town House went up in the flames. Some inhabitants, "monsters of wickedness" to cite Cotton Mather, had pillaged their neighbors' dwellings. Although theft never surfaced in 1723, the arsonist or arsonists responsible set the townsfolk on edge.[33]

Boston's wooden structures offered tempting targets for incendiaries. Fire inspectors and a fire society afforded modest protection, yet neither sufficed to save a building belonging to Dr. Elisha Cooke Jr., a prominent politician, land-lord, and physician, from destruction in March 1723. The building was located near the Long Wharf, Boston's most conspicuous artery of overseas trade. Storehouses occupied the nearly seven-hundred-yard structure, and any dam-age to them would have hurt Boston's economy. Jeremiah Bumstead, a local diarist, noted that Cooke's burnt building had also destroyed seven or eight tenements. Even so, this blaze may have been an accidental occurrence—stray sparks could easily ignite dwellings. Another fire on April 12, 1723, prompted Samuel Sewall to note "In the morning, between 6 and 7, the Bells ring for fire. Mr. Bridge his kitchen in King Street, near Madam Stoddard widow, is burned down. Progress of fire is mercifully staid!" Jeremiah Bumstead acknowledged the fire at Bridge's home, but added, "fire laid in several other places ye same day, vis. Judg Sewalls, Shrimpton, Hobbs, ye French Doctors & in the South meeting or Milk Street." Left unmentioned by both men was the growing pop-ular conviction that enslaved people of color engineered the calamities.[34]

Black slaves toiled as domestics, artisans, and laborers in Boston streets and households. As early as 1708, 400 blacks resided in Boston proper; by 1742, they numbered 1,374. Before 1720, black Bostonians had represented no more than 3 percent of the populace, albeit widely distributed among Boston professionals, businessmen, and artisans. The Reverend Benjamin Colman declared in 1723 that "Scarce a House but has one, excepting the very poor." Despite enslavement, African Americans could send their children to a free school, and the spiritually inclined could join the Religious Society for Negroes. However, social amenities could not obscure the stark conditions of black bondage—their mortality rate exceeded that of whites, and blacks comprised 16 percent of Boston burials between 1704 and 1749, twice their population share. Black funerals typically involved music, singing, and dancing at night, in contrast to more solemn white daytime interments. White Bostonians frowned upon noise and limited black funerals to one ringing bell in 1721. Nevertheless, segregated burial plots were unknown until 1744, so black Bostonians in the 1720s resided among their owners and neighbors in death much as they had done in life.[35]

Nevertheless, black resentment of their bondage surfaced. Slaves found after nine o'clock at night without a ticket from their master were sent to the House of Correction and whipped. "When a few of 'em had been served so," according to the Reverend Benjamin Colman, "fires were kindled about Town every day or night." Jeremiah Bumstead recorded on April 1, 1723, that Mr. Powell's house had been set afire by a black man. The *New England Courant* reported that a black man had confessed and been incarcerated. When the imprisoned black man accused five other African Americans, the authorities moved swiftly to examine and jail them. White anxieties continued to intensify, as the fires had occurred near the homes of prominent citizens. In response, a fifty-man militia was created to thwart feared black attacks against white firefighters. Political authorities evidently believed a conspiracy was afoot. For his part, Lieutenant Governor Dummer blamed "villains," "dissolute people," and "desperate Negroes" as arsonists. A fifty-pound reward was offered for anyone identifying the offenders. When Dummer's proclamation was announced, one black male was inspired to yell, "A bite, a bite," before being arrested. Notwithstanding these precautions, two more dwellings went up in flames over two nights. By April 18, the Reverend Joseph Sewell talked about the fires, which one listener admitted "were supposed to be purposely set by ye Negroes."[36]

Emboldened incendiaries set three more fires in May: one by a bake house near the Mill Pond; another on a house near Oliver's Bridge; and a third by the lower end of King Street. None did much damage, but the Oliver's Bridge arsonist had cleverly wrapped burning coals inside linen breeches. Suspicion began to extend to working-class whites, whose reasons for setting the blazes remained unannounced and hence unknown to us. However, one Winter, a shoemaker, spent time in the Bridewell as a suspect; the authorities also apprehended an unidentified servant on suspicion of arson. While borderland villagers worried about Abenaki raiders during Dummer's War, Bostonians worried about enemies from within.[37]

Boston residents experienced some relief when the apprehended black male, Dago, confessed to arson. Now there was a name and a face to the crime. The court sentenced Dago to death for firing Mr. Powell's house in April; it released the other five men he had named. Dago's July execution presumably drew a crowd—public executions were popular events and rarely missed. Others perhaps found satisfaction in observing Dago's swinging body, a warning to other would-be arsonists.[38]

No Boston newspapers had dignified the executed Dago with a name. For readers, he remained the unnamed black male, charged and convicted of arson. Yet Dago, as Bumstead privately identified him, could not have been unknown to residents, given his public trial and execution. That he may have been a free black man—Bumstead never mentioned an owner—probably compounded white fears. Slaves, presumably, struck out against bondage as an act of liberation. Free black arsonists were more unsettling. Like unidentified Abenakis who terrorized settlers and burned houses, Dago had assumed a similar symbolic status to city dwellers by threatening their lives and property. And Dago generally remained distinguished by race and sex, as did most Abenakis. Not surprisingly, newspapers gave no account of Dago's burial, his character being considered a bar to any description.[39]

Aside from the Abenakis and enraged African Americans, Boston faced threats beyond its docks and shoreline from pirates. These seafaring freebooters were often identified by white Bostonians. Newspapers trumpeted pirate captains by name, granting them a status seldom accorded African Americans. That pirates threatened Boston's commerce by waylaying merchant ships and stripping them of cargoes and men gave them added notoriety. Ironically, Dummer's War coincided with the high point of Atlantic piracy: between 1716 and 1726 close to five thousand pirates roamed sea-lanes and coastal waters, unleashing a wave of terror. In 1724, Benjamin Chadwell, captain of the captured schooner *Goodwill*, after rough treatment by the pirates, overheard them boasting that they would "sink, burn, and destroy all the fishing boats they could meet." Boston took such threats seriously. New England fishermen and fish merchants comprised an important cornerstone of the regional economy. To make matters worse, the boasting pirate leader, Captain John Phillips, possessed the means to carry out his threat, having recently run off from the Newfoundland fishing fleet. Phillips mounted two large cannons on his sloop; an accompanying pirate vessel mustered a far more impressive twenty-four guns. Together they could make short work of unarmed fishing vessels.[40]

The threat of execution hardly deterred pirates from their trade. One, Bartholomew Roberts, claimed as his motto a "merry life and a short one" untroubled by the future. As social bandits, pirates recruited underpaid, harshly treated merchant sailors who were attracted by the freebooting, egalitarian ethos of piracy; when that failed, pirates forced men into service. The distinction between willing and unwilling service could spell the difference between life and death for captured sailors. Depositions from merchant officers attested that pirates often seized unwilling sailors. In turn, these documents provided an escape from the hangman's noose. Several pirates even petitioned the king for pardon, announcing their intention in the Boston press. When the HMS *Grayhound* captured a pirate sloop in 1723, one man, Joseph Sweeter, a twenty-four-year-old Boston native, was listed as "forced" and saved from the gallows.[41]

Others were less lucky. In neighboring Rhode Island, the provincial government executed twenty-three of the pirates captured by the *Grayhound* on July 19, 1723. Cotton Mather implored his congregation to "consider the way that wicked men have trodden." What happened to the pirates' bodies was not disclosed by Mather. Pirates brought to Boston the following year provided Mather another opportunity for an execution sermon. Although the pirate captain, the aforementioned Phillips, had been slain earlier along with his mate, Burrill, their pickled heads attracted Boston's curious citizens. Two crew members from Phillips's ship, William White and John Ross Archer, were hanged. Afterward, the authorities conveyed the corpses to nearby Bird Island, where White was quietly buried and Archer gibbeted. The gibbet permitted the spectacle of death to be played out for an extended period until the body fell apart or was cut down.[42]

All this starkly contrasted with the deaths and burials of proper Bostonians. The bodies of executed criminals were publicly displayed as warnings to other evildoers; their actual burials generally went unnoticed. In contrast, prominent Bostonians had both an elaborate funeral cortege and a solemn interment. A coffin, pall, pallbearers, and other funeral accouterments, along with tombstone or vault, dignified their deaths. When funeral corteges traversed Boston streets, drawing marchers and onlookers, the body remained concealed. Any viewing would occur in the household prior to the winding sheet and closing of the coffin.

Increase Mather's passing on August 23, 1723, demonstrates Reformed Christian funereal culture during Dummer's War. A descendant of Richard Mather, an eminent first-generation Puritan divine, Increase had figured significantly in provincial affairs, been president of Harvard, and Massachusetts representative to England in 1689. During the Salem witchcraft trials in 1692 and 1693 his eventual moderate views tempered some of the more zealous emphasis on spectral evidence. By the early 1720s, Mather's deteriorating health was public knowledge, and his death when announced swept aside news of Dummer's War. Samuel Sewall described the stately funeral procession, which took in the North Meeting House and Mather's own home before the cortege reached the North burial ground. The Boston diarist Jeremiah Bumstead noted the "vast number at his funeral" and was suitably impressed by the turnout—as well he should have been, considering the fact that one hundred and sixty Harvard graduates and fifty ministers participated. Lieutenant Governor Dummer; John Leverett, president of Harvard; Samuel Sewall, the chief justice; and three ministers served as pallbearers. No one could doubt that Mather had been lavishly sent off.[43]

In contrast, the death of John Valentine, Esq., His Majesty's Advocate General for Massachusetts Bay, New Hampshire, and Rhode Island, in February 1724 presented a different, more controversial funereal aspect. Deceased royal officials might receive a certain level of pomp and circumstance. What complicated matters in this case was Valentine's mode of death at home. In Sudbury, Massachusetts, the Reverend Israel Loring wrote in his diary, "an aweful thing happened at Boston. John Valentine Esq., a famous lawyer hanged himself." In Puritan parlance, suicide constituted "self-death"—interestingly enough, a theme of a late seventeenth-century sermon by Increase Mather. Whether Valentine merited a dignified funeral aroused contention. Privately, Samuel Sewall fumed about the funeral—no one had consulted him or his acquaintances about the arrangements.

The resulting ceremony proved both typical and atypical of Boston funerals. Tolling bells announced the funeral as per custom, yet Judge Addington Davenport and Colonel Thomas Fitch, invited pallbearers, excused themselves after learning that the Reverend Samuel Myles, the King's Chapel rector, had balked at reading the office of burial. Four other pallbearers, including a leading lawyer, Robert Auchmuty, and Attorney General John Read, participated. Four justices, five ministers, and "much people" joined the funeral. Valentine's widow supplied a laudatory obituary and cited her husband's unsettled state, and Auchmuty swore an oath affirming Valentine's "distruction." The *Boston Gazette* simply noted that Valentine had been "decently interred."[44]

Cotton Mather and Samuel Sewall nonetheless conspired to have the last word. Despite the omission of the Anglican burial office, Mather and Sewall had serious reservations about Valentine's public funeral. Death by suicide prohibited normal burial, to their way of thinking. Seventeenth-century English practice had been to inter suicides in unconsecrated ground, typically at the crossroads of country lanes, occasionally with a stake driven through the body to pin down the corpse on the expected Day of Resurrection. Puritans did not consecrate ground per se, yet suicide transgressed Calvinist teachings, and Sewall inserted a Latin warning about Valentine in the *Boston News Letter* that, translated, read: "What is it to know countless things and to unravel cases / if you run away from what has to be done; if you do what should be run away from?" Mather and Sewall also published Increase Mather's earlier sermon against self-death. Although unable to stop Valentine's burial and laudatory obituary, the two men had sounded a warning against other would-be suicides being granted lavish interments. Mather's sermon, "A Call to the Tempted," had limited influence. When Hopestill Foster hanged himself at his home in 1724, Sewall fumed about being ignored regarding "the burial or anything else." That Foster had received a quiet evening interment failed to mollify the irate Sewall.[45]

Far different were the protocols and debates that arose over battlefield interments. Slain individuals could not always be properly buried; nor were tombstones, coffins, winding sheets, or the fashionable funereal accessories of mourning rituals in Boston close at hand. Recently created borderland settlements may well have lacked community burial grounds anyway. Dummer's War largely consisted of raids and ambushes emblematic of the "skulking way of war" that distinguished borderland conflicts removed from seaports. Swooping down upon unsuspecting settlers promised fewer casualties for attackers. Only rarely did larger Indian forces besiege forts or torch villages. New Englanders also maximized mobility and seldom fielded troops above two hundred men in any single campaign. But had New Englanders learned from the experience of King Philip's War, a vivid memory, in which men abandoned wounded comrades and left bodies unburied? Dummer's War would suggest that these lessons needed reinforcement, as slain soldiers and civilians sometimes fared little better than executed pirates or people of color.[46]

Little detailed information exists about the interments of slain settlers or soldiers during Dummer's War. The acknowledgment of death when announced in newspapers might suggest a place of repose but provide little in terms of specifics. Witness the case of Moses Eaton, the most memorable early casualty, whose bodily desecration horrified settlers but whose burial was barely mentioned. In Dunstable, the 1724 Indian kidnapping of two settlers led to a spirited failed rescue attempt, requiring compassionate neighbors to transport and bury the dead in a mass grave. But this account was rather exceptional, as no other instance of settlers assembling to bury more than several people reached the newspapers. More typically, slain individuals were simply "the deceased" and their burials went unrecorded. Fear of lurking Indians was another factor contributing to modest funerals. On August 27, 1723, attacking Indians torched a sawmill on the Mousam River and killed a settler named Jepsum. Two weeks went by before twenty men mustered the courage to locate the remains and inter them in an adjoining field.[47]

Security concerns also figured in tactical decisions regarding unclaimed Indian bodies. Normally, adversaries remained unburied, but in 1725 the existence of a half-dozen exposed Indian corpses produced a testy exchange among Massachusetts officials and military commanders. In King Philip's War, the Indians typically retrieved their dead; by Dummer's War, Provincial Secretary Josiah Willard wanted answers about why Falmouth, Maine, settlers had failed to position themselves near Abenaki bodies to shoot any returning Indians, for the site lay along a well-frequented Indian trail. All that would be necessary, thought Willard, ensconced in the relative safety of Boston, was a little effort on their part. From Falmouth, Colonel Thomas Westbrook cited the report's tardy arrival six days after the event and only a few hours before the Indians had attacked and killed two settlers. Venturing out was too hazardous and the logistics too daunting. As Westbrook tried to explain: "the place where ye dead bodies lay was sixty miles from them, so considering the Enemy's being among them judged it not safe to march so far from their several garrisons, for a small scout, at that Juncture, drawn out, would have very much exposed them."[48] Unburied Indian bodies were not enough to bait would-be ambushers, who were justifiably afraid they might be taken instead.

Conscientious commanders were more interested in interring their own troops properly if the means existed. Colonel Thomas Westbrook commanded an expedition in March 1723, searching for an Indian fort up the Penobscot River. On discovering it they burned the fortifications; the campaign had lost four men, however, one of them the expedition's chaplain, the Reverend Benjamin Gibson. These they carried with them and "interred in usual form." What "in usual form" meant and whether it included prayers, a few words of remembrance, a makeshift winding sheet or coffin, went unrecorded. Lacking a chaplain, the commander shouldered the responsibility, and Westbrook never described the funeral rite. That he had buried his men was sufficient, and the phrasing employed suggests an agreed-upon method of sepulture to follow. It remained for Samuel Sewall to place a Latin verse in the *Boston News Letter* commemorating Gibson.[49]

At other times, commanders attempted to retrieve the dead only to discover they were missing. Captain John Penhallow, stationed in Maine near Georgetown, reported an Abenaki ambush of several men who had left the fort. The slain men, Penhallow believed, had been butchered along with the cattle. Accordingly, he ordered a burial detail to search a one-mile perimeter around the fort; fear of waiting Abenakis explains the restricted zone of operations. Still, the bodies went undiscovered, encouraging Penhallow to believe that the Abenakis were holding the men for ransom.[50]

Circumstances occasionally rendered corpses unrecoverable. Soldiers lost to ambush expected comrades to retrieve them under fire by risking their own lives, but sometimes Abenaki attacks left no survivors to attempt such operations. The story of Josiah Winslow best illustrates this dilemma. A promising young man of parts, Winslow may well constitute Dummer's War most prominent casualty in terms of background and class. His family ancestry included Josiah Winslow, commander of the intercolonial force arrayed against the Narragansett stronghold, Mystic Fort, in December 1675. Colonel Isaac Winslow, the young man's father, had served as a provincial councilor. With such forebears, young Josiah Winslow had an impressive lineage to uphold.[51]

Josiah first gained attention while at Harvard. He and Joseph Belcher, a schoolteacher, became "involved in some difficulty," as a twentieth-century editor politely phrased the noisy dispute. Judge Samuel Sewall fined Belcher five shillings for cursing and added ten more shillings for disturbing the peace. Belcher posted a bond for good behavior. Sewall tersely noted that "Mr. Winslow's son did not appear." If Josiah had, Sewall might have slapped him with a fine and a bond for his role in the fracas. Was Winslow an excitable young man prone to loud outbursts? The answer appears to be yes. Was he willing to own up to his responsibility? That answer appears to be no.[52]

After graduation, Winslow followed the family path and turned to military service to better channel his energies. This time he won positive notice. Colonel Thomas Westbrook enthusiastically vouched for him, writing to Lieutenant Governor Dummer in April 1723 that, despite being "dropt" from the troop, he continued to contribute to it. Winslow marched with Westbrook to Penobscot, and his former commander added, "I doubt not but he will make a good Officer, & I hope your Honor will bear him in Mind when there is an opportunity to improve him." The opportunity soon came: in 1724, the newly promoted Captain Winslow received command of Fort St. George, a key Massachusetts bastion and site of earlier Abenaki attacks.[53]

Yet, Winslow chafed at the assignment. Safeguarding a fort meant assuming a defensive posture, and he had accompanied marching troops unofficially of his own volition. Not surprisingly, he seized the offensive, gathering sixteen men in two whaleboats along with some Indian scouts on April 30, 1724, his destination the Green Islands in Penobscot Bay, a popular Abenaki fowling place. Perhaps Winslow wanted to emulate Westbrook by taking the initiative. After all, scouting parties enabled aggressive commanders to surprise an enemy and gain an advantage.[54]

Winslow proceeded uneventfully to the islands only to find them deserted. He camped overnight and decided to depart on May 1 in the early afternoon. Evidently, he preferred a quick raid to waiting, but his absence from the fort also entailed the risk of the Abenakis suddenly descending on it in the absence of its commander. What Winslow and his scouts failed to realize was that the Abenakis were close by, waiting to spring their own trap. As the two whaleboats disembarked for home the distance between them steadily increased— the second boat, commanded by one Sergeant Harvey, had slowed down to shoot some river fowl. Fresh food for dinner was a mouth-watering prospect; but it also separated Winslow from the trailing boat by a half-mile. Two to three hundred Abenakis descended in canoes upon the surprised and out-numbered Harvey.[55]

Winslow hurried back to give battle. He could have retreated—Cotton Mather later claimed that thirty or forty canoes surrounded the captain—but his "manly, friendly, ingenious and courageous heart" rebelled at the thought. He fired from his boat at the approaching Indians; they responded in kind.

The tide of battle went against Winslow, the odds being too great and the canoes too numerous to fend off. English fatalities mounted. By nightfall Winslow and two or three surviving soldiers went ashore to continue the fight. When his shot and powder were exhausted, Winslow brandished his musket's butt end to repel the attackers despite being hampered by a broken thigh. Admiring Indians offered him quarter—the man had fought bravely and well, winning their respect. Probably, too, they wanted a captive to ransom. Winslow refused, preferring to "lay down his life in service of Country." Killed at age twenty-three, the "good natured young gentleman," in Cotton Mather's words, had honored his birthright by going to his comrades' aid.[56]

News of the calamity swiftly circulated. Although the entire English troop had been slain, Indian scouts had escaped, or been allowed to escape to recount the defeat. Colonel Thomas Westbrook informed Lieutenant Governor Dummer that "no less than thirty canoes" had assailed Winslow's force. More tellingly, Westbrook acknowledged the importance of retrieving the dead and his inability to do so: "We have not men to look for the dead bodies of our friends so that our Enemies have a double triumph over us." The choice of words here is telling. Victory came when one force defeated or drove off an enemy, but an additional victory—the "double triumph"—resulted when the bodies of the defeated were left unclaimed and subject to desecration and the elements.[57]

The death of young Josiah Winslow stung Massachusetts inhabitants more than any other Dummer's War death until Captain John Lovewell's. Unlike Lovewell, Winslow drew considerable attention from Boston's literary elite, reflecting his distinguished background. Not only had a young captain been slain, but his entire eighteen-man squad had been slaughtered—the war's largest single loss of life on the Massachusetts side so far. The tragedy inspired poets and clerics to take quill in hand. When the poet Mather Byles wrote "To the Memory of a young commander slain in a Battle with the Indians" in 1724, he never identified Winslow, the attackers, or the battle site. There was no need to, as people recognized the reference: "The sinking Youth drop'd fainting to the Ground / In quick short pants ebb'd out his quiv' ring Breath / while o'er his Eye-lids hung the Shades of Death." Cotton Mather identified Winslow in order to commemorate the "laurel of one who died fighting the battles of the Lord." Winslow's noted ancestry, Mather asserted, would have elevated him to a Master of Arms, a significant provincial office. He went on to instruct the survivors, and he must have been referring to the pamphlet-reading citizens, as there were no survivors from the troop save Indian scouts, to remember the "men who have deserved so well."[58]

Left unmentioned was Winslow's missing body. Its probable desecration was understood, given Indian practice and earlier newspaper references to dismembered corpses. Yet, in an attempt to provide emotional balm, Mather supplied the illusion of a funeral in the form of a published eulogy. Words were a poor substitute for pallbearers, marchers, and spectators, but they were the best Mather could offer; and in place of the missing tombstone, he furnished an appropriate inscription: "Dulce, pro Patria Mori / His ancestors did for their country lie / He'el of his Love a farther token give / Hopeless beyond them in a life to fly / He for his country takes the way to die / Titulo res digna Sepulibri."[59]

This was not the last word on the subject. John Adams, a poetically minded cleric, had felt Winslow's death also, writing verses that remained unpublished until five years after his death in 1745. Adams used King David's elegy to his intimate friend Jonathan killed in battle to establish the historical significance of Winslow's death. Then he confronted an issue never directly mentioned before—Winslow's unburied body. He wrote: "For who unmoved can see thy lovely Limbs / Stretch'd on the Ground and dy'd with Purple Streams / While with kind Insults dance the swarthy crew / About thy Corps, which when alive they slew." It was a distressing picture of enemies celebrating a death. Moreover, he held little hope for the body's recovery, remarking "now lost, perhaps, he lays unburied on / the Pagan Plains, burnt by the blazing Sun." Adams's private musings may explain the graphic reference to Winslow's corpse.[60]

The unburied Winslow lingered on in the popular memory, albeit less recalled than Captain John Lovewell. Nineteenth-century chroniclers acknowledged the sad reality—the want of men preventing interment—but perhaps, as one author mused, "our gallant little band were interred by the savages, or their flesh devoured by wild beasts and their bones left bleaching in the sun till concealed by the leaves of Autumn." The latter possibility was more likely. Further allusions to the unknown grave mentioned those who had died alongside Winslow, giving them belated due. As Cyrus Eaton, a nineteenth-century antiquarian intoned: "No column proud, no humble stone / To mark the spot, was reared for them / The evening thrush and beating surge / Performed their own requiem." At last Winslow's unnamed companions had received equal treatment in verse.[61]

Mourning the unburied Josiah Winslow and his comrades did not alter provincial battle tactics. Bodily dismemberment, or more specifically modified decapitation, featured in scalping; tearing off an Indian's hair represented a symbolic head severing, spurred by the opportunity to profit economically and collect a one-hundred-pound government bounty. The Indian practice of decapitation had evolved into a common New England war practice. The resulting bloodied, unburied Indian corpse merely reaffirmed the victor's prowess—a variation on the double-victory theme. Even if the aim had been to capture an adversary alive, battle's uncertainties altered the original goal, as the French and Abenakis both learned after Father Sebastian Rale's brutal death by invading provincial solders. Josiah Winslow would be avenged.[62]

In 1724, the fighting seemed endless. Indians had killed and captured settlers from Berwick, Durham, Deerfield, Saco, Chester, Groton, Arrowsic, Kingston, Portsmouth, and other New Hampshire and Massachusetts communities. Not only did men and women die, but the Abenakis slaughtered livestock and burned dwellings for good measure. In western Massachusetts, Grey Lock raided at will. The forts around Northfield meant to deter him afforded scant protection. Even coastal vessels and crews suffered assault. The Abenakis seized eleven fishing boats, killed twenty-two men, and captured twenty-three others in their maritime campaign. Small ships manned by Royal Navy sailors unsuccessfully swept the coast for them. On land, New Englanders had accomplished little: scouting parties pushing into Abenaki territory reported deserted villages; other expeditions turned back when conditions became too arduous. The often elusive Abenakis seemingly blended into the forest. In response, a General Fast, set for March 26, 1724, urged the avoidance of all recreation and servile labor, implored God to end His righteous judgment, and asked for victory against a "treacherous and bloody enemy and protect[ion of] our frontier from their barbarous insults and depredations."[63]

The crux of the problem, at least to some New Englanders, centered on Father Sebastian Rale. At Norridgewock, Rale lived among his flock and radiated opposition. Yet, if Rale could be captured, the war's dynamic might shift, and Massachusetts would hold an important bargaining chip perhaps sufficient to propel peace negotiations forward. Although the Abenakis were principally defending their own interests, many of them respected their resident missionary; his capture might give them pause. But could Rale be captured if attacked? Or would the aged missionary find martyrdom more appealing? No one could predict what scenario Rale might follow. Nevertheless, Norridgewock's destruction (with or without Rale) would provide a telling blow and scalps aplenty if the inhabitants could be caught off guard.[64]

In August 1724, Massachusetts gathered over two hundred men to reduce Norridgewock and seize Rale. The expedition included "backwoodsmen, who were adept in the arts of Indian warfare," along with Mohawk allies. On August 19, the men left Richmond fort and proceeded by whaleboat to the fall at Tecconnet. There a forty-man guard protected the boats at the mouth of the Sebasticook River. Using an old Indian path, the expedition marched into the Maine woods, avoiding the river to evade detection. Fortune intervened. The troop encountered three Indians, one of whom, Bomazeen, a noted warrior and chief, they shot while fleeing. His frightened widow gave the expedition directions to the village. Arriving unnoticed, the force attacked near the middle of the day on August 22.[65]

Confusion emerges about the actual assault sequence. Captain Johnson Harmon, the commander, positioned his company in the cornfield to cut off any retreat, perhaps convinced that another Indian encampment was nearby; if so, precautions needed to be taken. It fell to Captain Jeremiah Moulton to lead the remaining scouts against the village. He closed to within pistol shot, according to Samuel Penhallow, an early New Hampshire historian, before the Abenakis sounded the alarm. Some of the more resolute warriors gathered arms. Abenaki women and children tried to flee. During the exchange of musketry a noted and aged chief, Mogg, killed a Mohawk from his wigwam. In turn, another Mohawk shot him dead. Perhaps as many as one hundred villagers found safety in the woods; others drowned in the river or were shot by pursuing New Englanders. With the battle almost over, Captain Harmon led his company into the village.[66]

Where was Father Rale during the fighting? Penhallow noted that "the Bloody Incendiary," as he termed the missionary, had been slain, but acknowledged that "some say that Quarter was offered him." Obviously, this begs the question: was Rale permitted to surrender or killed outright? By refusing the offer of surrender—if indeed one was given—Rale was fair game to be shot. Other accounts claim that Rale fired from the structure while holding captive and wounding a Massachusetts boy. Lieutenant Richard Jacques, the nephew of Jeremiah Moulton and son-in-law of Johnson Harmon, entered the wigwam and dispatched the priest as he drew his gun. French authorities claimed that Jacques killed the unarmed Rale when his head appeared outside the dwelling. Who did what and precisely when rendered the narrative sequence cloudy.[67]

Thomas Hutchinson, later Royal Governor of Massachusetts and an avid historian writing before the Revolution, noted that French accounts drawn from escaping Indians had Rale meeting the New Englanders outside his home in the hope of drawing them away from his flock. On seeing the priest, the troops let out a roar and unleashed a hail of musket balls. Rale died in the village center by the cross, enhancing the aura of martyrdom. Moulton's forces expended two thousand musket balls during the Norridgewock attack, but it took only one bullet to dispatch Rale. The French listed thirty Abenakis killed and fourteen of them wounded.[68]

Sources do agree that the New Englanders occupied and plundered the village. Anything portable, from corn to blankets to communion plate, became booty. Most prized were scalps. At one hundred pounds apiece, the twenty-seven scalps taken, including Rale's, constituted a substantial payout. The occupiers removed the bodies to one central site, with Rale placed in the center and scalped—whether by Jacques or someone else it is impossible to say. Later French accounts insist that the priest's corpse was dismembered and abused, with his skull shattered in several places. Other soldiers shot musket balls into the corpse, mangled the limbs, and filled the mouth and eyes with mud to emphasize their disdain. Remarkably, the English suffered no casualties and their Mohawk allies lost only one man. To seal the victory, a Mohawk broke ranks and torched the village. Shocked returning Abenakis buried Rale and tribal members. Later generations of Catholics would honor the slain missionary with a monument at the site in 1833.[69]

For the Reverend Cotton Mather, the Norridgewock raid was cause to celebrate: the Abenakis had been trounced, their beloved shepherd killed and scalped. In his tribute to Winslow, Mather had proudly proclaimed, "the Hairy Scalp of that head of the House of the Wicked, paid for what hand it had in the Rebellion, into which he infuriated his proselytes." The Reverend Benjamin Colman seconded Mather, remarking, the "ghastly father of these perfidious savages like Balaam, the son of Beos, was slain among the enemy after vain attempts to curse us." In early eighteenth-century Puritan minds, Dummer's War was not only a battle between Indians and English, but between Catholics (the Antichrist) and True Reformed Christians. Hence, clerics expressed their jubilation in biblical tones. Layman Penhallow described it as "The greatest Victory we have obtained in three or four last wars; and it may be as noble an exploit (all things considered) as ever happened in the time of King Philip."[70]

A victory parade through Boston streets provided a celebratory capstone. After fast days and numerous proffered prayers, Bay settlement inhabitants could relax and shed their somber exteriors for a day. Spectators could salute the four companies led by Harmon, who won promotion to lieutenant colonel. Moulton received applause for leading the charge into Norridgewock. Any irregularities in Rale's killing failed to disturb the cheering citizens, clerics, or officials. At last, after the failure of previous raids against Norridgewock, the province could celebrate, and the men in the ranks participated in the tribute and collected the bounties for scalps. Only Samuel Sewall, the chief justice, implored God to "help us to rejoice with Trembling," perhaps signaling his concerns over the altercation. But then, Sewall was more sympathetic to Indians than other Puritans.[71]

Lieutenant Governor Dummer performed an official benediction in an address to the Massachusetts House of Representatives. After previous messages reporting indifferent results, he announced in November 1724 to the recently returned House of Representatives that the march to Norridgewock had "been attended with great success, in such a destruction of the enemy as had not been known in any of the late wars, and (as I hope) in the enforce[d] dissipation of the tribe." Even when referring to an unsuccessful march by Colonel Westbrook, who had led three hundred men in a failed raid that unearthed no Indians, Dummer's optimism persisted. Westbrook's soldiers, Dummer asserted, had become familiar with the woods, and surely their sheer numbers had frightened the Abenakis away.[72]

Celebration supplied the framework of "The Rebels Reward, or English Courage Displayed at Norridgewock," a poem published in Boston by James Franklin. The piece, according to Ann M. Little, bordered on a pornographic depiction of violence and brutality. The deaths of Rale and two Indians, Bombazene and Moog, were detailed in verse, along with an effort to procure bodies and scalps. That the English and Mohawk attackers had also looted the village drew approval as well: "Our men got stores of plunder / Both guns and blankets too / And drunk the Friars Brandy / Which was their honest due." That the verses should be sung to the tune of "All You That Have Good Fellow" was apparently not an attempt at irony.[73]

Father Sebastian Rale's death did not end Dummer's War or protect borderland settlements from assault. The Norridgewock had been destroyed, but many Abenaki warriors had been absent during the fight. If anything, the assault may have stiffened Abenaki resistance: Indian raiding parties continued to inflict damage, killing people at Northampton and Dover. Two Dunstable settlers kidnapped in September, along with the subsequent deaths of eight rescuers, evidenced Abenaki outrage. To add to New England's misery, the drought continued unabated and led, in Samuel Sewall's words, to a "year of great Scarcity." Even Lieutenant Governor Dummer acknowledged the "scorching drought" of the summer. Although Dummer proclaimed a general thanksgiving in October for the following month, specifically citing the Norridgewock victory, the war dragged on. The borderlands remained unsettled. Ironically, it would be a provincial fatality, John Lovewell's slaying at Pigwacket in 1725, that signaled the ebbing of hostilities. Winslow and Rale would be pushed to the sidelines in the New England public memory, superseded by the "brave Captain Lovewell," beneficiary of two determined chroniclers, the Reverend Thomas Symmes and Samuel Penhallow.[74]

CHAPTER 4
Scripting the Fight

In Bradford, Massachusetts, the Reverend Thomas Symmes sat at his desk, quill in hand and ink nearby, composing a sermon for May 16, 1725. For a cleric in early eighteenth-century Massachusetts, giving voice to God's Word from Holy Scripture defined the Reformed faith. Gathered congregants would listen respectfully but not always uncritically; judgments and assessments would necessarily follow. Especially memorable sermons might warrant publication, and Symmes believed printed homilies to be more "extensive and durable" than oral discourses. But before he could hunt up a publisher, the forty-eight-year-old minister needed to give voice to the tragic death of Captain John Lovewell in the Pigwacket, Maine, borderlands.[1]

Symmes rose to the challenge. His May homily emerged as the battle's literary and historical capstone. That Lovewell and company merited a sermon was understandable: Dummer's War, or Lovewell's War as many christen it, had upended northern borderland New England settlements for three years. Small groups of English and Abenaki scouts and raiders clashed, and Lovewell-led scalping parties had proven especially active. New Englanders donned the armor of righteousness while eyeing scalp bounties, intent on killing Abenakis whom they believed were in thrall to the popish French in Canada—New England's longtime adversary. Enough Old Testament battle texts existed to satisfy any Reformed cleric seeking parallels, and Symmes cited 2 Samuel, chapter 1, verse 27: "How are the Mighty Fallen, and the Weapons of War Perished?" References to 1 Samuel followed, with the Philistines, apt biblical bogeymen, standing in for the Pigwacket Indians. Symmes sought out survivors of Lovewell's Fight to construct a historical preface to the biblical lesson. *Lovewell Lamented, or a Sermon Occasion'd by the Fall Of the Brave Capt. John Lovewell and Several of his Valiant Company in the late Heroic Action at Piggwacket* was the result.[2]

Other New Englanders also found the battle print-worthy. For Samuel Penhallow, a New Hampshire merchant and government official, Lovewell's Fight comprised part of a larger chronicle of New England eighteenth-century Indian wars. When Penhallow dipped his quill into ink, it was typically to sign receipts and official documents, part of his job as a provincial official; at other times the prominent fish trader facilitated business transactions, invested in vessels, wharfs, and warehouses. If Penhallow spoke as a provincial judge, people knew to listen intently to his "strict, discursive, and even harsh" pronouncements, considered a veritable "terror to evil doers." Yet Portsmouth's wealthiest taxpayer turned diplomat when dealing with Maine Indians, and his son John, a militia officer during Dummer's War, provided him with military information. The end result, Penhallow's *New England Indian Wars*, touted Lovewell's Fight in a paean-filled ode while providing a broad-brush account of early eighteenth-century New England military engagements.[3]

Penhallow presumably researched Lovewell's Fight by drawing upon newspaper reports and word-of-mouth information. As a prominent member of the community, he was well positioned to receive accounts—news was a merchant's trade in coin, and government officials knew the value of information. Penhallow did imitate Symmes in one crucial aspect: he sought out a Lovewell fight survivor, Eleazer Davis, one of the four injured men left behind after the fight and among the last to reach a settlement. Davis supplied Penhallow with a poignant battle story spiced by descriptions of dying comrades left behind in the woods. When Symmes's pamphlet came out, Penhallow added (to him) some heretofore unknown information, courtesy of the minister's account. Benjamin Colman, a leading Boston cleric, helped to oversee publication, writing the preface to *The History of the Wars of New-England, With the Eastern Indians,* in 1726, the year of Penhallow's death. Like Symmes, Penhallow scripted the Pigwacket battle's outline, creating a benchmark account.[4]

Neither Symmes nor Penhallow, despite their independently crafted efforts, wrote in a vacuum. Both inhabited a New England where Dummer's War had roiled the populace, unsettled borderland communities, and divided provincial officials. This became New England's fight to win or lose—Great Britain stood on the sidelines. Some inhabitants questioned the war; many Massachusetts legislators balked at Governor Samuel Shute's requests for wartime funding. And Shute's hasty departure in late 1722 left Lieutenant Governor William Dummer to continue the fight. Clerics offered up a stream of advice-filled homilies, chiding New Englanders' moral shortcomings. Lovewell's Fight, although tragic, emerged as an essential battle narrative endowed with patriotic pride and religious faith; largely due to Symmes and Penhallow, Lovewell entered regional folklore, his name remembered as a New England worthy. Whereas Texans enshrined Davy Crockett and the Alamo, and white Americans in general memorialized Custer and the Little Big Horn, early New Englanders long ago appropriated Lovewell's Fight to serve their regional and cultural needs.[5]

Thomas Symmes had chosen to be the scribe who turned Captain Lovewell's death into a sermon. However, becoming a cleric for Symmes may have been less a choice than a family directive: his father, Zechariah, the son and grandson of clerics, loomed over him both physically and spiritually. Samuel Sewall described the elder Symmes as a "worthy gentleman, scholar, divine." Accordingly, Zechariah steered Thomas to follow in his footsteps. Recognized in the Harvard class of 1657 for his scholarly attributes, Zechariah gave Thomas his first Latin lessons in Bradford before sending him off to Cambridge in order to study with Mr. Emerson, a noted Latin tutor, thus keeping the goal of Harvard squarely before his son.[6]

Symmes indeed emulated his father, becoming a scholar of the first rank in his 1698 class. Puritans deemed excessive pride a sin, hence the elder Symmes applauded his son's achievement only quietly. Increase Mather, Harvard's president, proved more vocal. When assessing Thomas Symmes, Mather noted, "When at college, I observed real piety in him, and was then persuaded that the Lord would make him a blessing." Learning and piety were a potent mix to offer any congregation. Nevertheless, Symmes stayed in Cambridge before accepting a call from Boxford, Massachusetts, in late 1702.[7]

Boxford was a small northeastern Massachusetts community some twenty or so miles from Boston. For whatever reasons, Symmes's pastorate met "with uncommon difficulties," according to a town historian. The unidentified challenges were serious enough to motivate Symmes to consider leaving there by 1706.[8] Deliverance arrived when Bradford extended a call to him in 1708. With the elder Symmes's death a year earlier, and two possible replacement candidates who declined offers, the town turned to a favorite son. Symmes would see some changes in Bradford: the second meetinghouse, completed in 1705 and forty-two feet in breadth and forty-eight feet long, outclassed the earlier structure where his father had once preached. In addition, a new parsonage built in 1708 featured four chimneys—perhaps sufficient to take the chill off a Massachusetts winter. In any event, the congregation warmed to Symmes; membership grew steadily and at times almost explosively. Forty-six people came to Christ during a three-month period in 1720, twenty-five of them in one day. What a later age would label a revival occurred in Bradford before the Great Awakening erupted across New England.[9]

Challenges of different sorts still persisted. Success in the pulpit along with a new parsonage and church did not guarantee a comfortable livelihood. Thomas Symmes should have considered his late father's long unresolved contractual difficulties. The town did pay Symmes twice his father's salary; however, one hundred pounds in depreciated Massachusetts currency barely covered his expenses. Parsimonious parishioners often bedeviled Massachusetts clergy, and critics charged that Symmes, while better paid than neighboring clerics, had improperly budgeted funds. Ultimately, Symmes's children felt the pinch: two promising sons lost their chance to attend Harvard, ending the clerical line in that branch of the family tree. Additional financial assistance near the end of Symmes's life arrived too late to help.[10]

Thomas Symmes stayed on at Bradford despite straitened circumstances and a growing family of eight children. His talents, as the Reverend John Brown noted in a funeral eulogy, were shortchanged. The elder Symmes's library, although bequeathed to the son, proved old and out-of-date, compelling Thomas to borrow current books on history and divinity. Purchasing new tomes was apparently too expensive. Other challenges beset both parson and congregation. When divine service began, Symmes labored mightily (and unsuccessfully) to close the meetinghouse doors; worshippers who rested their heads on top of the pews or in their hands faced clerical rebuke; and church singers unaccustomed to musical notation produced a cacophony of unpleasant sounds—much to Symmes's dismay. Symmes took great pride in his singing ability, making him sensitive to badly sung psalms during worship.

Two of his sermons published in 1720 and 1722 emphasized the benefit of note singing. Anyone who disagreed about singing, or religious matters in general, might fall victim to the Reverend's "quick temper."[11]

Yet Symmes worked to correct misunderstandings, apologized when he was at fault, and displayed remarkable personal piety. What Increase Mather had praised about him at Harvard attracted people's notice. Displays of temper could not obscure the faith and intellect that these outbursts temporarily clouded. Symmes's colleagues did appreciate him. The Reverend John Wise, himself a champion of proper church singing, valued Symmes as an ally, writing to him that "when there were a sufficient number in a congregation, to carry away a tune roundly, it was proper to introduce that tune." Symmes also out-published most of his fellow clerics, his sermonic interests extending beyond church singing.[12]

For instance, the Ancient and Honorable Artillery Company, the oldest chartered provincial military organization in New England, provided a stage for a Symmes's sermon when, in 1720, they approached Symmes to speak. Sermons were an annual tradition of the Boston-based company; to be asked to preach before its prominent membership represented a singular honor, with a published sermon a distinct possibility.[13]

Just who in the company invited Symmes to Boston may never be known. We can say that individuals thought him worth hearing and that some wanted his words published. Almost certainly the Reverend Benjamin Colman, parson of the Brattle Street meeting and a leading Reformed clergy moderate, numbered among them. He may have been drawn to Symmes's unusually rich voice. In his preface to Symmes's sermon, Colman judged the effort "pleasant in the hearing," and the diarist Samuel Sewall, a company captain, applauded Symmes's delivery as a "great refreshment and comfort as to the afflicted estate of the Church of God." The printed word could not reproduce Symmes's intonations; still, *Good Soldier, Described and Animated,* carried clear words of advice easy enough to discern. Readers learned that adversaries were best met by settlers proficient in arms, steadfast in calling, and Christian to the core. The sermon chided settlers who acted the part of soldiers without knowing their role. As Symmes ruefully remarked, "The Good Lord pardon our Training Day Sins." What was the source of this reference? Obviously, too much time spent drinking over long winter months had eroded martial virtues. Further moral admonishment would flow from Symmes's pen with Captain Lovewell's death.[14]

Samuel Penhallow's path toward historical narrative differed from that of

Symmes. English born, Penhallow attended a Dissenting school run by the Reverend Charles Morton, a noted educator. Classes there focused on science, politics, and culture. A republican, even radical, atmosphere pervaded the academy with students voting on school decisions. Although the academy closed in 1686 as a result of ecclesiastical pressures from the Church of England, Penhallow accompanied Morton to New England, planning to study at Harvard for one or two years. English Dissenters offered Penhallow twenty pounds sterling per annum to learn the Indian languages, a sum that would increase to sixty pounds if he ministered to them. In Massachusetts, Penhallow met Samuel Sewall, then a young man of parts, and corresponded with Cotton Mather, a rising clerical figure. But Penhallow shelved any ministerial plans, went to Portsmouth, married Mary Cutt, daughter of a prominent New Hampshire merchant, and transformed himself into a prominent fish trader and merchant.[15]

New Hampshire was a rougher, less polished version of Massachusetts. Instead of the "City upon a Hill" championed by John Winthrop and his Puritan descendants, New Hampshire became synonymous with ship masts, furs, and fish. Faith necessarily coexisted with profits. A smattering of non-Puritans inhabited the province, and even the Anglicans had a toehold there from the early 1600s. Massachusetts treated New Hampshire as a younger sibling, occasionally errant yet not without promise, and the New Hampshire lieutenant governor reported to Massachusetts's chief executive. Meanwhile, Samuel Penhallow attended the Portsmouth church, rising to deacon by 1707. For him, as for many Reformed Christians, faith and profits went hand in hand. While Symmes struggled financially, reliant upon his parishioners' uncertain generosity, Penhallow enjoyed relative comfort in a brick house at the head of a Portsmouth pier.[16]

Movement up the political ladder followed. Wealth opened doors to society, and society opened doors to politics, so provincial offices fell within Penhallow's grasp. That Penhallow aligned himself with the Portsmouth political elite led by the Wentworth family in 1716 underscored his status. He advanced from the provincial assembly to the council. In 1714, he became a superior court judge, attaining the post of chief justice three years later. He also served as colony treasurer. Samuel Penhallow, Esquire, as he styled himself in correspondence, ranked among a bare handful of New Hampshire's favored elite able to employ that title.[17]

As a prominent official, Penhallow could expect to become embroiled in

Indian affairs. New Hampshire's location north of Massachusetts and west of Maine put it on the front lines of Native American–English interactions. In 1703 Penhallow sailed to Maine on a delicate mission, hoping to defuse a crisis with the Penobscot Indians. New Hampshire traders needed Indians for the fur trade. They also knew that gifts wisely dispensed helped to ensure peaceful relations. Goodwill had evaporated when New Hampshire men abused Indians—in this instance, one Chadwell, who had robbed and killed a member of the Penobscot nation. Warfare already engulfed Europe, and Maine's fluid borders, inhabited by English settlers, French missionaries, and Abenaki natives presented a potential tinderbox ready to ignite. Penhallow temporarily restrained the Penobscots, earning their gratitude by announcing Chadwell's imprisonment. Nevertheless, when a French and Indian raiding party attracted some Abenaki recruits in August, killing eight people in Casco and Wells, Massachusetts declared war, undoing Penhallow's placatory work.[18]

Penhallow could rejoice when the Eastern Abenaki signed a peace treaty in 1713. Along with Governor Joseph Dudley, chief executive of both Massachusetts and New Hampshire, Penhallow and several councilors from the two provinces traveled to Casco, Maine, to affirm the treaty. A celebratory mood capped by the exchange of gifts followed, though Penhallow observed enthusiastic younger Indians, unswayed by the sachem's authority, stealing his presents. In 1717, Penhallow accompanied Governor Samuel Shute of Massachusetts and Samuel Sewall to Georgetown, Maine, participating in ceremony-steeped Indian negotiations. The climax came when the Indians, at the governor's insistence, draped themselves in the British flag to symbolize their allegiance to the king.[19]

Penhallow's other notable Indian experience involved running afoul of Massachusetts law. As a successful merchant and trader, Penhallow necessarily diversified his operations. The fishing trade and ship ownership furnished the means to deliver the goods and hunt up markets. His importation of Indian slaves from Carolina into the colony aboard his ship, the *Neptune*, in 1712 revealed his seamier business dealings. The action violated a recently passed law prohibiting the introduction of Indian slaves and servants into the province. Penhallow claimed ignorance and asked that the fine be remitted. His old friend Samuel Sewall simply acknowledged the incident in his diary without noting its outcome.[20]

Dummer's War recalled earlier settler conflicts with Native Americans. Steadily building border tensions exploded into full-scale war by 1722, leaving

Penhallow to ponder the violence of his times. Outraged at "the cruelty and perfidy of the Indian enemy," he had, it seems, kept records. But Penhallow had intended to write a private memoir until he was convinced to publish a chronicle "by some whose judgment I pay a deference unto." Accordingly, he lambasted the Indians as New England's scourge—this was standard Reformed Christian rhetoric—but also chastised New Englanders' feeble efforts at conversion. "We have rather aimed to advance a private trade," Penhallow noted wistfully, "then to instruct them in the principle of true religion." Was he displaying a twinge of conscience, suggesting a more nuanced view of the Abenakis that did not descend to Indian hating? If so, it was brief. Penhallow portrayed eighteenth-century New England wars in a glow of provincial patriotism that evinced scant empathy for Native Americans. John Lovewell and company would aptly symbolize this narrative line.[21]

John Lovewell attained recognition as a successful scalp hunter from his first two expeditions against the Indians. The fatal third expedition against the Pigwackets drew considerably more publicity in both official and private circles. News about John Lovewell's death spread rapidly across New Hampshire and Massachusetts. When the first party of men reached Dunstable on May 11, led by the deserter Benjamin Hassell, a grim Colonel Eleazer Tyng forwarded the gloomy message to Boston the following day. By May 13, Samuel Sewall had heard Lieutenant Governor William Dummer report Lovewell and many company members killed. That same day the first survivors reached Dunstable, adding to the story, and Seth Wyman led a second group of Lovewell men to the settlement on May 15. Some of these men, after departing Dunstable, talked to newspapers.[22]

That Symmes wrote a sermon about the battle by May 16 should be no surprise. The image of desk-bound clerics tediously drafting Sabbath-day remarks ignores how many clerics were capable of writing discourses from notes in less than a day. Symmes had done so on at least one occasion. Mastery of biblical passages helped too—Old or New Testament texts learned long ago became foundation stones for constructing future lessons. The first report about Lovewell sent to Dummer from Dunstable, perhaps augmented by the accounts of returning troopers on May 13, could have reached Bradford by May 15. Symmes had all of Saturday, May 15, to construct a sermon on the available information. What he most likely heard, if short, would have detailed

John Lovewell's death, the loss of men, Hassell's desertion, and the Indians slain. Additional specifics would come later. And, as we shall see, Symmes's sermon contained grimmer details than his later published version.[23]

Lack of precise details of the battle would have troubled Symmes little. After all, his much praised 1720 sermon elaborated on faith, soldiers, and God in broad brushstrokes. Moreover, Symmes's colleagues had fashioned Dummer's War into a platform that portrayed the war in theological terms: Catholic versus Protestant, the French against the English, with the Abenakis as French pawns, emerged as available themes. Cotton Mather and Benjamin Colman wrote British contacts that French Canadians and their Abenaki allies were besieging Protestantism, New England, and by extension Great Britain. Europe's peace still held, but New England clerics imbued the borderland conflict with Atlantic and divine significance.[24]

Before local audiences, New England clerics employed pulpit and printing press to bewail the sorry state of affairs. The Reverend Benjamin Wadsworth blamed New England's recurring drought, recent pirate attacks, and the 1721 smallpox epidemic on the citizenry's moral shortcomings. Dummer's War fit nicely into the spectrum of misfortunes. The Reverend Thomas Foxcroft, a much published Boston cleric, linked Indian depredations to lackluster religious faith—a theme Symmes would play upon. In Northampton, Massachusetts, the Reverend Solomon Stoddard targeted New England's failed missionary works. In assessing Captain John Lovewell's downfall, Symmes could draw on his colleagues' blueprint, needing only an appropriate biblical text for emphasis.[25]

Symmes employed 2 Samuel, focusing on a distraught David grief-stricken by the deaths of King Saul and his son Jonathan, David's closest friend. Here memory of the Bible was helpful. Symmes praised David's distress-filled elegy for its elegance and tenderness. David's "Brave and Manly" lamentations, in Symmes's words, inspired the Israelites with "zeal to prosecute the War against the Barbarous Philistines, and to avenge the Death of their Sovereign, and several of the Royal Family, and many other Gallant Soldiers, and to defend themselves, against their Insults and Depredations." If lamentations in biblical wartimes served a valued purpose, they might also work well in early eighteenth-century Massachusetts. Lovewell stood in for Saul and Jonathan. The tragedy, if properly broached, could inspire the righteous to continue the fight and right the disaster.[26]

Except for the sermon title, John Lovewell was unmentioned until the homily was nearly three-quarters done; the scripture and the lesson had provided the intellectual thrust. When referring to Lovewell and company, Symmes admitted that he was unfamiliar with most of the men. Yet, in his estimation, their prior actions in successfully stalking Indians on two occasions without casualties bespoke their character. Long marches in winter or summer did not fatigue them; their intimate knowledge of Abenaki hiding places served them well. However, lest people attribute Lovewell's early success and later death to the "fortune of war," namely a fickle bit of happenstance, Symmes pointedly reminded his listeners that "the Finger of God" was responsible.[27]

Symmes emphasized the mishaps that had befallen Lovewell's last mission. That the captain had left so many men behind to succor one sick man; that a cowardly soldier prevented timely aid from the rear guard; and that Lovewell ventured into the woods with so few men in the spring, when the "Enemy are capable of better Subsisting in Bodies," underscored (in Symmes's judgment) God's displeasure toward the captain. And why was this so? "God," Symmes proclaimed, "is loudly calling upon us to amend our ways & doings." It was New England's sins that destroyed Lovewell and companions, just as "David slew Uriah the Hittite by the Sword of the children of Ammon." This was vivid, disturbing imagery starkly drawn. Prior calls from the pulpit and the press, reinforced by many election sermons, had supplied warnings "against the Provoking Guilt of the Land!" Now, Symmes insisted, New Englanders must shake off their spiritual lethargy if they wished to fight anew. Arms must be in good working order, ammunition nearby, and marksmanship practiced. Those thus prepared and emboldened in faith should search for Lovewell survivors and bury the dead, just as the men of Jabeth Gilead had done for Saul and Jonathan.[28]

Symmes also reminded his listeners and readers of the importance of sepulture. This theme had been sounded in previous wars. Body parts represented war trophies: both Indians and English collected scalps and otherwise desecrated bodies. The recovery of bodies for proper burial fulfilled Christian interment traditions. The men of Jabeth Gilead, outraged by the Philistines' abuse of the slain Saul and Jonathan, formed a troop, entered the pagan temple, burned the bodies, and interred the bones under a tree at Jabeth. New Englanders, thought Symmes, should emulate them, taking a "sufficient Number, as far as Pigwacket, only to cover the Dust, the Valuable Dust of our Gallant Soldiers, that there kept the Field, lest the Dau'ters of the uncircumcised rejoyce."[29]

Yet Symmes went beyond admonishment and prescription to offer a sliver of hope. New England's tragic loss had nonetheless averted a far worse disaster: the Indians' slain, according to Symmes, numbered triple Lovewell's losses, and among them was Paugus, a fierce Indian leader. Paugus's death at the hands of Lovewell and company had saved many more English lives. Grieving congregants, if smarting from Symmes's earlier criticisms, could draw some consolation from this message—if the minister in fact had presented this specific scenario.[30]

No doubt Paugus's death provided New Englanders with some emotional compensation for the loss of Lovewell. However, Symmes could not have known that Paugus died on May 16. Returning troopers never named Paugus; they described Indians dropping and being carried away by comrades. Colonel Eleazer Tyng's rescue party, departing Dunstable on May 17, the day after Symmes's sermon, uncovered Paugus's battlefield grave several days later. Not until June 10 did the *Boston News Letter* alert readers to this fact. Unless the Bradford cleric had heard rumors, Paugus appears to have been a later Symmes's addition for publication. The Volunteer's March, a heroic ballad about Lovewell and company published by May 31, cited Seth Wyman as having killed Paugus, suggesting that word-in-the-street information was a possibility here; however, no original copy from the 1725 ballad survives. Whatever the Bradford congregation heard from the pulpit, Symmes had satisfied himself that his homily merited publication.[31]

For Symmes, that meant a trip to Boston, home to publishers, several printers, and three newspapers. He turned to Samuel Gerrish, a prominent bookseller responsible for printing five of Symmes's six published sermons. Gerrish approached Bartholomew Green. As printer and publisher of the *Boston News Letter,* the quasi-official newspaper of Boston, Green could offer better credentials than James Franklin, the *New England Courant* publisher, whose edgy articles ruffled officials' feathers. Yet Gerrish wanted more than a jeremiad-laced sermon—he asked for a historical narrative to balance the homily. Symmes scurried to find newspaper fight accounts before encountering Seth Wyman, the acknowledged hero, and several others "of good credit, that were in the engagement," namely Ebenezer Ayer and Abiel Asten. Wyman came from Woburn, and Ayer and Asten hailed from Haverhill, Massachusetts, a neighboring town to Bradford. Symmes wished to list the combatants, hoping to bequeath their names to posterity, while intending some "enlargements" in the battle narrative.[32]

Symmes listened to the men's accounts and then began writing. In the case of the troopers whose names were at hand, the heroic could be individually

highlighted and praised; the others were simply identified by name. The coward Hassell remained conspicuously omitted. We cannot know how long the
writing took, but Gerrish's bookstore offered the May 16 sermon, with its historical preface, for sale by July 1. Moreover, Symmes had asked Wyman, Ayer,
and Asten to sign an attestation of the account for publication. Perhaps the
sonorous-voiced minister had been less than pitch-perfect, for the three men
endorsed the product cautiously: "We whose names are hereunto subscrib'd,
having had the Proceeding Narrative carefully Read to us (tho we can't each
of us indeed, Attest to every particular article and circumstance in it,) yet we
can and do Aver that the substance of it is True, and are well Satisfy'd in the
Truth of the whole."[33]

Why the three men registered uncertainties about particular details while
acknowledging the overall depiction is a mystery. Preston Tuckerman Shea,
who has studied the topic thoroughly, labeled the attestation "curious"; to
him it suggested disagreement and subsequent negotiation between the three
men and Symmes over the battle account. Perhaps Symmes's editorializ-
ing embarrassed them; or the fact that Symmes had heard "reports, (as I'm
informed)"—in his words—about Eleazer Davis and the other three men left
behind. Talking about abandoned comrades raised a sore point. Nor could
Wyman and company testify to Davis's account, since they had been long
separated from him by that time. Symmes cast no blame on them—Hassell
conveniently served as the unnamed villain—but the suffering of Davis and
the others could cause readers to apportion blame to others.[34]

The resulting product passed muster with the public. In effect, Symmes's
historical ode to brave men balanced the sermonic elegy he had originally
offered. Gerrish possessed at least a polite interest in things military, holding
the rank of sergeant in the Boston Artillery company. Of course, as a member
of Old South Church and a prominent publisher, Gerrish appreciated religious works, but marketplace interests could not be gainsaid, especially since
Lovewell's Fight was on everyone's tongue. Information-hungry Bostonians
craved publications on current topics.[35]

Gerrish probably noticed, and if not Green might have seen, a *New England
Chronicle* advertisement on May 31 for "The Volunteer March," the aforementioned ballad whose verses saluted Lovewell and company. James Franklin
labeled it an "excellent new song." As well he should, as Tom Law, a popular ver-
sifier, most likely authored the account, and his ability to turn out popular pieces
guaranteed their circulation. Broadside ballads could be hawked in Boston

streets, posted on building walls, and sung in taverns. Some even reached rural towns courtesy of peddlers, a fact Cotton Mather bewailed as early as 1713. This being so, Gerrish needed Symmes to tap into the popular mood with something more than a general call to reform. Lovewell's Fight packaged as historical chronicle would complement Law's ballad and draw readers.[36]

This so-called strategy produced dividends. Bookseller Gerrish needed people to stop by his establishment near the Brick meetinghouse in Cornhill, Boston, hence his July 1 advertisement in the *Boston News Letter* alerting readers that "This day is published, Historical Memoirs of the late Battle at Piggwacket, between Capt. Lovewell & Company, and a number of our Indian Enemy." For one shilling a copy or ten shillings a dozen, readers could learn about the battle "well attested by several that were in that fight." Mention of Thomas Symmes's sermon followed. Gerrish artfully moved the titles around. Although *Lovewell Lamented* headed the title page, the advertisement emphasized the historical prologue. The battle took precedence in form (as the prologue did to the sermon) as well as in advertising substance. The pamphlet soon sold out.[37]

Flushed with success, Gerrish moved ahead with a second edition. The *New England Courant* on July 10 alerted Bostonians to the forthcoming new edition. This was the first time a Symmes's sermon had required a second printing. Then again, none of them had targeted a military battle before. The second edition, entitled *Historical Memoir of the Late fight at Piggwackett, with a sermon, occasion'd by the fall of the brave Capt. Lovewell,* positioned the battle prologue to dominate the title page. The type was reset too. Yet both the *New England Courant* announcement and the *Boston News Letter* advertisement in July 15, 1725, started with Symmes's sermon before mentioning the "particular account of that heroic action." Perhaps the ads targeted more religious-minded readers. The new title carried the note *The Second Edition Corrected,* which may have been intended to lure second-time buyers.[38]

Symmes as chronicler/historian barely needed to cloak his ministerial persona. Writing history was not terribly different from writing a sermon. True, Lovewell and company were not historical biblical figures, but nonetheless parallels could be drawn. What Symmes did do was temper some of the harsher, jeremiad intonations that distinguished the sermon: God would still hover in the background, but more discreetly; Saul and Jonathan went missing. In their place, other triumphant biblical figures could be linked to Lovewell and his men.[39]

Symmes started with Joshua, in fact a more successful Israelite warrior than Saul, drawn from the sixteenth chapter of Exodus, to lead off the prologue. Lovewell and Joshua, however indirectly linked, provided a telling biblical image. Scripture related that Joshua had stopped the sun from setting and set Jericho's walls tumbling. In this instance, Symmes related how Joshua "discomforted" the enemies of Israel, the Amaleks, "with the edge of the sword," assisted by Moses, who invoked God's help from afar. The success of those fighting the Lord's battles, Symmes related, is "very proper to be commemorated, for the honor of God and encouragement of his servants in future expedition and military actions."[40]

The battle sources—Wyman and his comrades—followed, with the soldiers and their settlements named. Hassell, as always, remained deliberately excluded; unnamed, he descended into historical oblivion, his fall from grace complete. The account then set the parameters leading to the battle. On May 8, a Saturday, according to Symmes, after prayers the men spotted a lone Indian near the Pigwacket pond. Lovewell warned of a possible trap; the troop refused to be intimidated and responded in a Greek chorus. To return home, they thought, would brand them cowards. The Indian was shot. But Lovewell's fears proved correct when a subsequent ambush saw the two sides clashing, with guns ablaze. Casualties mounted, prompting the English to retreat to a defensive position, a "vast service" that spared lives. The wounded chaplain, Jonathan Fyre, drew special attention in the Symmes's narrative, fighting courageously until he was wounded, at which point he offered prayers above the din of musket shots. Symmes ignored newspaper claims that Frye had killed five Indians, content to emphasize his religious character rather than his military feats. By evening, the battered troop had compelled the Indians to leave.[41]

Now Symmes faced a moral conundrum more aptly suited to a pulpit discourse. How to handle the story of the wounded left behind? In his May 16 sermon, he had emphasized finding survivors and burying the dead. Now the story of the abandoned men and the company's fragmentation needed telling. This was sensitive historic terrain. During King Philip's War the unrecovered dead and the abandoned wounded had spurred ministerial indignation. Time and again, clerics insisted on burial and rescue. Hassell's desertion at the beginning of the fight provided a solution. Symmes noted that Wyman and his men had separated from the seriously wounded scouts—Frye, Farwell, Davis, and Jones—after a short march because they were convinced the rear guard from the fort would rescue them. Frye and his companions agreed.

The exhausted troopers broke up into three companies, allegedly to throw off Indian pursuers, with two of the groups later meeting up at the empty fort. Hassell could be blamed for the deserted camp. The troopers then pressed onward and reached Dunstable by May 13.[42]

What Symmes did was to offer words of thankfulness: Psalm 107, "O that Men would Praise the Lord for his Goodness, and for His Wonderful Works toward the Children of Men," provided his theme. The men had survived! And the next paragraph mentioned Seth Wyman's safe return on May 15 with several others. The trouble was Frye and company were still out there—how would God's mercy manifest itself when the hand of man had seemingly failed?

The Reverend Symmes avoided ready-made biblical verses. Instead, Eleazer Davis's voice, drawn from reports he had heard firsthand, informed the narrative. It was a grim tale. The four men despaired of aid after days of waiting. Despite infected wounds and lack of food, they began to march. Several miles later Frye stopped and instructed Davis to inform his father of his calm readiness to die. Farwell followed shortly afterward, heralded by Symmes as one "Deservedly Applauded" in battle. Jones turned up in Saco, Maine, after separating from Davis. Symmes resolved the dilemma of the unrecovered soldiers by listing them as casualties "lost by the way," almost implying that they were misplaced, not abandoned. Symmes insisted that the returnees (and indeed all brave soldiers) embrace the motto of Moses on his altar of gratitude: "The Lord is my Banner."[43]

Symmes measured out moral censure selectively. Hassell bore the entire burden of the blame. Indeed, he became a kind of sacrificial victim; his actions seemingly absolved all others of any questionable behavior. The returnees from Pigwacket who neglected to wait for Wyman at the fort? That rated no comment by Symmes. The four men left behind, of which two later separated? No blame there either. Even Solomon Kies, who informed Wyman of his impending battlefield departure, severely wounded and unable to stand, found himself "wonderfully strengthened," by the time he reached the fort to find his comrades—with nary a criticism from Symmes. Was Kies really that different from Hassell? And Jones had left Davis without reprimand from Symmes.

The second edition of the fight continued to hew to this line. Symmes added a missing trooper's name, dropped an incorrect name, and inserted a lengthy footnote on the second page. In *Historical Memoir*, Symmes described a day of prayer before the battle had occurred: "Agreeable to which, upon intelligence of great numbers of Indians coming down on the frontiers, and the march of several of our companies in search of 'em; at the motion of his honour, the Lieutenant Governor and the ministers of Boston, the public lecture there, on April 29 was turn'd into a day of prayer, which was but nine days before the fight at Piggwacket: the success whereof should there have been ascribed with thankfulness and proved to God as a gracious answer of the humble prayers of his people, and improv'd as further encouragement."[44]

In thanking the lieutenant governor and the clergy, Symmes was perhaps polite; yet reminders about prayers' efficacy and God's role blended religion and battle reporting, and compensated for any unintended slight of the Almighty. Symmes's verdict on the battle had evolved; it was now called a "success." Previously, tragedy and repentance had distinguished the sermon. Although still present, that message was now relegated to the latter half of the pamphlet behind the historical prologue, necessitating an extended footnote to keep readers focused on the divine.[45]

Whatever readers took away from the pamphlet, Symmes had little time to ponder its impact, for he died in late October. In framing the battle narrative, he had provided a lodestar to guide future chroniclers and historians. They could revise and challenge his account; they could expand and embellish the story in their retellings; but his effort could never be ignored. Would that have pleased him? Perhaps the Reverend John Brown's 1726 memorial account of his life would have been more to the minister's liking. Brown portrayed Symmes as a faithful, sometimes temperamental, cleric of great piety. Then again, a notice in that pamphlet identifying Gerrish as the publisher of the *Historical Memoir* and *Ashton's Memorial* might have gratified Symmes too. *Ashton's Memorial* told of a Marblehead man and companion who escaped pirates to survive sixteen months on a deserted island. Marblehead minister John Barnard composed and added a sermon to the tract. An exciting adventure involving men and the environment was followed by a sermon with lessons to teach in *Ashton's Memorial*. Now *that* Symmes could appreciate. It was a format he had employed himself.[46]

Samuel Penhallow wrote a more encompassing historical narrative less wedded to the eighteenth-century jeremiad in tone and substance. The length and breadth of Queen Anne's War, which included the bloody Deerfield raid, followed by Dummer's War, provided plentiful details. Names of soldiers and settlers abounded, set alongside treaty terms and ceremonies. In writing about

Dummer's War, Penhallow castigated French missionaries, especially Father Sebastian Rale, applauding the successful 1724 Norridgewock raid that ended that "bloody incendiary" life. But Penhallow remained mindful of God, and the Reverend Benjamin Colman, his sponsor, would be sure to emphasize the Almighty's role in the preface, though how much of it Colman wrote aside from biblical insertions remains questionable.[47]

Colman's job may have been to get the manuscript to press. As a leading, well-published cleric, he would find printers' doors open to him, at least wider than they might be to first-time author Penhallow. As its sponsor, Colman had a direct stake in the work and approached Samuel Gerrish and Colonel Daniel Henchman, solidly established Boston publishers. Gerrish we know from Symmes's sermon, but Henchman, according to Edward Wheelock, who edited the 1924 reprint of Penhallow's Indian Wars, was "the most eminent Boston bookseller of his time." Gerrish had published more than fifty books; Henchman, along with Benjamin Eliot, printed seven hundred and fifty copies of the Reverend Samuel Willard's eleven-hundred-page tome in 1726—the longest book published in Boston. Not surprisingly, it was Henchman and several others who established New England's first paper mill. Thomas Fleet served as Penhallow's printer. London born and trained, Fleet produced work of indifferent quality, employing worn typefaces. Penhallow's book, which Wheelock described as an example of "unskillful and inconsistent typography," was unfortunately representative.[48]

Either Garrish or Henchman could stock the book in their respective stores. But how many were printed? That question cannot be answered, except that we can infer that the seven hundred and fifty copies of Willard's work, A Complete Body of Divinity, probably exceeded Penhallow's Indian Wars by a wide margin. Besides, Willard had many subscribers; Penhallow just had Colman, an important minister yet not a guarantor of large sale numbers. That relatively few copies of Penhallow's work survived may indicate as much.[49]

Enter the mysterious Edward Wheelock. As the 1924 editor and all-round scribe who deciphered Penhallow (and possibly Colman's insertions), Wheelock left meager traces of himself. He likely republished Penhallow's book himself—no publisher was listed in the 1924 copy—and Boston, the city of publication, may have been his home. But this is just conjecture. We do know that Wheelock was an assiduous researcher, pouring over the original manuscript and Penhallow's research notes. One question that Wheelock addressed was the extent of Penhallow's authorship and Colman's editing. The actual manuscript contained numerous errors. What Penhallow had written in draft was in fact quite unpolished and critical. Some passages were omitted from the final product. While Wheelock offered a line-by-line analysis comparing the rough manuscript to the published text, he admitted that only the "more important variations from the printed text" made the notes of his 1924 reprint. Evidently frustrated, he reported: "so many and so various are the discrepancies that their transcription would require more space than their interest warrants. Not only are there some differing spellings of places and persons, but many serious omissions of places and persons; but many serious omissions of statement of facts; conversely there are found a few additions in the text seemingly added in proofreading, it may be by another hand."[50] Wheelock believed that the Reverend Colman had toned down Penhallow's prose, corrected errors, and substituted more refined Latin words for "homely Anglo-Saxon." What Colman polished, others buffed. Subsequent 1824 and 1859 editions saw different stylists tailoring the work.[51]

What Penhallow did provide was a chronicle of events from 1703 to 1725. The names of political worthies, especially Governor William Dummer and the oft-controversial Governor Samuel Shute, materialized in print; however, Lieutenant Governor Dummer received nine citations to Shute's three despite the latter's longer term of office. Governor Joseph Dudley, the chief executive during much of Queen Anne's War, garnered five mentions, but four of these involved listing his name on treaties. Penhallow also knew enough to exercise tact: in describing Shute's unexpected hasty departure from Massachusetts, he gently explained it as "His Excellency's Affairs now calling him to Great Britain." Left unsaid were the contentious political battles between Shute and the legislature, as well as the possibility that Governor Shute had departed in fear for his life. For Dummer, a born and bred Massachusetts man, praise rang loud: this was a man "whose prudence and good conduct have made him acceptable unto all."[52]

Of equal interest, however, is Penhallow's ranking of military leaders. The names of dead, wounded, attacked, or lost civilians furnished much of the coverage; this was more a chronicle and less a modern piece of historical scholarship. Names mattered, especially when readers might know them. Commanders in the narrative occupied the high ground. Benjamin Church, the King Philip's War scout, received a cameo mention for raising men at the start of Queen Anne's War. Captain John Penhallow, Samuel's son, garnered several references in a display of parental pride. But Caleb Lyman, an early scalp hunter from 1704, won inclusion if only to make a point underscoring provincial stinginess. Penhallow reprinted Lyman's original account listing seven Indians killed and six scalped. That Lyman and his Indian allies received just thirty-one pounds from Massachusetts outraged Penhallow: "I beg the Country's leave to observe, How Poorly this bold Action, and great Service was rewarded; No doubt they looked for, and well deserved, eight times as much; and now the province would readily pay eight hundred pounds in the like Case." At least Lyman, by 1726 a Boston church elder and respected citizen, could receive spiritual succor, in that a "gracious God has recompensed to the Elder, I trust, both in the Blessings of his Providence and Grace." Merchant Penhallow, familiar with government treasury disbursements, expected proper payment for good work.[53]

Scalp bounties by the time of Dummer's War met Penhallow's criteria better, with one hundred pounds being allotted for an adult scalp. Consequently, Captain Harmon's August attack on Norridgewock netted twenty-seven scalps that received prompt and proper provincial payment. Moreover, Rale was scalped and killed and several Indian captives safely returned. The published work lauded Norridgewock as the "greatest Victory we have obtained in the three or four last Wars; and it may be as noble an Exploit (all things considered) as ever happened in the time of King Philip." In the manuscript Penhallow heaped additional praise on the expedition's surmounting difficult travel conditions, in which the men ventured 120 miles into the Indian country, "thro so many swarms of flyes, gnats, and mosquetoes." He also proved more circumspect in private, for the manuscript notes claimed no action compared to the Norridgewock victory since the Narragansett defeat in King Philip's War.[54]

Had Colman excised the passage? Or was Penhallow so awash in provincial pride that he decided to forgo the reminder of an earlier New England assault? That constitutes the mystery. Colman almost surely added phrasing, but did he persuade Penhallow to remove passages? Stylistic considerations perhaps dictated Colman's hand, or perhaps he eliminated praise that he deemed excessive. In any event, Colman may have been piqued that Penhallow had neglected to remind readers of God's intercession, a role that the Boston minister cited in the preface when he lauded the Norridgewock escapade as "the wonderful victory obtained August 12, 1724," due to the "singular Work of God; And the Officers and Soldiers piously put far from themselves the Honour of it. The plain hand of Providence and not their own Conduct facilitated and

quickened their march." Much as Symmes reminded listeners and later readers of God's finger directing events, so did Colman credit divine power.[55]

Captain John Lovewell inspired less editorial oversight. His buildup in
the history, starting with the first raid, depicted a public-spirited Dunstable
resident whose company of thirty volunteers shot one Indian and captured
the other, pocketed one hundred pounds, and earned two shillings five pence
per day. By his second expedition, Lovewell easily surprised the ten sleeping
Indians. The scalp bounty totaling one thousand pounds went unmentioned;
for Penhallow, the Indians' brand new guns that fetched seven pounds apiece
seemed more worthy of being recorded for posterity.[56]

The third expedition received the most detailed treatment. If Symmes
created the first blueprint about Lovewell's exploits, Penhallow only learned
of it in mid-July 1725, when the second edition of Symmes's work appeared.
Penhallow complimented the cleric as the "ingenious Mr. Symmes." Still, certain events related by Symmes surprised him: Lieutenant Robbins's desire to
have a gun in order to shoot one last Indian was unfamiliar to him; nor had
he heard of Solomon Kies's remarkable battlefield escape. Neither the Boston
newspapers nor Eleazer Davis, Penhallow's main informant, mentioned
these events. Penhallow registered mild surprise without directly challenging
their accuracy. Sharp-eyed readers could draw their own conclusions—what
Symmes had announced did not always square with other accounts.[57]

Even so, Penhallow's depiction paralleled much of Symmes's description of
the battle, including Lovewell's troopers rejecting their captain's advice about
the lone Indian spotted before the shooting. The Reverend Jonathan Frye,
whom Symmes commended for heroically praying while wounded, came off
more modestly. Newspapers claimed that Frye had scalped several Indians,
whereas Symmes asserted that he had scalped the lone Indian before the battle. Penhallow also omitted mention of Frye the combatant, instead focusing
on Frye the severely wounded survivor who died alone. Here Eleazer Davis
furnished Penhallow with eyewitness testimony; Symmes had only heard
accounts reported by Davis. While Symmes emphasized the dying Frye's brave
declaration to his father, Penhallow left any paternal message unrecorded—
perhaps because there was none to record.[58]

Davis the abandoned trooper provided Penhallow with information
unknown or unheard by Symmes. Both chroniclers agreed that Wyman's
assumption of command was crucial. Yet not everything Davis related made
the editorial cut in Penhallow's work. For instance, he asserted that Wyman

had killed five or six Indians while concealed behind a tree. This certainly accords with Wyman's later accolades, suggesting he was both a take-charge leader of men and a marksman. More modestly, Davis claimed that he himself "had many a fair shott, and saw several fall; he lost one joynt off of his thumb, had his gun broke in two." These accounts were struck from the finished version. Had Penhallow thought Wyman's accomplishment too heavily gilded? Or had Colman exercised his pen? We cannot tell.[59]

Colman's overall editorial role cannot be discounted. Wheelock judiciously acknowledged the possibility when perusing the manuscript. Almost certainly, as Wheelock posited, Colman expounded on Penhallow's text, supplying biblical citations, namely the men of Jabeth Gilead, who recovered the bodies of Saul and Jonathan and also prepared a decent burial for them. This could almost have been lifted from Symmes's publication. Perhaps biblical accounts interested Penhallow less than they did Symmes. And burial issues, although significant to laypersons, more easily stimulated clerics to display their scholarly background by citing chapter and verse.[60]

Penhallow next underscored the official response to the missing and dead troopers scattered in and around the battle site. Official reaction had been swift and forthcoming; consequently, Colonel Eleazer Tyng's burial detail formed part of the official narrative. Penhallow targeted the fifty absent New Hampshire troopers sent to assist Colonel Tyng. As a New Hampshire official, Penhallow was understandably embarrassed by their actions. Readers of Penhallow's book learned that the well-equipped New Hampshire men "were not so happy as to find them," a technically true statement, as the troopers never rendezvoused with Tyng. In reality, fear overcame the New Hampshire men so that, although well-armed and provisioned, a point Penhallow's manuscript notes stressed, the men "were so miserably terrify'd that in a most shameful and cowardly manner they returned without searching the wounded or dead, or making the least discovery." This damning judgment rivaled any pulpit jeremiad; it may well have resembled Judge Penhallow's sharp-tongued court pronouncements. In any event, Edward Wheelock, after examining the manuscript and the printed version, found them telling enough to include in his notes. Editorial scrutiny deleted Penhallow's heated remarks lest they undermine the heroic motif created.[61]

Penhallow ended the Pigwacket battle on an upbeat note, associating Lovewell and company with British professional soldiers. Although Penhallow admitted that no detachments in Dummer's War could hope to match those of British forces, "which have caused the World to wonder," yet to ignore the "braveries of these Worthies, who died in the Bed of Honour, and for the interest of their Country, would be a denying them the Honour that is due unto their Memory, and a burying them in Oblivion." The glory of the empire manifest in military feats united Britons across the Atlantic, and Lovewell and company's sacrifice vouchsafed Massachusetts's position in a greater political entity. The patriotic glow of empire also made it easier to overlook the moral quagmire of abandoned solders.[62]

We do not know what Penhallow thought of the final book. Apparently, no advertisement in any of the Boston newspapers informed potential readers of its publication. Perhaps people were more interested in other books, such as the steady stream of annual almanacs. Still, Penhallow's account did attract buyers. One Joshua Hempstead, who was interested in eighteenth-century Indian wars, apparently picked up the book in 1728. That the owner of the book fell asleep, causing the work to fall into a fire, as Edward Wheelock suggested, seems far-fetched, though it does explain the copy's damaged condition.[63]

What did survive was the story of the ambushed Lovewell troopers withstanding a tenacious foe. What Symmes and Penhallow chronicled, others built on and embellished. Edward Wheelock, for instance, pointed to the sporadic publishing history of Penhallow's work, which gave people the opportunity to continue to add notes to subsequent limited editions. Yet, the men most familiar with the battle, Lovewell's surviving troopers, added little about the fight. Wyman, Davis, and a few others talked about it, but they were the exceptions. Those who spoke about the conflict were generally seeking to remind listeners of their sufferings, highlight their wounds, and press for monetary compensation, and the best means of doing so was to petition government officials. Wounded ex-Lovewell troopers, maimed or still recovering, hoped for sympathy and recognition; bones shattered by musket balls or limbs improperly set might persuade frugal-minded legislators to loosen their purse strings. Even healthy survivors wanted payment for their service. How skillfully the Lovewell troopers crafted their personal narratives would go far in determining the extent of government compensation.[64]

CHAPTER 5
Social Welfare and Lovewell's Men

On June 4, 1725, Hannah Lovewell, the widow of Captain John Lovewell, petitioned the General Court of Massachusetts. Widows occasionally appealed to the government, but rarely with the endorsement of Lieutenant Governor William Dummer, who days earlier had urged the House of Representatives to show compassion toward Hannah. Lovewell's death, a provincial tragedy, had shaken the family. Suppliers were demanding payment for the hogsheads of bread, canoes, and ammunition procured for the company's expedition, and Hannah Lovewell was uncertain "whom suppliers delivered to so as to demand what is due for them." The court, recognizing the "extraordinary service of Captain Lovewell and company in the actions of Pigwacket," furnished twenty pounds directly to Lovewell's estate and allotted additional funds for canoes, ammunition, and bread. No legislator expected Hannah Lovewell to bear this burden.[1]

Hannah's petition is testimony to the financial impact the war had on a borderland hero's family. Outstanding bills had to be paid and debts honored. Hannah Lovewell's grasp of business and military affairs may have been shaky, but with two young fatherless children to raise and a third on the way, she knew enough to ask for assistance. The two-hundred-acre Lovewell estate, which included several buildings and a half-interest in a sawmill assessed at four hundred forty-four pounds, five shillings, and sixpence in November 1725, along with property in Chelmsford, Massachusetts, valued at fifty pounds, could not be sacrificed to creditors. Even so, despite additional government compensation beyond the twenty pounds, Hannah Lovewell faced still more financial demands. She petitioned the General Court again in June 1726, citing Lovewell's "considerable cost in maintaining volunteers for the service against the Indians" and imploring the legislators for help "as to their great goodness and bounty shall seem meet." The court granted her fifty pounds but rather testily added that these funds represented "in full for any demand on this province for any service done by the said Capt. John Lovewell"—in other words, further requests would be unwelcome.[2]

The Pigwacket battle between Anglo-Americans and Abenakis in 1725 represented the last major engagement of Dummer's War. It enshrined Lovewell's name in the pantheon of New England heroes and weakened Eastern Abenaki autonomy. It also left Pigwacket veterans and their families having to deal with a host of subsequent issues, financial and otherwise. For some individuals, the loss of a loved one at Pigwacket left them grief-stricken, emotionally distraught, and filled "with bitter lamentation or with deep concern."[3] Little wonder, as exposed corpses had awaited battlefield burial for days and other bodies were never recovered. Economic worries compounded the families' grief. How would debts be paid? Could the farm or business be maintained without a husband or father? Hannah Lovewell was not alone in raising such issues—other widows also pleaded for help, citing their fatherless children and desperate financial straits. Injured Pigwacket survivors complained about wounds and medical bills, and the seriously maimed requested provincial pensions. It fell to the General Court of Massachusetts to balance compassion with fiscal constraint, seeking to assess financial and human costs.[4]

Naturally, not every Lovewell expedition survivor or bereaved family member confronted the same challenges or even approached the General Court. Rewards bestowed by a grateful province often eased financial worries, enabling many people to resume normal lives. Widows might remarry and Lovewell soldiers start life anew. A few continued to see service in future wars; others never again shouldered arms in combat; and some virtually disappeared from the historical record. Yet, whatever their circumstances, Pigwacket veterans and widows were linked to an epic (by colonial standards) battle that endowed them with a certain social identity—they were Lovewell men or Lovewell widows, basking in Captain Lovewell's heroic aura and more easily recognizable than other Dummer's War veterans. If they needed help, like Hannah Lovewell, their connection to Lovewell and the Pigwacket fight might prompt legislative action while also testing the limits of government compassion.

Classical Western literature addresses the challenges faced by the returning soldier. The long-suffering Odysseus encountered one-eyed monsters, bewitching sirens, and wrathful gods before reaching Ithaca ten years after the Trojan War's end. At home, Odysseus discovered suitors besieging his wife and despoiling his halls. The disguised and outraged Odysseus revealed himself and exacted a bloody revenge by slaying the would-be suitors. At this point the story more or less ended, at least insofar as Homer was concerned, leaving the subsequent fate of Odysseus and his family blank. Other Trojan War veterans fared worse in Greek and Roman literary accounts. Agamemnon, the Greek army commander, died shortly after reaching home, murdered by his wife or her lover or both; Ajax the Locrian dared to defy the gods and drowned; Diomedes reached home to discover an adulterous wife. In short, few notable Trojan War veterans found a quiet life afterward.[5]

No bard plucked a lyre to relate tales of homeward-bound colonial soldiers taking revenge in the manner of Odysseus. And certainly none struck up a song about veterans' subsequent domestic lives. Colonel Benjamin Church's memoir, which puffed his King Philip's War exploits, divulged little about hearth and home but concentrated on outlining tactics and stratagems for defeating Indians.[6] When fighting ceased, most borderland soldiers swapped muskets for farm tools, worked crops, and raised families. By contrast, Pigwacket survivors and bereaved family members approached the government armed with memorials and petitions as their weapons of choice, intent on compensation or outright assistance.

Lieutenant Governor William Dummer, the acting chief executive since January 1722, championed the Lovewell troopers. Unlike his ill-fated predecessor, Governor Samuel Shute, Dummer worked with the legislature to ease political strains. It was a wise strategy. With the Eastern and Western Abenakis disturbing borderland settlements, the lieutenant governor needed legislative support. He directed the war effort, corresponded with commanders, and offered military advice, scolding and praising. Most important, he kept the legislature informed and approached representatives gingerly for funding—the legislature would express concern about war payouts to no-show soldiers. Indeed, colonial assemblies, concerned about unnecessary taxes, took their role as guardians of the public purse seriously.[7] Nevertheless, when citing the war's improved outlook in a May 26, 1725, speech to the General Court, Dummer singled out the Lovewell expedition: "I recommend to your compassion the widow of Capt. Lovewell and those of his men who died bravely in the late action of Pigwacket in the service of their Country. And I make no doubt but you will distinguish by a suitable reward such officers and soldiers as have distinguished themselves by an uncommon bravery."[8] As the acting chief executive, Dummer expected Lovewell's men and his widow to be suitably compensated for their loss and suffering.

What Dummer requested followed a government tradition of assistance to war veterans and widows. Prior colonial conflicts had featured substantial monetary outlays to raise and supply troops followed by more modest charitable expenditures. Wounded soldiers and widows regularly appealed for help. Soldiers' petitions covered an assortment of reasons—anything from lost possessions to medical bills to debilitating injuries to time spent in service underlay requests. Widows typically required payments to support themselves and any offspring. Dummer's War, although dwarfed by the better-known French and Indian War, was no exception. However, Lieutenant Governor Dummer's personal plea for Lovewell combatants (and one family member) marked his first executive foray in this direction. That the tragedy involved the death of a war hero gave it added urgency.[9]

The Massachusetts House of Representatives oversaw public expenditure. Along with the smaller, more elite provincial council, the House responded to appeals and memoranda from towns and individuals, generally holding two or three legislative sessions per year. In a single day, the House could act on several or more memorials; at other times the House let the Committee of Petitions handle requests from former soldiers, widows, and concerned inhabitants. Indeed, when not handling tax or budgetary issues, the House of Representatives took up the hundreds of petitions submitted before them. Such business was usually settled quickly in several days. Less often, a petition might reappear months later. When Thomas Bradbury, a former soldier in Dummer's War, requested nine pounds, two shillings, for a "fit of sickness contracted by an ill habit of body" while serving in the army, the House sent it to the petitions committee on August 29, 1723. By August 31 they dismissed the petition. As they thought the "ill habit of body" Bradbury cited could have been a disguised reference to venereal disease, they declined to touch it. Only a push made by Captain Joseph Eaton of Salisbury in December 1724 urging the committee and the House to agree to disburse fifteen pounds for Bradbury's doctor bill resurrected the affair. Physicians had to be paid regardless of Bradbury's uncertain condition or morals.[10]

In 1725, Colonel John Stoddard of Northampton headed the Committee of Petitions, seconded by Colonel John Chandler, Jonathan Remington, Nathaniel Paine, Esq., and Timothy Lindall. Stoddard, the politically ambitious youngest son of the Reverend Solomon Stoddard of Northampton, had entered the assembly at the tender age of twenty-four. A hard-nosed official, Stoddard had advocated harsh tactics against the Abenakis, at one point urging that dogs be set upon them. Jonathan Edwards memorialized him more kindly as a man of parts, distinguished by "strength of reason, greatness, and clearness of discerning and depth of penetration." His judgments, according to Edwards, were arrived at after careful deliberation.[11] What Stoddard thought about provincial combatants and their widows remains less clear—the committee never recorded its votes or kept minutes. Any wheeling and dealing or lively debate among members hence remains impossible to discern. What we can say is that Stoddard knew enough to ingratiate himself to Dummer and subsequent royal governors, which compensated for his uncertain speaking abilities and limited legislative popularity. In this regard, Lovewell expedition members and bereaved spouses could breath easier: what the governor requested, Stoddard typically endorsed.[12]

For her part, Hannah Lovewell, the first Lovewell widow to petition the legislature, remains a shadowy, vague figure obscured by her husband's martyrdom. Generations of genealogists and antiquarians have failed to uncover Hannah's family name; all we can assume is that Lovewell married a woman of modest background. That being said, Hannah's petition expressed gratitude toward Lieutenant Governor Dummer for mentioning her, "as well as the other widows who were bereaved of their husbands." Dummer had never referred to these widows directly. Rather, Hannah was reminding legislators that other women had lost their husbands and needed assistance.[13]

The grief-stricken, destitute widow figured as a familiar figure in the sphere of public welfare. Next to orphaned children or maimed soldiers, such women elicited perhaps the greatest degree of sympathy, and war widows dating to as early as King Philip's War had received support from the General Court. Dowry rights in estates were protected and outright grants of assistance dispensed. Economic intervention by local communities occurred if no other support proved forthcoming.[14] While Alexander Keyssar found affluent eighteenth-century Woburn, Massachusetts, widows still on tax rolls, their indigent sisters typically were removed from them—in itself a form of assistance as well as recognition of their situation. Yet, as Keyssar observed, rising welfare expenditures targeting widows occurred in 1708-9 and 1712-13 during Queen Anne's War. Dummer's War produced a similar spike in rates for the 1720s.[15]

Cotton Mather called attention to the widows' plight from his Boston pulpit. Scanning the congregation, Mather concluded that a fifth of his listeners were widows. Spousal death from natural causes and sickness no doubt explained the high number; also, Boston sailors lost at sea left widows in their wake. Whatever the causes of their situation, widows needed succor: "let your liberal alms fall as the showers of Heaven upon them," Mather urged. For the Widow Dorothy Frizzel, whose husband and son had both died in 1724, Mather asked compassion; whereas "the man that shows no pity to the afflicted is no friend unto them." The Reverend Mather practiced what he preached, emptying his pockets to aid the indigent he encountered in Boston streets.[16]

What Mather prescribed and what Puritans rose to sometimes conflicted. Early eighteenth-century Boston was struggling in a maturing Atlantic economy distinguished by cycles of war and peace that alternatively pumped and drained money in and out of the seaport. Economic ripples extended beyond Boston to provincial settlements. A depreciating provincial currency added to fiscal and political woes. Amid the economic fluctuations, poor relief remained a constant expenditure that, while seldom excessive in peacetime, could spike in wartime as more individuals sought assistance. Latter-day Puritans by the early 1700s increasingly blamed the poor themselves, targeting idleness and intemperance as root causes. Since few private charitable bequests existed, towns necessarily devised public solutions, ranging from home relief to poor houses. Boston had a poorhouse for the most destitute; most rural villages boarded out the poor, reimbursing the people who kept them. Communities subscribed to local care of resident poor, a cornerstone of English welfare laws, by screening residents from nonresidents, but poorer communities such as Dunstable, where Hannah Lovewell lived, welcomed provincial assistance whenever possible. Troops had protected Dunstable during Dummer's War. Could not Massachusetts safeguard Dunstable from rising poor rates?[17]

Hannah Lovewell was the ideal candidate to present a petition before the General Court of Massachusetts. Singled out by Lieutenant Governor Dummer, she had assumed the role of the most publicized war widow, her property in no way precluding provincial assistance—at least not at first.

Representatives acknowledged the "sorrowful circumstances of the widow of Captain John Lovewell as well as other widows who lost their husbands in the late action of Pigwacket." By June 12, the petition committee chaired by Stoddard had received the appeal. Bestowing charity underscored both compassionate and political concerns; it would ease suffering among veterans or bereaved family members and "encourage such like brave and gallant actions for the future."[18] In other words, provincial benevolence in the aftermath of tragedy satisfied both popular feeling and government wartime needs.

Not surprisingly, Stoddard's committee recommended relief to troop members and widows, and the House voted hundreds of pounds in payouts. The three slain Indians found by Colonel Eleazer Tyng at the battlefield qualified the Pigwacket fighters or their heirs to receive three hundred pounds. Admittedly, the "scalps were not produced," yet that technicality was easily passed over. To the thirty-three men (or their surviving heirs) present at Pigwacket—the deserter Benjamin Hassell being conspicuously omitted— were granted 990 pounds on June 17, 1725. All shared equally regardless of rank. In addition, immediate family members of slain Pigwacket fighters received death payments. The House approved thirty pounds each for Josiah Farwell, Jonathan Robbins, Jacob Fullam, Jacob Farrah, and Elias Barron's survivors. Deceased Pigwacket fighters without spouse or children effectively lacked heirs anyway—siblings and parents did not count. Captain John Lovewell's family garnered sixty pounds, the highest sum and a reminder that rank did indeed convey privilege.[19]

Hannah Lovewell's petition had yielded substantial results. The one-hundred-dred-pound-plus settlement should have largely covered the debts owed suppliers; in fact, Hannah Lovewell's subsequent remarks suggest that it did. The only fly in the ointment involved household debts unrelated to the Pigwacket venture. At the next legislative session in late autumn, Lovewell asked for additional funds to pay a government bill for ten pounds, seventeen shillings, and nine pence, contracted by her husband for bread stores during his second expedition. Hannah reminded officials that John had ambushed ten Indians in that action, and with "some small children to bring, in poor circumstances," she hoped the General Court would remit payment. Hannah's wording here may have been ill-advised: citing the ten Abenakis killed would remind cost-conscious legislators of the earlier one-thousand-pound payout. To claim poverty might appear rather excessive. In fact, Colonel Stoddard's committee denied Hannah Lovewell's petition.[20]

Hannah Lovewell had discovered provincial charity's limits. Dummer's plea for assistance delivered in the aftermath of the Pigwacket battle had spurred committee members to act promptly; now they just as quickly refused to supplement the disbursement. True, the sum requested by Hannah Lovewell was significantly less than the first, but the governor had selected only the victims of the Pigwacket battle for benevolence. To bring up an earlier, successful expedition as a reason for being granted more money played poorly among cost-conscious legislators.

Hannah Lovewell had the winter months in which to brood and ponder. The lengthening shadows outside and the flickering fire inside the family hearth signaled the change of seasons and fortunes. In the Lovewell household, the children gathered round the hearth, and one of them, an infant, was either suckled or placed in a cradle. There was no husband to offer warmth in the marital bed now. How much Hannah Lovewell could rely on her friends or extended family can only be guessed. She needed bills paid without sacrificing the estate. A glimmer of hope appeared with Colonel Stoddard's departure from the assembly: the sometimes venomous local politics in Northampton had reconfigured the committee, which might permit a more charitable intervention. The new petition committee chair, Thomas Lindell, was a prominent Salem merchant and Harvard graduate, first elected in 1717, who stood down in 1721 and then accepted election again in 1725. His 1760 obituary in the *Boston News Letter* described him as the "Spirit of integrity and virtue." Such qualities, however, did not help the Widow Lovewell—at least not at the moment. On June 2, 1726, she asked to be released from fifty pounds' interest on a 150-pound bond Captain Lovewell had posted from a county loan application. The eager captain had encumbered his estate to procure funds for launching the Indian raid. The House raised the question "Whether the prayer of the petitioner should be granted?" The answer came back no. In fact, Lindall's committee never received the petition.[21]

John Lovewell's exploits and martyrdom had initially elicited legislative compassion toward his family, resulting in the single biggest death payment to any member of the expedition. Still, monetary compensation had to be linked to the Pigwacket battle rather than Lovewell's prior debts, which remained Hannah Lovewell's responsibility. Five days after the legislature's rejection, Hannah presented yet another request—this time emphasizing John Lovewell's overall provincial service. In effect, Hannah was altering her plea's narrative arc by citing Captain Lovewell's "considerable cost and expense for the encouragement and raising of volunteers to pursue and destroy the Indian enemy, and [the fact that he] raised several companies of able and effective men, who with him marched out against the enemy in the service of the country, that thereby left his estate very involved and encumbered so that the petitioner cannot pay the debts due from the estate without selling the estate."[22] Only the assembly's compassionate intercession could avert the pending financial disaster.

This petition's patriotic cast more neatly aligned with Lovewell's heroic image than had Hannah's earlier requests for financial relief. By stressing her husband's personal sacrifice, his repeated efforts against a provincial enemy, and his overall service to the province, this time she managed to strike a more responsive chord among the assembled legislature. That male champions helped her seems possible, judging from the legislative verdict: an additional fifty-pound disbursement went to Colonel Eleazer Tyng and Captain Henry Farwell, prominent regional residents, in response to Hannah Lovewell's request. Both men knew about petitions and memorials: after requesting compensation, Farwell had received burial expenses for several Dunstable men killed in 1724; and Tyng, the town representative, had handled various reimbursement requests—some successfully, some not. Even so, the assembly insisted that no further monetary assistance to Hannah Lovewell would be forthcoming.[23]

Hannah Lovewell never approached the House of Representatives again and receded into the provincial background. Yet a rural widow with young children hardly had time to perform both household and field tasks. Heavy lifting was man's job in the colonial world; cords of firewood from the family sawmill, if that was the fuel source, had to be delivered, cut, and split. Was Hannah capable of sawing, splitting, and carting the wood from nearby wood-piles? Could she also tend the livestock—a horse and several cows—when bur-dened with innumerable domestic chores and children too small to be much help? Perhaps these were factors in Hannah's decision, made after 1728, to leave Dunstable for the nearby town of Merrimac to marry Benjamin Smith. A loving spouse, Smith raised Captain Lovewell's children; they in turn honored their father's memory: daughter Hannah married Captain Joseph Baker of Pembrook in 1739, and son Nehemiah Lovewell went on to command a ranger company in New Hampshire. Attraction to military affairs and military men ran deep among the Lovewells.[24]

Hannah Lovewell's postwar experiences show the challenges military widows faced when asking for financial assistance. That she was the bereaved spouse of the war's most famous casualty gave her a certain advantage, to be sure, but not automatic help, requests for which were subject to close scrutiny by the legislature and its respective committees. Wartime fiscal concerns would factor into assemblymen's decisions. Other Lovewell troop widows had already been rewarded with death payouts. And if Hannah Lovewell was obliged to beg and cajole, strategically reframing her requests in attempts to gain additional compensation, would other Pigwacket widows fare likewise?

Priscilla Barron was among the first Lovewell widows to follow in Hannah's footsteps. Her husband had wandered from the troop into the forest—his body was never recovered—and the thirty-pound death payment and thirty-pound service allotment granted her proved inadequate. Priscilla's three small children added to her financial woes. Elias Barron had left his family an unfinished house frame atop a sixty-acre tract, meaning, presumably, that they were living elsewhere. This was a smaller estate than Hannah Lovewell's. In addition, the Widow Barron's December 21, 1726, petition noted a sixty-pound debt against her husband. Given the sums she had already received from the government and the amount of her husband's debt, Barron begged the government's permission to sell some of the land to pay the obligation, keeping the rest of it to support her children.[25]

Priscilla's petition cited Elias Barron's connection to Lovewell, highlighting his death at Pigwacket. Lovewell and Pigwacket—the two were seemingly inseparable in the public memory—provided provincial officials with telling imagery. More significantly, Priscilla Barron's petition posed fewer difficulties than Hannah Lovewell's, and the legislature quickly approved the request—after all, no money needed to be dispensed by them. The Widow Barron retained a one-third interest in any proceeds; her children would receive the other two-thirds. Priscilla later gained additional emotional and financial satisfaction by marrying Jonathan Mead on March 2, 1729.[26]

The Widow Sarah Wyman approached the government on December 24, 1726. Her husband, Seth Wyman, had barely had time to enjoy his promotion to captain before raising an expedition to search for Abenakis. With silver-hilted sword at his side, the mark of an officer and a gentleman, the thirty-nine-year-old Wyman showcased to raw young volunteers the rewards that lay within reach of the brave. Valor alone could not repel disease, however.

That summer Wyman and company were struck by an outbreak of dysentery, the scourge of early American armies careless of sanitation and camp conditions. Wyman's death on September 5, 1725, in Samuel Penhallow's words, was "very much lamented." As Seth Wyman had been substantially rewarded after Pigwacket, his widow had to embroider reality to entice the government to supply funds.[27]

Sarah Wyman offered a particularly compelling, albeit inaccurate, justification for her receiving assistance beyond her obvious loss: Seth Wyman, she claimed, had participated in all three Lovewell expeditions. However, other sources suggest that only Lovewell, Farwell, and Robbins, the first three officers, had served in all three scouting parties. Artful recrafting of events to depict Wyman as a veteran Lovewell stalwart could only strengthen the plea. That Wyman had provided food and clothing for his own company of troops, saddling his estate with a twenty-pound debt before dying of illness "contracted by hard marches against the Indian enemy," explains the subterfuge. Creditors demanded payment, and the General Court responded with twenty pounds. Yet any personal relief it afforded his wife proved short-lived—Sarah Wyman died on November 5, 1727.[28]

The next petitioning widow, Eunice White, bereaved spouse of Captain John White, possessed a shakier tie to Lovewell. Like Wyman, dysentery had claimed Captain White in 1725. Two years later his widow pressed the government for money; yet Captain White had neither marched to Pigwacket nor been a member of the ten-man rear guard at Ossipee. Eunice White reminded representatives that her husband had been Lovewell's lieutenant in the second expedition, "when he slew the ten Indians," received a thousand-pound bounty, and garnered public acclaim. This tactic had initially failed to impress Hannah Lovewell's listeners. However, Eunice White reminded legislators about Captain White's efforts to form a company to bury Captain Lovewell at Pigwacket, "which he performed in a very difficult season of the year." To be sure, Colonel Tyng had commanded the interment operation at Pigwacket, a fact the petition omitted to mention, but sepulture evoked memories of Symmes's popular pamphlet urging the burial of dead soldiers. Penhallow noted that Colonel Tyng, "with Captain White who went afterward," had interred the twelve slain Lovewell troopers. Good Christians buried fallen comrades just as the ancient Israelites had done. If White was such a good soldier, should not the legislature extend charity to the captain's seven fatherless children?[29]

Eunice White's petition employed two crucial symbols—Lovewell and

Pigwacket—to stir legislative emotions while stressing the importance of sepulture. Captain White had not been a Pigwacket veteran, so his widow's narrative had to transform him into a company member by symbolic extension. Had Captain White not served alongside Lovewell before? Did he not trek to Pigwacket to perform a final service? Affirmative answers to these questions might cloak White's true role from closer legislative scrutiny. Besides, the Widow White's plea had stressed her husband's abundant patriotism: the captain had tried to raise Mohegan Indian troops in Connecticut before dying of dysentery. In effect, he had sacrificed himself for Massachusetts—if not in actual fighting than in preparing to fight. That he had been the village blacksmith showed how war could raise humble individuals to prominence. Eunice White asked for 250 acres to help educate her seven children. The General Court responded with one hundred pounds for "good service done for the province."[30]

In August 1728, Margaret Robbins, widow of the slain Lieutenant Robbins, petitioned the government. The badly wounded Robbins, according to the Reverend Thomas Symmes, had stayed behind, gun in hand, in hope of dispatching another Abenaki warrior. His widow asked for assistance in light of her five small children and "little or nothing to support." Robbins's service in all three Lovewell expeditions went unmentioned. The province granted her thirty pounds, and Margaret soon found additional emotional support from William Shattuck of Groton, her next husband. One of the children from this union, Captain Job Shattuck, would serve conspicuously in the American Revolution and Shays' Rebellion.[31]

The stories of these Lovewell widows, although few, reveal their concerns and petition tactics. Virtually all the women cited financial embarrassment and fatherless children as reasons for assistance; emphasis on their husbands' service records was common too. If some exaggerated their spouses' contributions, like Widows Wyman and White, they had ample motivation to embellish reality: Hannah Lovewell had been turned down more than once until her dogged persistence and artful narrative reframing finally paid off. As petitioners, these women temporarily transcended the domestic sphere to politick. Lovewell and Robbins, deputy husbands when their spouses were away, perhaps felt emboldened to claim provincial assistance as their rightful due. Or maybe male relatives insisted on their taking this tack. Cash was not a given: the government typically provided cloth to "widows . . . as a death payment for their husbands' service," according to Jack S. Radabaugh. But women familiar with looms and spinning wheels could still barter goods in local village economies. And given the vagaries of provincial paper money, cloth probably represented a sounder, more recognizable medium of exchange.[32]

What happened if a male family member requested compensation for a lost son? Then the appeal's dynamic changed slightly. Jonathan Frye, the unofficial expedition chaplain and the third and only surviving son of Captain James and Lydia Osgood Frye's eleven children, came from a locally respectable family. The twenty-year-old Jonathan, a Harvard graduate, was the only college man among the raiders. He was also romantically linked to Susannah Rogers, the thirteen-year-old daughter of a Boxfield, Massachusetts, clergyman. Captain James Frye disapproved of the connection, his parental outrage fueled by issues of age and class. In a bit of youthful rebellion, Frye had enlisted in Lovewell's Pigwacket expedition to earn enough money to marry.[33]

A grieving Captain Frye, dissatisfied by the thirty-pound service payout, insisted on more proper compensation in a December 17, 1725, petition. Jonathan Frye, according to his father, had been the company chaplain, and hence entitled to greater rewards. This was untrue; Frye balked at his son's lowly rank as private. Other chaplains such as Jonathan Pierpont, attached to Colonel Thomas Westbrook's expeditions, had received close to forty pounds in 1725 for scouting service. Frye had also lost a gun valued at four pounds. As Jonathan was not yet twenty-one, Captain Frye expected what "the wisdom and goodness of the court shall seem meet," in terms of service and lost property. Family honor demanded as much even if Jonathan Frye was unmarried and childless. The Committee of Petitions concurred, and by December 20, 1725, the House agreed that the public treasury owed the captain compensation. How much money Jonathan received was unstated; it remains difficult to believe that Captain Frye took payment in cloth.[34]

Nevertheless, a footnote needs to be added to the Frye family saga. Susannah Rogers, Jonathan Frye's intended, could not present a claim before the General Court, as she was unmarried and underage. Yet, aware of Captain Frye's disappointment, Rogers turned to poetry, writing that Jonathan was "Wounded and famishing all alone / None to relieve or hear his mourn / And there without all doubt did die." In her gloomy verses Rogers urged Frye's parents to have faith: their son, she intoned, "is gone beyond your cares / And safely lodged, in heaven above / With Christ, who was his joy and love." Captain Frye still preferred monetary compensation in addition to the comfort of his Reformed faith. Susannah, too, recovered, marrying at the age of twenty-three, her poetry career thankfully short-lived.[35]

Other Dummer's War widows, unconnected to Lovewell and Pigwacket, encountered a mixture of legislative responses. In fact, few of them submitted memorials to the provincial government. Some widows needed to settle estate issues; others sought business licenses to support themselves. Both these requests were easily granted. Widows whose husbands had died fighting might have turned to local relief in any case. Still, Margaret Hilton, whose husband, Captain William Hilton, had commanded a foot company until "he died of the distemper that was prevailing in the army, after a fit of sickness of nine weeks," approached the provincial government. Medical attention, nursing costs, and various sundries had left Margaret in "distressing circumstances." She implored the "compassionate consideration of the court" in her August 23, 1723, petition. The assembly rejected the plea. On November 13, 1725, Elizabeth Coggin, bereaved spouse of Captain John Coggin of Woburn, Massachusetts, had her petition sent down from the Massachusetts Council to the House. The wording stressed Coggin's provincial service, hopeful that the captain's contribution would "be had in remembrance." The bill failed to win House approval.[36]

Moreover, high rank entailed no assurance of assistance; the notable or the obscure could be aided or denied by legislative decree. Thus, Widow Hannah Kibby, whose late husband had served in a military whale boat, asked for his back wages. This seemingly simple request for funds due was buried in committee—at least no subsequent record emerged in the records. On the other hand, the Widow Susannah Scales's June 1725 legislative request mentioning her five children "in low and distressed circumstances," won ten pounds from an often parsimonious government. Her husband had been killed by the Abenakis the previous April, and the government instructed Major Samuel Moodey, the representative of Falmouth, to pay the petitioner and her children, "in consideration of their great loss."[37]

Surviving family members represented only one group of potential Lovewell expedition claimants. Injured veterans often required (and demanded) more government attention—their claims could continue for years despite generous subsidies. Indeed, as Lovewell's exploits imprinted themselves on the public memory, injured veterans continued to request funds, crafting verbal images of suffering that potentially might overcome legislators' cost reservations. But not all Lovewell veterans were wounded or participants in the

Pigwacket battle. The ten men stationed at the Ossipee fort until Benjamin Hassell's arrival sent them fleeing never received the service payments granted the thirty-three combatants and their heirs. Yet they had followed Lovewell's orders, deployed themselves in readiness, and tended an injured comrade. Hassell's tale may have unmanned them, but the rear guard had left very welcome provisions for the fragmented company survivors. Shouldn't such men receive compensation?

When Lieutenant Governor Dummer requested legislative compassion toward Lovewell expedition members in late May, he deliberately excluded the rear guard. In private, he blasted them as cowards on a par with Benjamin Hassell. Sergeant Woods, the fort commander, had informed his superiors about the men's insubordination and refusal to stand their ground. Perhaps Woods felt that this action would protect him from criticism. Accordingly, he approached the legislature, his June 9, 1725, memorial asking recognition of service for the ten-man group. Strictly speaking, this was not a petition for assistance—none of the men had suffered wounds from fighting. Instead, it represented a hope "that some further allowance be made for their service than what had already been ordered to be paid out of the Public Treasury." The memorial also informed legislators that Woods and his co-petitioners had been left at the fort by Lovewell's order.[38]

The memorial never reached Stoddard's committee. Instead, the House decided on June 9, 1725, to pay the sum of five pounds, twelve shillings, and six pence to Zachariah Parker, John Goffe, Isaac Whitney, Obadiah Astin, and William Ayers, the company surgeon. The other rear-guard members went unlisted in the petition. An oversight or legislative snub kept Woods from receiving money, and he never contested the legislature's decision.[39]

William Ayers still had unfinished legislature business. Doctor Ayers practiced his profession in Haverhill, Massachusetts. Among the younger Lovewell recruits at age twenty-three, Ayer's medical career had barely begun. He may have wrapped wounds, applied splints, removed limbs, and bled patients— versed in Galen's medical philosophy—but the title surgeon conferred only modest experience or expertise on one that young. Still, Ayer's petition for eight pounds in medical and overall expenses on June 11 won assembly approval. This was less than the generous payouts to the thirty-three Pigwacket fighters and their families; it may have also irritated the young surgeon. In time, Ayers would formulate a plan to ensure rewards to all Lovewell expedition members, not just the Pigwacket fighters.[40]

Meanwhile, the legislative session concluded its business in June. During this interval injured Lovewell veterans slowly recognized that compromised limbs and joints might not heal; musket balls impossible to extract could serve as painful reminders. Money bestowed by a beneficent legislature for service and scalps would eventually run out. Doctors wanted bills honored, and people sheltering injured Lovewell veterans expected payment. Not surprisingly, a new round of petitions bombarded the legislature during its November session.

William Davis and Thomas Bullfinch received three pounds from the House of Representatives on November 10, 1725, for riding to Billerica, Massachusetts, to attend and doctor the dying Seth Wyman. It represented a single day's work. Nevertheless, Davis and Bullfinch felt shortchanged, asked for a reassessment, and lost their bid—the assembly refused to sweeten the original disbursement. After all, they were not expedition members, but doctors rendering a service. That the House was concerned about rising medical expenditures became clearer several days later, when several members questioned doctors' bills at Boston's Fort William. The House instructed Boston representatives to form a committee to prevent any reoccurrence.[41]

This tougher stance toward medical reimbursement did not signal a whole-scale rejection of charitable requests. Rather, the House wanted to exercise greater scrutiny over payments rendered. This meant even questioning the board, the lieutenant governor and the council, when the assembly was out of session, to ensure that military disbursements followed the letter of the law. Neither Dummer nor the council welcomed the remonstrance sent them by the House. It does show, however, that expenses and charity were expected to be balanced and carefully assessed.[42]

On November 11, 1725, Samuel Whiting and Solomon Keyes, both Billerica residents, asked for compassionate compensation. The two Pigwacket veterans had already drawn thirty pounds each; their doctor's bills ran to almost eighteen pounds apiece, including provisions, medicines, and nursing. Yet treatment left them "unable to do any work for their subsistence; [and] praying the compassionate consideration of this court and to their wisdom and justice shall seem meet." As volunteers, provincial law guaranteed them medical treatment. That same day John Kitteridge, the Billerica surgeon, asked for forty-four pounds and sixteen shillings for attending the wounds of and applying medicines to Samuel Whiting, Solomon Kies, and Josiah and Noah Johnson. Both requests went to committee, and two days later Colonel John

Stoddard recommended that Kitteridge be fully reimbursed. Whiting was granted fourteen pounds, fourteen shillings, and Kies twenty pounds, twelve shillings. It would appear that the government recognized differing levels of aid after reviewing joint petitions. However, when Benjamin Johnson, the father of Josiah and uncle of Noah, along with Samuel Pierce, asked for assistance for boarding and feeding two Lovewell soldiers, presumably Josiah and Noah, they received forty shilling each.[43]

Some requests described more thoroughly the injuries received. Legislators had heard earlier war veterans detail wounds, deliberate and accidental. Men in arms suffered from inadvertent falls or accidental gunshot wounds, not just injuries inflicted by an enemy. At least one soldier was shot while asleep in a barn while his comrades practiced target shooting! Another was accidentally killed when he pointed the muzzle of his gun at himself and a twig caught the cock and set it off. Most requests revealed more serious reasons for injuries, however: eighteenth-century Massachusetts soldiers more often experienced injuries to arms, hands, legs, thighs, eyes, and thumbs; less frequently the collarbone, chest, ribs, shoulders, and knees were cited.[44]

None of the Lovewell veterans confessed to accidental injuries. When Josiah Jones forwarded his November 8, 1725, petition, he adopted the typical tenor of such claimants, requesting aid as "the wisdom and justice of the court shall seem meet." That was standard boilerplate. But Jones added that "he received a musket ball, which yet remains in his body; and that by reason of the said wound he is rendered a cripple and unable to labor for his support and livelihood." That gave his plea an added poignancy. The House referred it to the Committee on Pensions, which accepted the fact that Jones was in considerable pain. By December 17, Jones bemoaned his lengthy sixteen-week convalescence, which had cost him over twelve pounds in food and clothing. His wound having already been described, Jones cited his nineteen-day trek in the woods that involved his "suffering great hardships and heavily in danger of perishing" before reaching Falmouth. Graphic language gained Jones eight pounds, seven shillings, and six pence, nonetheless less than his cited expenses.[45]

Jones had left Eleazer Davis, Jonathan Frye, and Josiah Farwell behind in the woods. His departure meant that Davis had to watch Frye and Farwell steadily decline while struggling to keep himself alive. Like Jones, the injured Davis had undergone an exhausting emotional and physical ordeal; unlike Jones, he nursed his companions along, urging Farwell to eat and march. Davis's November 8, 1725, plea before the House of Representatives mentioned the loss of a thumb joint, and, like Jones, he reported a bullet lodged in his body. Unable to labor after a lengthy convalescence, Davis appeared to be a worthy recipient. Colonel Stoddard's committee requested the sum of twenty-five pounds. The House paid out thirty-five, citing Davis's loss of time, past suffering, and expenses.[46]

We should be cautious about judging the government responses to Jones and Davis. Different payouts could easily reflect legislative judgments about injuries described and amounts requested. That one applicant received less and one more than requested may signify little. Yet, just possibly, Davis aroused greater sympathy, his loyalty to dying companions contrasting with Jones's abrupt departure. The story of Pigwacket, as told by the Reverend Thomas Symmes, gave legislators a context for their monetary judgments as much as the tone of the two men's petitions. Any word-of-mouth information (perhaps derived from Penhallow's interview with Davis?) would have further redounded to Davis's credit.

Other wounded veterans approached the legislature to address their sufferings too. Men such as Timothy Richardson, a Woburn resident, complained of several unspecified wounds while admitting to great pain in a December 17, 1725, appeal. Several days later the committee of petitions recommended eighteen pounds; the actual amount received, by the decision of the House, was five—this despite the fact that a bullet had gone through the trunk of Richardson's body and a bone, leaving him disabled and hard-pressed to support his family.[47]

Josiah and Noah Johnson had a different experience with the legislature. Both were severely hurt in the Pigwacket battle, receiving considerable doctoring and nursing. Their petition noted several wounds "whereby they are so crippled, that it is doubtful they will ever be able to get their living by their labor." Few petitioners had yet to proclaim themselves maimed for life. They asked for thirty-six pounds, one shilling; the committee on petitions recommended that Noah receive twenty-one pounds, seventeen shillings, and Josiah thirty pounds, two shillings—considerably more than the sum requested. Lest anyone think the committee overly generous, however, the members broke down Noah Johnson's request, with twelve pounds allotted in consideration of "past suffering, pain, and loss of time, he having of late received pay and subsistence from the Province." The rest covered his expenses. Josiah experienced the same sort of accounting although receiving greater sums. Clearly, the committee judged requests remaining mindful of past awards.[48]

The House of Representatives found the Johnsons petitioning again on June 9, 1726. Wounds in both hands left Noah unable to support himself; searching for a cure to close the wounds, he had futilely spent three pounds, sixteen shillings, and six pence, and hence required further assistance. Josiah's petition reached the legislature by June 15, 1726—his wounds, too, remained open despite four pounds and fourteen shillings' worth of medical expenses. The Committee of Petitions, headed by Timothy Lindall, responded on June 10, 1726, with money for Noah's doctor bills, plus ten pounds in consideration of the pain caused by the reopened wounds. On June 16, Josiah won reimbursement for doctor bills plus ten pounds in basic maintenance from the Committee on Muster Rolls, headed by a Mr. Lewis. Why two different committees handled similar requests remains unclear; however, both displayed compassionate concern toward Noah and Josiah Johnson.[49]

Legislators must have recognized that some Lovewell veterans would never recover. Accidental injuries happened naturally enough in farming villages and seaport communities—people fell down, broke bones, crushed limbs, suffered ruptures, and found subsequent manual labor difficult if not impossible. Laborers or artisans could emerge as town charges, especially if no family members could support them. Because of their wartime service, however, Pigwacket veterans held a claim upon the province. That they were scalp hunters, would-be entrepreneurs enticed by bounties, in no way weakened their petitions. To refuse them charity would be to deter future recruits; it would also leave towns, in particular borderland settlements, to pony up the funds or provide basic maintenance costs. The Johnsons' financial travails would reveal the workings of provincial compassion.

Come the winter of 1726, the House of Representatives heard again from the Johnsons. Noah evoked John Lovewell's name and cited his service against the "Indian enemy" when referring to his broken right wrist. The public treasury paid out ten pounds. Josiah Johnson, now residing in Woburn, Massachusetts, mentioned the Pigwacket battle as well, receiving eight pounds "in consideration of his loss of time" and fifty shillings for doctor bills. Apparently, Josiah still had hopes of mending—Noah no longer offered that excuse. By the spring of 1727 other requests for assistance would appear, and by the 1730s and 1740s pleas from the Johnson men continued. Noah Johnson, now of Suncook, New Hampshire, citing his wounds in Pigwacket, "where Captain Lovewell was slain," received three pounds, ten shillings, in 1744. Josiah Johnson gained an annual six-pound pension for five years in 1743. These sums were less than before, perhaps reflecting their propertied status, but still evidence that the province felt obligated to honor the Johnsons' request. That the legislature resorted to pensions only underscored the seriousness of the men's injuries.[50]

Pensioners ranked among the rarest, and at times most distressing, aid recipients. Spared the embarrassment and toil of continually having to present charitable requests, pension recipients might enjoy funding either for a set period of years or until they died. In England, pensions were typically bequests of royal favor dispensed as a reward for service. Colonial governments employed them as military recruitment aids: Plymouth in 1636 passed the first such law promising care for injured or disabled soldiers; it also covered families of the fallen who were unable to support themselves. Massachusetts followed suit by 1676 during King Philip's War, overwhelmed by the number of dead or wounded soldiers and their stricken families. Several other colonies were doing the same by the early eighteenth century. Yet, despite the flurry of legislation, colonial pensioners themselves have remained understudied, their subsequent lives revealing little more than names, dates, and sums in a ledger. Lovewell veterans, by contrast, occupied a more prominent sphere in the public consciousness, being known to contemporaries for their exploits and studied by antiquarians.[51]

Of these pensioned folk, Noah Johnson showed how such individuals could transcend physical limitations. Johnson's injured right wrist compromised strenuous activity: pushing a plow, handling tools, holding reins, or indeed any two-handed tasks presented challenges—one antiquarian account described him as "partially incapacitated." Nonetheless, Johnson married, and his children later served in the French and Indian War alongside Major Robert Rogers, the famed ranger commander, perhaps literally following in their father's footsteps. Johnson himself proved surprisingly energetic. In 1735, he moved to Suncook, later Pembrook, New Hampshire, where he owned property, undeterred by the "disability of the hands and arms." There Johnson served as the town proprietors' clerk; responsible for record keeping, he helped to hire the town minister, the Reverend Aaron Whittemore, and did a stint as church deacon. In 1736, Johnson, along with Henry Lovejoy and James Moor, basically managed the settlement's political business. As one chronicler noted, "he was the most prominent man in the conduct of affairs." Such affairs also included resolving town disputes: a vocal minority of townsmen opposed the Reverend Whittemore in the pulpit because they believed him to be insufficiently Presbyterian. This boiled over into the proprietors' meetings, where embittered Presbyterians continued to stew over the installation of the Congregationalist Whittemore. Noah Johnson and Benjamin Holt petitioned the General Court, related their side of the controversy, and won the right to keep Whittemore in the pulpit.[52]

Pembrook was only one stage in Johnson's life odyssey. He left for Dunstable by 1746 and apparently spent the next several decades there, paying taxes as late as 1781. Johnson retired to Plymouth, New Hampshire, a property-less resident responsible for only a poll tax and lodging with his daughter and her husband, Colonel Joseph Senter. The last living Lovewell veteran, Johnson had beaten the odds, surviving ambush and injury to enjoy a long productive life. Not surprisingly, he had ample time to reflect upon the Pigwacket battle, and a popular story highlighted Johnson's battlefield injury. When trying to drink from a stream during the fighting, he discovered that the liquid was seeping through a bullet hole in his left hand! At some point, the old soldier returned to the battle site, escorted by the local minister in the newly settled town of Fryeburg, the Reverend Mr. Fessenden. They found the battlefield and Johnson broke down in tears after showing the "place where his comrades fell." Johnson's age at his death, incorrectly listed by the (Boston) *Columbian Centinel* in 1798 as one hundred and four, added five years to his life. No matter. The ninety-nine-year-old veteran garnered praise for having "engaged in the famous battle of Lovell at the place now called Fryeburg; and had three or four years been the last survivor who engaged in that memorable transaction."[53]

Josiah Jones, identified along with Noah Johnson and Eleazer Davis as the three most seriously disabled Lovewell veterans, followed a different social trajectory. Jones stayed in Concord, found a wife, Elizabeth, raised three children, and died before his fortieth birthday on June 4, 1741. He left little imprint on town affairs. This should not surprise us: most New England household heads might attend town meetings, vote, and never attain local office; or, if elected, they might hold posts as constables, fence viewers, or overseers of the highways, modest offices in keeping with men of modest status. That Jones was a man of modest means is suggested by his petitions to the provincial government. He requested, and received, a five-pound-per-annum pension for three years in 1736 in recognition of his injuries and service. In 1739, the government renewed Jones's stipend for five years; and in 1741 the legislature, acknowledging the "necessitous circumstances" of the Widow Elizabeth Jones and her three small children, extended it by four years. Although Concord had no poorhouse until 1753, Jones and his bereaved family thus avoided becoming public charges, the stipend a welcome addition to the family income.[54]

Eleazer Davis carved a more prominent community niche for himself. By 1732, he had married the eighteen-year-old Sarah Willard, a native of Lancaster, Massachusetts. Restless in Concord, Davis relocated to nearby Groton, Massachusetts, attained residency in the newly formed town of Harvard that had hived off from Groton, and dove into town affairs. He was among the first assessors chosen at the initial Harvard town meeting in 1732. He occupied the post several more times over the next decade and a half. By 1744, town residents chose Davis to be their selectman; it was an office typically reserved for older, experienced men respected by their neighbors. Davis won reelection in 1745 and 1746, later returning for one-year terms in 1754 and 1758. Even so, he received a public pension of four pounds per annum for five years in 1738. Age and injuries may also explain why Davis turned to inn keeping in 1759; it enabled him to sell liquor from his farmhouse, so long as he followed the law and removed tipplers by 9:00 p.m. Who would begrudge a license to one of Lovewell's injured men, a former selectman no less? When Davis died in 1762, the town lost not just a farmer but a respected resident, local businessman, and good citizen.[55]

Many Lovewell veterans surmounted their injuries and never requested pensions. Yet, if damage to reputation could be considered a disability, then one otherwise conspicuous Lovewell veteran, Benjamin Hassell, at first stayed in the shadows. No petition from Hassell reached the House of Representatives; nor did a payout for service similar to those distributed to the thirty-three Pigwacket fighters or their heirs arrive at his door. The Reverend Thomas Symmes had cast Hassell out of the company both physically and symbolically, citing "Their Names [those of Lovewell's company] that made up this Company (excepting his that started from them in the beginning of the Battle, and ran back to the Fort, which I'd be excus'd from mention[ing])."

For good measure, Symmes later referred to the unnamed company deserter at the beginning of the fight. But the severest reproof emerged when Symmes announced that dying honorably in battle was to be preferred to abandoning comrades; men who left their fellows behind, as Hassell did, would "live with disgrace; and for their cowardice have the offer of a wooden sword, and be branded with the infamous character of a coward, even by the weaker sex." Samuel Penhallow described the unnamed Hassell as the man who "was so dreadfully terrified that he ran away." Perhaps Hassell's hidden identity protected Lovewell's good name—Hassell was his cousin, after all—but Hassell the Dunstable deserter could hardly hide from kin and neighbors.[56]

Time might have healed these painful memories. Dunstable residents, damning Hassell at first, came eventually to think better of him. The Hassell clan were among the earliest Dunstable settlers, victims of Indian attacks, and otherwise accounted solid citizens by neighbors. Borderland inhabitants well understood that these attacks created situations where men had to save themselves first and comrades second. Frederic Kidder, a noted nineteenth-century chronicler, after dutifully pouring over the available records, opined, "It is said, that, at first, there was much feeling against him [Hassell], as being the cause of so much suffering and disaster, but it was forgotten, and he regained the favor of his neighbors." Hassell relocated to Merrimack, becoming a "useful and respected citizen." A later twentieth-century chronicler argued that his options at Pigwacket had been limited: if separated from his fellows, Hassell had wisely saved himself by fleeing; to stay exposed and alone on the battlefield would have been suicidal. Seen in this light, Hassell's actions made sense.[57] And perhaps Hassell's account of disaster to the rear guard could also be understood in this context. The ten-man rear guard had believed themselves outnumbered and unable to do much good for already dead or dying comrades.

Uninjured Lovewell veterans had no claim for pensions. Service payouts and scalp money provided their compensation, and some relived their accomplishments and quite possibly varnished the truth beyond Symmes and Penhallow's accounts. Whatever stories they passed down certainly became grist for embellishment, especially by friends or descendants. After his death John Chamberlain drew attention as the alleged killer of Paugus, the Indian leader slain at Pigwacket. Neither Symmes nor Penhallow named Chamberlain as Paugus's slayer; however, subsequent generations of family members and antiquarians championed him, noting that Chamberlain and Paugus, who had allegedly known each other, had agreed to clean out their fouled muskets by the pond. It was said that Chamberlain killed Paugus after a brief exchange, earning the nickname Paugus Chamberlain. Years later, according to this story, a vengeful son of Paugus attempted to kill his father's slayer, only to be slain himself by the ever vigilant Chamberlain.[58]

Isaac Larkin, a Lovewell veteran promoted to ensign after the battle, allegedly related a similar tale. Like Chamberlain, Larkin confronted a vengeful Indian years after the Pigwacket battle. Charles Wooley told Samuel A. Green, a nineteenth-century Groton antiquarian, that an Indian was noticed suspiciously lurking near Larkin's log house by the Nashua River in the north part of Groton. Larkin instructed his wife to open the door, aimed his musket at the Indian, and promptly shot him dead. He then carefully buried the body, keeping the incident quiet. Only years later did Charles Wooley reveal the secret, constructing another layer of narrative. For people such as Chamberlain and Larkin, the fight transformed itself into rather tall stories of vengeful Indians, perhaps illuminating the dynamic of New England folklore more than the actual battle at Pigwacket or its aftermath. That other individuals who lived later passed these stories on is suggestive. Whereas Lovewell was the recognized martyr and the promoted Wyman the official hero, others relied on the passage of time and narrative retellings to claim a place in the tale.[59]

In contrast, other Lovewell men eschewed stories of vengeful Indians. What they had experienced required no embellishment. Nor did they challenge the general depiction of the fight except to supply a few additions to it. Josiah Johnson, for instance, lived with his wife Elizabeth's family during his last years and "often told the story [about Pigwacket] and always told it alike, agreeing with the printed accounts in general and adding some particulars." We do not know what Johnson said precisely, but Eleazer Davis told his grandson about using moccasin strips and a fish hook to catch fish in a brook for the Reverend Frye. Still another anecdote, attributed to an unnamed wounded Lovewell trooper, described him lying down to die in a hole from a blown-down tree, only to rejoice when his faithful dog came upon him and urged him onward.[60]

Some men preferred to let their actions speak for themselves, venturing forth to fight again. Solomon Kies enlisted in the French and Indian War, dying at Lake George in 1758 at the age of fifty-seven. John Goffe, part of the ten-man rear guard, rose to the rank of colonel in the Seven Year's War and enjoyed a long life into his eighties. The Melvin brothers, Eleazer and David, joined the Massachusetts expedition besieging Fort Louisbourg, the mighty French fortress off Nova Scotia in 1745. A revival-like burst of patriotism, abetted by hope of French plunder, had swept the province, fueling zealous New Englanders' hope to cast down the Antichrist (the Popish French) while discreetly nodding to mammon. Whatever their motivation, the Melvin men shared in the victory and the subsequent English occupation of the fort that turned into a disaster. Nine hundred Massachusetts men died from disease and exposure in the winter of 1745/46 after Louisbourg's surrender. No plunder was allowed.

An injured Captain David Melvin went home to Concord, dying on November 17, 1745, at the age of fifty-five. His half-brother Eleazer, twelve years younger, proved more fortunate: a lieutenant in his brother's company, Eleazer became a captain at Louisbourg and by 1748 was commanding a company of New Hampshire rangers. In 1754, he led a company to Norridgewock, an Indian encampment prominent since before Dummer's War, before dying at home in October. Linked to both Pigwacket and Louisbourg, Eleazer Melvin could encourage recruits or reassure unsteady scouts by virtue of his wartime experiences. He was one of the Lovewell men accorded recognition, and perhaps even awe, by younger troopers familiar with the story of the heroic captain and the Pigwacket battle.[61]

Most Lovewell survivors, however, never again responded to the call to arms. A home and farm were more attractive to them than fighting Indians and leading troops; even better would be to acquire more land and supplement their provincial payouts and pensions—if their province could be persuaded to grant them land. And here precedent worked in the Lovewell troops' favor. Early Massachusetts settlers in the 1630s had forged both a reformed faith and an economic identity based on land. True, a few rural artisans plied trades, yet they often tilled acreage as well. When hard coin was scarce and paper money unpredictable, land endured as a valued commodity. Rewards of real estate built upon Indian conquest enticed officials, traders, and ex-soldiers to buy and sell and speculate. Indeed, much of Massachusetts history could be described as the process of land acquisition by conquest and redistribution, as speculators and settlers competed to form towns and secure profits.[62]

The idea of turning Pigwacket into a prospective land boom may have originated with the aforementioned Doctor William Ayers. Though left behind at the fort, Ayers refused to be left behind in terms of any future gains. Joined by David Melvin, Ayers put a proposal for land before Lieutenant Governor William Dummer. Some of the other Lovewell veterans had clearly been exchanging information and devising tactics for exactly this purpose. In the petition submitted on May 31, 1727, Melvin and Ayer noted that it was "for ourselves and at the instance and request of others of our company to the number of thirty," roughly the number of battle survivors. They reminded Dummer that Lovewell's men had "performed many fatiguing marches in pursuit of the Indian enemy and went through many hardships, perils and dangers, more especially in the engagement with the enemy at Pigwacket." Veterans unable to work or provide for their families needed property, and tracts near Pennecook situated along both sides of the Merrimack River, "free from all grants to any particular persons," provided the prize.[63]

By August 5, the House of Representatives approved a six-mile-square tract of land on each side of the Merrimack River. This property was near territory being disputed with New Hampshire. In addition, the House expanded the number of recipients to include all forty-seven individuals (or their legal representatives) who had first started out with Lovewell. Even Benjamin Hassell the deserter could expect to receive a share of property. Also favored were the first thirteen people from Lovewell's first expedition, provided they properly settled the land. An additional three shares of land would go to support a minister and a school. Surveying commenced by the autumn.[64]

Even so, petitioning and procuring land required Pigwacket veterans to be patient. What had started in 1727 still needed to be reaffirmed and resolved— no easy task as it turned out. On July 29, 1728, the House of Representatives received another petition from Daniel Melvin and William Ayers, in which they and "sundry other soldiers in the service of the province under the command of Captain Lovewell" asked for a tract of land next to the town of Pennecook. The matter of land grants soon became amended to include the troopers from Lovewell's second expedition, not the first. It also attracted people who had no Lovewell association, for which reason the Massachusetts government struck men off the list. Land applications had multiplied in the 1720s, not just for Pennecook, but for areas in Maine, New Hampshire, and western Massachusetts. Settlers in more densely settled regions clamored for acreage. By accommodating the Lovewell expedition members, the General Court hoped to provide both a compassionate response to veterans and a means of settling outlying areas.[65]

In Suncook, the arrival of settlers slowly enabled a town to develop. Surveys showed the Lovewell men (or their heirs) all present and accounted for during the first division in 1729. This even included Toby the Indian and William and Jonathan Cummings, cousins—three men who had been sent home during the expedition's early stages. Toby and William were injured; Jonathan went as company to William. The business of settlement forming slowly progressed. By 1732, Eleazer Melvin again strode to the front of the line as part of a committee to lay out with a surveyor and chain men sixty-one grants of land, which would include at least "forty acres of the best land." Even Benjamin Hassell benefited, his name duly recorded, although spelled differently according to the uncertain phonetics of the day. Hassell contracted for Lot Number One, agreeing to build a sawmill and a gristmill for the town's benefit, and receiving a sixty-pound advance. In partnership with Benjamin Parker, apparently one of the settlement's movers and shakers, Hassell had "arrived" both geographically and socially, reborn as a village promoter and perspective miller. Sadly, his reach exceeded his grasp, as the deal for the gristmill and sawmill never materialized.[66]

This soon proved the least of the town's worries, however. A village without a mill might survive if another was in reach, but settlers with uncertain land titles faced more serious challenges. And that was precisely what bedeviled Suncook. Land disputes with neighboring New Hampshire materialized: the province had granted the proprietors of Bow land in the Massachusetts grant. Fistfights broke out between contending settlers by the 1730s, and the Bow proprietors sent out two militiamen to warn off trespassers. By 1732, New Hampshire informed London of Massachusetts' infringement of title. In 1737, a royal commission arrived in New Hampshire to investigate the dispute. As the wheels of imperial power slowly turned, the case went against Massachusetts by 1740. It fell to Suncook proprietors to appeal to New Hampshire for aid, as Indian attacks threatened their existence. The ever active Noah Johnson kept his interest in the land, especially once New Hampshire's title became clear, negotiating and petitioning. In 1773, Johnson petitioned Massachusetts for yet another grant of land, joined by a number of other disgruntled shareholders.[67]

Whatever Johnson and company said to the Massachusetts legislature proved effective. No longer did they mention the name of Lovewell, but as property holders whose titles were invalid they could sound the alarm over land rights. It was sufficient in 1774 for the legislature to grant the petitioners new land in Maine—New Suncook—in order to reestablish themselves. In time, the settlers would establish a new community, incorporated as Lovell, Maine, in 1800, a fitting tribute to the man whose exploits had made it possible.[68]

Much of this was of no immediate concern to Lovewell veterans or their descendants. Only Noah Johnson chose to retain his holdings in Suncook; others had viewed it as an investment opportunity rather than home. And life in general returned to a degree of normalcy insofar as veterans could return to life. The injured could display their wounds and relate tales to interested listeners. Stories would circulate and build just as other battle stories from other conflicts developed and grew. Passing years would thin veterans' ranks and leave others to relate their accomplishments. Pigwacket would be remembered and its battle retold as both a fireside tale and a chapter of Massachusetts history; in Samuel Penhallow's mind, it elevated provincial soldiers to a status comparable to British professionals, whose record needed no embellishment. It was quite an achievement. Next to the subsequent payouts of money and land, it provided a richer reward in granting Lovewell veterans a degree of immortality in the public memory.[69]

The memory of Captain Lovewell and his troop at Pigwacket thus came to symbolize bravery under trying circumstances. Yet, such a construction required artful manipulation, as not everyone had acted heroically: the battle's aftermath saw comrades abandoned, with the degree of their consent to be so at times uncertain. And who was it that would survive in memory? The Abenakis, who were struggling to hold onto their land, saw their former home on the battle site being gradually invaded and occupied by New Englanders. Would anyone tell their tale? New England settlers saw the site as undeveloped land, a prospect that promised the possibility of a future settlement, if it could be exploited. Over time, the formation of a community there would indeed provide a usable memory: visitors to the site could observe growing town pride. But time is a fickle mistress who seldom bestows favors equally, and the town of Fryeburg would be alternatively remembered and forgotten, much like Captain Lovewell's legacy. Pigwacket, Captain Lovewell and his troopers, and Fryeburg, Maine, would jostle for primacy within the public memory.

CHAPTER 6

Remembering Lovewell through the Centuries

On May 31, 1725, the *New England Courant* advertised a newly composed ballad, "The Volunteer's March," that promised a "full and true account [of] the bloody fight which happen'd between Capt. Lovewell's Company, and the Indians at Pigwacket." Several weeks earlier that battle had riddled John Lovewell's thirty-four-man company, left twelve people dead or dying on the battlefield, and three more to perish in the woods. For New Englanders, the "excellent new song," contained verses that, in one version, touted "Our worthy Capt. Lovewell among there did die" along with "Young Fullam too . . . because he fought so well / Endeavoring to save a man, a sacrifice he fell." And Seth Wyman, a subordinate officer, "who shot the old chief Paugus, which did the foe defeat." With heroes aplenty, the ballad highlighted New England valor and went on to enjoy a long-lasting popularity, enshrining Lovewell and the Pigwacket battle in the popular memory.[1]

In 1849, Henry David Thoreau elaborated upon this memory, albeit in ways quite different from the intention of the ballad. Building on an 1839 trip he had taken along the Concord and Merrimack rivers, Thoreau referred to the "Volunteer's March" as "the old nursery tale, sung about a hundred years ago." Town histories filled the gaps in his knowledge. In *A Week on the Concord and*

Merrimack Rivers, he identified Dunstable, Massachusetts, as the home of the "famous Captain Lovewell." This became a segue to the 1725 battle between Lovewell and the Pigwacket: the English troops' exploits, as Thoreau noted, had furnished them victory laurels and land grants in Pembroke, New Hampshire. In addition, Eleazer Davis and Josiah Jones, two severely wounded troopers, had survived their daunting wilderness treks and gone on to receive provincial pensions. But what was the fate of the Indian combatants at Pigwacket? They had fallen "so thick and fast," according to the ballad, that "Scarce twenty of their number, at night did get home well." Thoreau wondered "how many balls lodged with them . . . and finally what pension or township was granted them, there is no journal to tell."[2]

These two accounts show memory construction at work. The advertised ballad, based on early newspaper accounts, had sung the praises of brave Englishmen defeating an Abenaki adversary. Commentators considered the Pigwacket battle an important moment in New England borderland history, which evolved into an oft-repeated fireside tale passed down through generations. Thoreau, on the other hand, deployed the ballad and local histories of the fight to challenge and recast people's memories. The Abenakis had been wiped out and their war whoops silenced, as he noted, yet "What if the Indians are exterminated, are not savages as grim prowling about the clearings today?" To Thoreau's way of thinking, New England's past and present demanded more critical scrutiny and fuller inclusion of others. He would be neither the first nor the last to expand upon Lovewell's 1725 battle.[3]

Ballads set to popular tunes competed with more established printed works. New England singing centered more on psalms and church hymns than on provincial events set to English airs. Probably most locally composed verse was performed as read poetry rather than as sung ballads. By the 1720s polite poets had material enough to inspire: Mathew Byles for one, the unofficial Massachusetts poet laureate, used Captain Josiah Winslow's death at the hands of the Abenakis in a 1724 composition. That Winslow's body had gone missing made the tale more poignant to recite. The Reverend John Adams also mentioned Winslow's unclaimed body in private verse. Winslow had been an officer of promising parts and respectable lineage. Quickly dashed off squibs and poems about recent tragedies were early eighteenth-century staples; even the young Benjamin Franklin had tried his hand at them. Whether in verse or prose, Boston area bookstores and presses complemented Boston newspapers, supplying a range of materials.[4] The "Volunteer's March" began the popular commemoration of Captain Lovewell and his men. The written accounts by Thomas Symmes and Samuel Penhallow in 1725 and 1726 had provided a historic record based on survivors' verbal ones. In contrast, the "Volunteer's March" was a popular oral outlet whose easily recited verses, if not sung aloud, could be passed down independently of the printed source and lodged in the popular memory. The 1724 Norridgewock raid during Dummer's War that resulted in Sebastian Rale's death attained similar contemporary popularity as a ballad, "The Rebel's Reward: or English Courage Display'd." Both it and the "Volunteer's March," later popularly referred to as "Lovewell's Fight," incorporated the English air "All ye that Love Good Fellows." Boston verse maker, Tom Law, its probable author, was an in demand but now obscure individual whose name popped up in 1720s correspondence. The Norridgewock ballad even inspired a satirical riposte, suggesting that people noticed Law's work.[5]

The "Volunteer's March," although developed from public information, contained questionable assertions. That Lovewell had died bravely was apparent enough—all accounts bemoaned his lose. That Wyman had risen to the occasion as the de facto commander was accurate too. But whether Wyman had actually killed Paugus is speculation, as no newspaper had reported this fact; Symmes and Penhallow simply mentioned Paugus's death without attribution. Nevertheless, Symmes did credit Wyman with slaying an Abenaki powwow at a crucial moment. That Paugus could have been a corruption of "Pow Wow" for the "Volunteer's March" balladeer remains a distinct possibility.[6]

Wartime verses drew readers during the 1720s. Dummer's War had prompted campaigns and scouting sorties, in response to Abenaki raids and killings that stimulated a sense of provincial pride. Great Britain had stayed out of the conflict, leaving Massachusetts and New Hampshire to soldier on alone. Garrisoned towns, scalping parties, and backcountry expeditions complemented provincial diplomatic efforts. The French in Canada, although officially neutral, had Father Sebastian Rale active among the eastern Abenakis, alarming provincial Massachusetts authorities. Dummer's War reverberated especially among northern New England borderland inhabitants. Theirs was a war against a perceived French proxy, the Abenakis. Balladeers and Penhallow promoted Massachusetts as a loyal partner in the British Empire. Indeed, Penhallow allowed that, although Lovewell's troops were not British soldiers whose exploits "have caused the world to wonder," nonetheless the men had nobly died "for the interest of their country." The "Volunteer's March" reaffirmed this bravery more directly in verse.[7]

Even the Lovewell family sought to preserve and perhaps even profit from the captain's wartime memory. Several years after Dummer's War, the elder John Lovewell, Captain Lovewell's father, appeared in court for nonpayment of debt. He had contracted in 1736 with Joseph Jewett of Groton to write two ballads about his son John. One production cited his successful second expedition that had yielded ten Indian scalps; the other highlighted the 1725 expedition "when Capt. Louell was kill'd." Neither of these works has survived; nor does Jewett seem to have had any additional publications. How Lovewell met Jewett likewise remains a mystery. We do know that John Lovewell promised Jewett five pounds or delivery of twenty copies of each ballad to Jewett's house by the end of 1736. Lovewell did not honor the agreement, lost the suit brought by Jewett in Concord's Inferior Court of Common Pleas in 1738, and failed in his subsequent appeal before the Superior Court of Judicature in Charlestown in 1739. Lovewell's five-pound costs ballooned to seventeen pounds in damages and court fees.[8]

What Tom Law had done for Boston, Lovewell and Jewett might have hoped to do for rural villagers. Legal difficulties aside, Lovewell and Jewett evidently believed a market for historic verses existed. That Jewett would accept twenty copies of each ballad in lieu of cash is suggestive. Dunstable was home to Lovewell and the slain Lieutenants Jonathan Robbins and Josiah Farwell. Groton men had volunteered and died in the Pigwacket adventure as well. The ballad citing Lovewell's death may have left other fatalities unidentified, but townsfolk's memories of the battle would nevertheless be stoked, and sales might just result from the new compositions based on an iconic wartime event.[9]

Coincidentally, in 1736 a Concord resident, Joseph Stow, also penned verses about Lovewell's Fight. Stow remains a cipher—Stow family members resided in Concord, and Joseph and Elizabeth Stow had lost their two children, Joseph and Hannah, a day apart in October 1727. Obviously, Stow knew about the Pigwacket battle: his manuscript copy entitled "The brave Capt. Lovell of Dunstable" bears the notation "written in Concord, November 27, 1736." Actual publication seems to have occurred in January 1740, as indicated by the Houghton Library manuscript at Harvard University. That Stow wrote about Lovewell and company more than ten years after the battle underscores the captain's continuing hold on the popular memory. Heroic tales of battling

provincials in particular, those who died nobly while outlasting Indian adversaries, inspired amateur verse makers to take quill in hand.[10]

Stow's composition introduced a new wrinkle by identifying a different
Paugus slayer. The "Volunteer's March" had named Seth Wyman as doer of
the deed. Stow boldly penned that "Paugus was shot by Chamberlain / he saw
and did shout / This damp'd the Heathen as he fell in middest of the Rout."
Chamberlain had gained a place of honor—the only survivor Stow named.
The other scouts listed in the manuscript were the already dead, those close to
death, or those left to die in the woods; Wyman was totally ignored. Lauded
by Symmes and rewarded by Massachusetts, Wyman would certainly have
been known to Stow. Nonetheless, Stow thrust Chamberlain atop Wyman's
lofty perch, presumably because of stories he had heard. Popular memory was
clearly conflicting: Was it Wyman or Chamberlain who shot Paugus? Stow's
championship of the latter, although previously unknown, may explain later
efforts to designate Chamberlain as the marksman who felled Paugus.[11]

Stow's work resembled a sermon in verse. He told survivors of the fight:
"pray watch against all sin / Our Land also; and serve the Lord / Who did
Salvation bring." Be obedient to God and ever vigilant while honoring thy faith
lest salvation be jeopardized—this was standard enough latter-day Puritan
advice. Stow minced few words in his description of fatalities: those left
dying at Pigwacket were "lying in their Gore / And left with mortal Wounds."
Some of the walking wounded were little better off: "When helped they had
been / And travel'd in the lonesome woods / But home they could not win."
Assistance could not guarantee a homecoming for these unfortunate men.
Stow identified Frye, Farwell, and Barron, while reaffirming that Farwell "was
found where he did die." As with the "Volunteer's March," Stow never appor-
tioned blame or alluded to the deserter Benjamin Hassell, whose story had
unnerved the rear guard into leaving any possible survivors unaided. Some
memories were best forgotten by simple omission.[12]

Lovewell and his men also occupied a memory niche in the aftermath
of Dummer's War imprinted in verse and song. Until King George's War
erupted, resulting in the 1745 Anglo-American seizure of the French fortress
of Louisbourg, no local military event had attracted comparable interest. As
Nathaniel Ames, a Boston almanac editor intoned in 1745, it had been twenty
years "since our New England Hero, Lovell dy'd / Whilst victory lay bleeding by his side." Lovewell shared space with the provincial captains who took
Narragansett Fort in 1675, worthy companions by New England standards,

placing him in the colonial New England pantheon. That Lovewell had been named and the others not indicates whose name was on people's tongues.[13]

A younger generation also heard about John Lovewell in ordinary everyday conversation. True, the "Volunteer's March" ranked among New England's most popular songs, as different versions circulated in the eighteenth and early nineteenth centuries. But even Timothy Dwight, president of Yale College, praised Lovewell and reaffirmed his popularity as a conversation piece. Dwight hailed from a family of Yale men and civil leaders, among whom numbered a major and a colonel. They could include a borderland captain like Lovewell in their talks and pay homage to his exploits. Dwight's silence on the subject of the popular Lovewell ballad can be explained by the facts that he was a patrician (by New England standards) and that the kind of tunes that interested clergymen were primarily those sung during worship. His posthumously published four-volume New England and New York travel tome concerned itself with current and historical descriptions. At Dunstable, Lovewell's birthplace, Dwight summarized the battle by acknowledging Lovewell as "This gallant man, whose exploits were the theme of frequent conversations when I was a boy."[14]

Later Lovewell chroniclers echoed Dwight. Frederic Kidder, a noted nineteenth-century antiquarian, informed readers in his 1865 Lovewell expedition book that perhaps no other pre-Revolutionary military event could match the Pigwacket campaign. Indeed, to his way of thinking it aroused people's sentiments and was remembered by the elderly as an emotionally stirring tale often told in childhood fireside settings. But Kidder was no clergyman, for he added that the aged "can also call to mind how they have listened to hear their grandmothers sing one of the crude songs of that day, of which those heroes were the theme." Rough verse alien to Dwight's childhood upbringing was fondly remembered by others of his generation.[15]

Naturally enough, the battle site itself enhanced Lovewell's memory. Landscape and memory could be mutually reinforcing—people visited battlefields to connect to a remembered past celebrated in prose or verse. That some battlefields still contained visible relics such as bones, bullets, or equipment gave them a physical, felt dimension as powerful as any memorial. Indeed, such objects could mark sites for years or even decades to come. Protruding bones or skulls washed up by the rain could commemorate the fallen in grisly fashion. The Pigwacket battle represented a small-scale engagement by European standards, its site lacked visible human remains, and its distance from settlements at first also deterred people from going there. Nevertheless, occasional visitors chanced upon the site and recalled its history.[16]

Before the conclusion of Dummer's War, in the late summer and early fall of 1725, Captain Samuel Willard led one of the last scouting parties to reach Pigwacket and discovered the abandoned campgrounds. Some of the battle-scarred Pigwackets had relocated farther north, closer to Canada; others most likely sought shelter in the White Mountains, more or less unnoticed except when hunting. A rough 1726 census listed forty Pigwacket males over sixteen, but that number was an approximation based on a single point in time. Still, Pigwackets remained a presence. In 1741, Walter Bryent, surveying the New Hampshire–Massachusetts boundary, carefully ventured toward the site, notching white and pitch pine trees after every mile; after all, he was on the king's business. Cold, snowy weather impeded Bryent and his men, so an abandoned logging camp offered a makeshift refuge for one night. Otherwise the men camped out in the woods.[17]

Then, on Sunday, March 22, at 9:00 p.m., two Indians, Sentur and Pease, warily approached and hailed Bryent's camp. The ensuing exchange convinced them of Bryent's peaceful intentions. Still, the setting near Pigwacket prompted Sentur to reminisce over the 1725 encounter, which had left him wounded and blind in one eye. Sentur warned that other approaching Indians might be less friendly. Indeed, when Bryent later returned to a previously marked tree, he found "on said tree a Sword handsomely formed grasped by a Hand." Was this yet another warning? If so, it appeared that wartime memories lingered among the Abenakis as much as the English. Bryent continued surveying, uncovered deserted Native American campsites, and espied Lovewell's pond across the Pigwacket plains before his men halted and compelled him to leave. Soft snow combined with broken river and brook ice were the stated reasons, although Bryent also attributed some of it to "backwardness" among his men. The fear of Abenaki warriors may well explain this "backwardness."[18]

In 1747, as King George's War roiled New England, Bryent returned to Pigwacket and stood on the battle site. What he recorded was short yet memorable: the bullet-ridden trees revealed that the battle's fury was as yet unclaimed by nature, with faces carved on the bark to commemorate the fallen. New England tombstones sometimes sported death's-heads with angel's wings or hourglasses marking the end of life, and by the middle of the eighteenth century more cherubic angelic faces slowly began to appear in New England burial grounds. But these admittedly crude attempts at portraiture went beyond those traditional standards, suggesting that an anonymous engraver had gone to some trouble to memorialize the deceased scalp hunters. The graves went unnoticed by Bryent; by the time of his visit to Pigwacket the ground had obviously settled and been covered over by vegetation.[19]

Settlement of the northern New England area advanced slowly. Shortly after King George's War ended in 1748, the brief interlude of peace was shattered in the Ohio River Valley when Virginia challenged French claims to the region, prompting the first firefight in 1754. Great Britain and France formally declared war in 1756. British and provincial troops sought to capture and retain key military fortresses. Native Americans weighed options and chose sides. Borderland settlers learned to be careful lest a musket ball or tomahawk end their lives. Many simply fled their homes. As for the British, they learned to enlist ranger companies. Major Robert Rogers, a larger-than-life latter-day version of John Lovewell, showed what fighting Indian-style entailed: attacking the Native American community at St. Francis in 1759, he massacred a largely defenseless group of old men, women, and children, narrowly avoiding his angry pursuers, as some of his starving men turned to cannibalism to survive. Over time the British prevailed, prompting the French in 1763 to sign away their North American mainland territories. Native Americans adjusted to the changed political dynamic. Some were too decimated to offer much resistance; others continued to assert their independence. In northern New England, however, Indians posed few obstacles to ex-soldiers seeking to extend the borderlands with land bounties.[20]

Colonel Joseph Frye of Andover, Massachusetts, a relative of Chaplain Frye of Lovewell fame, was a man with military plaudits to his credit and an eye for opportunity. In 1755, he had helped expel the French Acadians from Nova Scotia, torching homes until one village rose up against him, forcing a hasty retreat. Yet Frye's officers presented him with an engraved silver tankard in 1757—somehow he had managed to keep their respect. That year, Frye also survived Fort William Henry's botched capitulation. Angry French Indian allies demanded the right to booty, whereas the French wished to preserve European protocols of surrender, which allowed the adversary to withdraw honorably without harm. The result was disaster. Believing themselves protected, English and provincial soldiers soon discovered otherwise; in the ensuing chaos an Indian captor stripped Frye of his outer clothing before he could make good his escape. Frye later petitioned Massachusetts for a land grant, receiving a six-mile-square tract at Pigwacket in 1762. The broad valley along the Saco River, which boasted ponds and fields with pine, birch, oak and maple trees, afforded arable, well-timbered land.[21]

Joseph Frye set about creating a community. Tracts went for twenty pounds sterling, and settlers needed to construct a house and till land for several years or lose their portions. Atop the town's highest hill, Frye's home physically and symbolically dominated the infant settlement named after him. The town store inside the house further underscored the prominence of his position: here, the colonel conducted his business attended by a black slave while settlers paid court and begged favors; many borrowed saws, chisels, and plows, some of which they never returned until a memorandum book put matters to right. "Before I made this book," Frye ruefully noted, "people borrow[ed] tools of me and would bring them home by means whereof I lost tools and was at great expense at times to look up those I save."[22]

Did anyone ponder Lovewell's Fight while engaged in settlement building near the pond that bore the captain's name? If newcomers hailed from neighboring New Hampshire, as some indeed did, the colony's 1761 map of northern New England might have been familiar to them. "An Accurate Map of His Majesty's Province of New Hampshire in New England, 1761," made for the British Secretary of War, described Pigwacket as "famous for Captain Lovel's fight with the Indians in 1725, who commanded scout of 34 men was here surprised by 80 Indians in ambush & in a most obstinate Indian skirmish ever known was killed with 15 men." Lest British officials fret about the outcome, the map patriotically reported that the English had retained the field.[23]

At least one early settler, John Evans, knew about Lovewell and the battlefield. As a former ranger, Evans appreciated Lovewell's experience—he had served alongside Major Robert Rogers and narrowly survived the 1759 raid on St. Francis. By the winter of 1762/63, Evans arrived in Pigwacket and was soon operating the town gristmill by Lovewell's Pond. He built roads across Maine in the 1760s and 1770s, his reputation as a first-rate axe man and surveyor being known far and wide. When he wasn't working, Evans encountered Indians from the historic 1725 battle—they preserved a presence in the region. Perhaps Sentur had lived long enough to talk to Evans, or maybe Old Philip, a guide to Rogers' Rangers, had related stories to tell. Certainly, the bullet holes on the trees offered reminders of the fight. Scanning the terrain and listening to the stories nonetheless left Evans puzzled: why had Lovewell instructed his men to drop their packs after spotting a solitary Indian? Why did the Abenakis leave off fighting at dusk when they held the better ground? No one could answer his questions.[24]

The Reverend Paul Coffin, Buxton, Maine, Congregational minister and Harvard graduate, wondered about the Pigwacket battle too. Familiar with ancient languages and recent history, including Symmes's account of Lovewell's Fight, Coffin would find his knowledge tested when he rode to Pigwacket to preach and baptize in the autumn of 1768. In his journal, Coffin referred to Pigwacket as a "fine pitch pine plain," with upper Fryeburg, "extremely pleasant. Nature has formed here the desirable rural retreat which poets described as the most amiable situation in life." Coffin dropped in on Colonel Frye, who was busily planning a new home. The convivial Frye related his Fort William Henry exploits, but his Pigwacket battle stories contradicting Symmes's account caught Coffin's attention.[25]

Perhaps it was this that spurred Coffin to visit the battlefield on October 6 and reflect on Colonel Frye's battle account. Frye disagreed with Symmes over the number of Indians there: although Lovewell's men had spotted a single Indian, Frye insisted that originally two Indians (one unobserved by the scouts) had been present. Moreover, Frye claimed that the two Indians held an English captive—no history had even hinted at that. The second Indian popped up again, in Frye's telling, to report the battle's aftermath to the English, at first claiming that all of Lovewell's troopers had been killed and only two or three Indians were dead. Asked again, the Indian responded, "Now me say true—forty Indians." Frye asserted that there were sixty Indians in all, a number Coffin accepted as valid, although Symmes had reported that there were more than twice the number of Indians than English, putting the number closer to seventy, if not eighty. Frye insisted that the two Indian bands did not converge immediately upon Lovewell men; only after the initial attack by Paugus did "Nath" lead a band of twenty Indians into the fray.[26]

Scanning the battlefield, Coffin questioned the practicality of the defensive position of Lovewell's men, who were placed so the Indians could shoot at them from the west or the north: if a trooper positioned himself against one wave of fire, he was exposed from another angle. Also, the number of trees available for cover was small even by 1768, prompting Coffin to lament "the poor breastwork of the English." That any men had survived surprised Coffin and led him to conclude that the English and Pigwacket stood farther apart than he had realized. He also thought Lovewell's initial attack on the lone

Indian was ungallant. Nevertheless, he praised Lovewell's men for outlasting their numerically larger opponents.[27]

The unnamed second Indian, the basis of Colonel Frye's information, remains a mystery. Where could Frye have heard this story? The surviving Abenakis were one possibility. Coffin never saw Indians in Fryeburg, but John Evans had heard Abenaki battle accounts; the Abenakis, moreover, valued oral memory and storytelling. Tales could have reached Colonel Frye, an inveterate storyteller himself, later to be circulated among visitors. Conversations with Indian battle participants, as Bryent and Evans had discovered, reaffirmed or challenged popular memory, and among the Abenakis, Molly Ocket related her share of memorable stories.[28]

Molly Ocket claimed an area for herself that transcended borderland New England cultural boundaries. Born around 1740, Ocket wandered through northern New England and Canada, turning up in Fryeburg and Bethel, Maine, among other settlements, where she ministered to the sick. Roots, herbs, and bark were Ocket's stock-in-trade, poultices a favored remedy. Stories about her kindness to settlers were legion. So, too, were stories about her fondness for rum and beer. Molly received a warm welcome from white inhabitants in an age when memories of Indian attacks lingered. (Bethel had witnessed an Indian raid in 1781.) In between her ministrations, she told stories about her lineage, at one point announcing that she was the daughter and granddaughter of chiefs. Tales of Lovewell's Fight were also on offer. What precisely she said about it remains unknown, except that "She was certainly very familiar with the events of Lovewel's fight and the war next proceeding," according to one settler's recollection. Molly Ocket was not the only source of Lovewell lore, as we have seen, but she embodied the art of Abenaki storytelling and enjoyed access to settlers. Colonel Frye's account of an unrecorded Indian describing the battle could easily have come from such a source.[29]

Popular memory about Lovewell's Fight, in Fryeburg at least, diverged from Symmes's account. How much Symmes had learned from the three returning Lovewell troopers—Seth Wyman, Ebenezer Ayer, and Abiel Asten—and how much he invented can only be speculated. Without Abenaki accounts Symmes's tract obviously remained incomplete. Individuals, however, visited the battlefield, assessed the terrain, and forged their own conclusions. Stories from Abenakis would enter into their narratives, albeit indirectly and perhaps unaccredited. Hence the Reverend Coffin's knowledge, drawn from Symmes and later challenged by Frye, prompted his own investigation that resulted in a private journal narrative. Other individuals interested in the 1725 battle and exchanging information would layer the story further. An added Indian or two or an unrecorded battle incident would hardly be out of place.

Narrative re-creation (whatever the actual source) gave Lovewell's Fight an organic quality. It could grow and extend in different directions only to wither and fade when neglected or overturned. In fact, other episodes might entrench themselves and modify the dominant story line. Lovewell and company's heroism—the repeated refrain in retellings—shrouded Benjamin Hassell's desertion and the rear guard's hasty retreat. Those incidents became seldom mentioned, easily marginalized aspects. Officials might have murmured about them in 1725, but Symmes and Penhallow had kept Hassell nameless. Later chroniclers and verse makers underplayed or completely omitted to mention Hassell and the rear guard in favor of John Lovewell, Paugus, Seth Wyman, Jonathan Frye, and one or two others they deemed worthy of remembrance. Heroism, not cowardice, emerged as the dominant, remembered theme.[30]

Lovewell's Fight, however, faced competition in the form of other popular memories. A stirring battle story with hardy survivors might be dwarfed by a larger battle or wartime tragedy. New events inevitably crowded out past episodes from people's memory. The American Revolution furnished battles and heroic figures galore, which were embraced by regional and national audiences in story and song. Lexington and Concord, for instance, captured popular imaginations in Massachusetts, relegating Lovewell's Fight to a conversational topic among the aged by the mid-nineteenth century, as one Lovewell chronicler admitted. Why would Bostonians recall Lovewell's Fight, when hills named Breed and Bunker stood nearby to jog memories and tongues? Would Portland, Maine, residents tell tales of Lovewell and Paugus, or relate the British firebombing of their community in late 1775? Localities acquired and elevated different memories according to their proximity and identification with events.[31]

The Reverend Jeremy Belknap tried to position Lovewell's Fight more squarely in the historical canon by means of his carefully researched three-volume New Hampshire history. When exploring the White Mountains in the company of clergymen and guides in the summer of 1784, Belknap observed historical venues and striking terrain. Hence, to him the Ossipee River was not just a piece of geography but the location of Lovewell's fort (now a decaying ruin of rotten wood) where the rear guard had been posted. John Evans guided Belknap into Fryeburg and offered his observations; at the battlefield, Belknap saw the still visible bullet holes and initials carved on a tree. The troopers' exposed position stood out too. Evan's musings informed Belknap, who remarked, "It is astonishing the Indians ever left the ground."[32]

Belknap's resulting history debunked Thomas Hutchinson's claim that the lone Indian sighted by Lovewell's men had been a decoy. Hutchinson had authored a provincial history of Massachusetts prior to the Revolution; but as a onetime Massachusetts royal governor, loyalist Hutchinson was easily ignored by patriotic Americans. Moreover, Belknap's assertion raised scant popular attention due to his work's modest sales. New Hampshire's not inconsiderable history, populated with explorers and officials from the 1600s onward, left Lovewell with one chapter in the second volume devoted to Dummer's War. In other words, Lovewell's Fight represented just one tale among many in a largely unread work.[33]

Elijah Russell revisited Lovewell's Fight and suffered much the same fate as Belknap. A printer by trade, Russell headed to Fryeburg to start *Russell's Echo or the North Star* in February 1798 after operating a Concord, New Hampshire, newspaper. Russell was taking a gamble: though Fryeburg proved historically rich, the town's interest in current events remained untested. Could farmers and loggers afford the one-dollar-fifty-per-annum fee for his newspaper? Or would they opt for the reduced seventy-five-cent rate to be paid in advance upon purchase of the first issue? Perhaps residents simply did not care. Russell scurried to line up subscriptions, arranging for out-of-town patrons to pick up their papers. He capitalized on Fryeburg's link to Captain John Lovewell, publishing in 1799 *The History of the Fight of the Intrepid Captain John Lovell [Lovewell] which took place on the eighth day of May on the beach at Lovell's Pond in Fryeburg in the District of Maine.* Russell intended to improve on the Reverend Symmes's 1725 account and alter certain narrative strands.[34]

Russell extolled the Lovewell troop's exploits: "Never was a battle sustained with more fortitude and courage than was this on the part of Captain Lovewell and his men." Their march into the Abenakis' domain opened the region to "settlement and civilization." Russell also saluted Fryeburg's early residents, in effect linking their community building to Lovewell's achievements. Much as Lovewell's troop had marched to war, such men as Samuel Osgood, Moses Ames, John Evans, Jedediah Spring, and others "encountered the hardships, the fatigue, the suffering, and the losses of the first settlement of this new country." They persevered sufficiently to install a minister and incorporate an academy. Such flattery was meant to yield commercial returns, as leading families basking in Russell's laudatory introduction might be moved to purchase the work. Anyone who subscribed to Russell's newspaper would aid its publication by buying a "Lovell Fight or some other little book . . . the expense a mere trifle." If not, Russell related the consequences: "But as 'without the rain from heaven, the corn shall wither on its stalk' for also without the oil of public aid, printing presses will creak with rust.—That this may never be but that the wilderness may continue to bud and blossom as the rose shall be our 'Constant Prayer.'"[35] The newspaper closed later that year; its readers too few or too uninterested to heed Russell's plea even with Lovewell's Fight as the lure.

Russell's commercial failure nevertheless enlarged the official public memory of the Pigwacket ambush. This marked the first work since Symmes's 1725 sermon history to specifically target the clash between Lovewell and the Pigwacket. More important, Russell championed John Chamberlain as the slayer of Paugus. Joseph Stow had credited Chamberlain decades earlier, yet subsequent chroniclers had never cited this work. How Russell chanced upon this information remains unknown: Did he see Stow's effort, or did Chamberlain's descendants and friends circulate tales? We can only speculate. In Russell's retelling, Chamberlain shot Paugus after the two men had washed their befouled muskets together and exchanged words. Years later, Paugus's vengeful son stalked his father's killer in Groton, Massachusetts, according to Russell, only to be dispatched by the ever-vigilant Chamberlain. This sidebar to the memory of Lovewell's Fight over who killed Paugus added a new twist to the story. But before any more narrative strands could be added, Lovewell first needed to be anchored more securely in the public memory.[36]

Historical memory during the early republic usually centered on the American Revolution. Leading patriots easily seen as titans of independence became the honored dead. If partisan divisions between Federalists and Republicans led to selective retellings of the past fueled by class and ideology, Americans could nonetheless celebrate July 4 in a display of nationalism. Parades and speeches followed by food and drink emerged as annual rituals. As an anniversary celebration, Independence Day held an unrivaled position. Localities might commemorate particular Revolutionary incidents—Evacuation Day in Manhattan or Bunker Hill in Boston, for instance—but the overall Revolutionary focus overshadowed the nation's earlier colonial past, threatening to leave Lovewell's Fight lost in the fog of obscurity.[37]

Despite Revolutionary commemorations, however, Lovewell's Fight continued to register discreetly in early republican New England. Groups and individuals found myriad ways, some of them rather tenuous, in which to link or contrast the battle to current concerns. Close to Fryeburg, a recent settlement, New Suncook, became incorporated as Lovell, Maine, in 1800. That the settlers had bought land grants originally given to Lovewell's men easily explains the naming. An 1818 Portland, Maine, reprinting of Symmes's narrative by an anonymous Fryeburg resident took a different path to the Indian fighter. The pamphlet's introduction bemoaned the state of religion, partisan politics, and misbehaving public officials during the so-called Age of Good Feelings. Even so, the "delights of the present" shone brightly in Fryeburg, home to a church and a fine academy; its citizens graced pulpits, sat on the bench, and practiced medicine. Driving off the Pigwacket in 1725, as Lovewell's men had done, evidently made possible these events that led to Fryeburg's public-spirited residents. An 1819 Boston reissue of Symmes's account, whose publisher found the rising generation's love of fiction disturbing, urged readers to favor history and biography instead. Lovewell's Fight exceeded "the description of a general battle, the destruction of a whole fleet, or the final triumph of one nation over another."[38]

Literary figures also kept Lovewell's Fight before the public. Before becoming a Bowdoin college professor, peace advocate, and faith-and-science-blending psychologist, Thomas C. Upham penned verse on Fryeburg's past. The *Boston Colombian Centinel* offered readers a poem in November 1819 described as a work "from a young gentleman of Maine, occasioned by a visit to the very memorable battle ground near Lovell's Pond." No further identification of the site was necessary—Bostonians understood the reference. Even more remarkable, Upham's untitled poem omitted Lovewell, Wyman, Frye, and Paugus entirely. Instead, it eulogized the departed Indian warriors reduced to "lifeless form." Gloating played little part in the composition, as whatever "hellish Vengeance" the Pigwackets had "robed in blood" was atoned for by their grisly demise. All that remained was the site:

> The lakelet waves come murmuring to the Shore
> And curl in luster round the forms they Lave
> Whisper farewell—proclaim the battle o'er
> And hymn a requiem round the Red-man's Grave.[39]

That same year a poem entitled "Lovellspond" appeared in Upham's *American Sketches*. Again, strident bellicosity was absent, and the dead—Abenakis and New Englanders—are unnamed; only Lovell's Pond, the subtitle referring to "The scene in 1725, of a desperate encounter with the savages," supplied a marker. But here it was Lovewell's men, not the Indians, who earned a eulogy, hailed in the last line as the "heroes of Lovellspond slumber'd in gore." It was a less than triumphant sendoff.[40]

Upham also wrote "The Birchen Canoe" in 1819, based on Solomon Kies's escape from the battle; Kies had reached the rear-guard fort after first spotting an unoccupied Abenaki canoe. In Upham's verse, the nameless occupant of the canoe, "the pale bleeding soldier," dies in the craft, which becomes his coffin, as "the murmurs of Lovellspond sooth him to rest." Instead of heralding Kies's escape, Upham preferred to add him to the death list, albeit in the best poetic fashion.[41]

Henry Wadsworth Longfellow memorialized Lovewell, and hence Fryeburg, as well. Longfellow remains best known for "Paul Revere's Ride," "Hiawatha," and several other popular nineteenth-century poems, but the young poet's first effort in 1820 dealt with Lovewell's Fight—a very American topic for a very American poet.[42]

Young Longfellow had spent summer days at his Grandfather Wadsworth's farm in Gorham, Maine. Wadsworth was a Revolutionary soldier and born storyteller; his tales of capture and imprisonment by British soldiers (capped by a successful escape) delighted his grandchildren. Gorham's proximity to Fryeburg and Lovewell's Pond, recalled by Longfellow's younger brother, Samuel, evidently inspired young Henry. When leafing through Upham's *American Sketches*, Longfellow left a penciled comment noting the error about the unnamed soldier who the poem said died in the canoe: "great mistake—soldier did not perish thus. He reached the shore badly but not mortally wounded & lived on many years." The thirteen-year-old Longfellow confidently composed *The Battle of Lovewell Pond*, inspired by local history and perhaps by Upham's poetic license.[43] The result of his effort, published in the *Portland Gazette*, complemented Upham's work. The youthful Longfellow did not think names were necessary: "They are dead: but they live in each patriot's breast / And their names are engraven on honor's bright crest." Longfellow had earlier written that no markers distinguished "where their ashes repose / Nor points out the spot from the graves of their foes," recognizing that their sepulture was incomplete.[44]

John Farmer and Jacob B. Moore, editors of the *Collections, Historical and Miscellaneous, and a Monthly Literary Journal,* also pitched Lovewell to their readership. Farmer was an avid researcher, a corresponding member of the Massachusetts Historical Society, and an all-around genealogist. The publication he coedited with Moore targeted military history, New Hampshire biography, and statistics. Accordingly, in 1822 the journal built on Symmes's work and identified Chamberlain as Paugus's slayer. Two years later the periodical supplied Lovewell family information and reprinted the Lovewell Fight ballad. When publishing the 1823 *New Hampshire Gazetteer* together, Farmer and Moore enthused that accolades for Captain Lovewell and his "coadjustors often resounded from the humble cottage of the poor and the stately mansion of the opulent." Here was a democratic hero for all citizens of the early republic.[45]

It remained for the *North American Review,* arguably the nation's premiere literary journal, to bestow a blessing on Lovewell and company. The January 1824 issue described Lovewell's Fight as a popular New Hampshire nursery tale: "there is scarcely a person that lives in the eastern and northern part of the state but has heard incidents of that fearful encounter repeated from infancy." The periodical's intellectual heft provided ex-Federalists with a literary platform; it also served to inform and instruct high-toned readers about New England's history. The *Review* reported that Fryeburg was "often visited with interest to this day, and the names of those who fell, and those survived, are yet repeated with emotions of grateful exultation."[46]

All Fryeburg needed was a town celebration to reaffirm their link to the oft-praised Captain John Lovewell and the 1725 battle. For that, Plymouth, Massachusetts, where Forefathers' Day celebrations had turned Plymouth Rock into a national icon by 1820, offered a precedent. The Plymouth bicentennial ranked among the earliest bicentennial observances in the young republic—no mean feat, as the Revolution more typically fueled historical inspiration. Daniel Webster, a rising lawyer and politician, offered a stirring and lengthy oration—elevating the Pilgrim Fathers into the company of New England's democratic, liberty-loving founders—that burnished his own speaking credentials. In 1825, Fryeburg prepared for the Lovewell Fight Centennial. That the battle had predated actual town settlement mattered little; anniversary observances were occasions to trumpet a community's identity and showcase values, and what better event than the bloody 1725 fight between Lovewell's troop and the Pigwackets?[47]

Fryeburg local worthies set to work. Ebenezer Fessenden Jr., Robert Bradley, Stephen Chase, James Osgood, Asa Charles, and Joseph Colby—the committee members were movers and shakers: all of them save Colby had or would serve as town selectmen. Anniversary celebrations usually demanded a public address, the better to instruct listeners about the occasion's purpose, so the committee hoped to snare Daniel Webster, a teacher in the village academy in 1802. Webster had blossomed politically, argued cases before the Supreme Court, and won oratorical renown. But he turned down the centennial invitation. Instead, Fryeburg summoned Charles S. Daveis, a Portland lawyer and well-connected politico who, as the *Portsmouth Journal* noted, was a "most able and accomplished scholar," to do the honors.[48]

What Daveis delivered was less a paean to Lovewell than a discourse on classical and recent history, evoking comparison to ancient Greece and Rome, Great Britain, the American Revolution, and the early republic. Fryeburg received a brief nod as "this thriving and thronging hive of industry and animation." Lovewell and Paugus were cited more than once in the resulting sixty-four-page pamphlet—the only Pigwacket battle figures to be so honored. Chaplain Frye received one brief acknowledgment, but Chamberlain, Paugus's alleged slayer, went unmentioned. Daveis acknowledged Americans' rightful pride in their heroic forbears, yet also noted that the numerically decreased Native Americans, their war whoops now extinct, merited consideration. That Daveis mentioned them at all illuminates a paradigm shift in the making.[49]

New Englanders had an excellent vantage point for observing firsthand the declining numbers of Native Americans. The American Revolution had ended disastrously for most Indians; many had relocated or ceded large tracts of ancestral lands. In New England, the native population remained a pale shadow of those in decades past, exciting little concern or apprehension among white residents unless they became public charges. William Tudor, in *Letters on the Eastern States,* an 1820 tome, wrote: "There are few things connected with our history that have occasioned more declamation or more opposite statements." Some Americans subscribed to the belief that Native Americans possessed remarkable virtues; others, according to Tudor, attributed "dishonesty, perfidy, and ferocity" to them. In Maine, the remnants of Indian nations primarily inspired curiosity. Their Saco River encampments drew onlookers, who noted their modest circumstances; attired in a combination of native and modern dress, and reliant on a largely barter economy based on hunting and fishing, Native Americans eked out a livelihood while struggling to maintain their identity.[50]

When Charles Daveis spoke in Fryeburg, he likely addressed a town with few if any Indian residents. The last Indian claim to the region had been deeded away in 1796, and Molly Ocket had died in 1816. No comparable Indian figure attracted notice among Fryeburg white residents. For his part, Daveis reminded listeners of Indians' terror-based warfare that "no power of description will ever be able to parallel." This was strong stuff in line with earlier anti-Indian attitudes. Yet Daveis blamed the French and the English— those "active and vindictive foreign agents," in his words—for instigating these Indian tactics. Now declining, the Indians could be more dispassionately evaluated, and Paugus, admittedly a "cruel and merciless enemy" when roused by passion or "Canadian artifice," had in fact been welcome among the settlers, according to Daveis, including the man (Chamberlain or Wyman?) "from whom he received the fatal bullet. Paugus might justly appeal to any man if he ever came to his cabin hungry and cold and he gave him an inhospitable reception." Sympathy for Paugus also existed elsewhere: the New Hampshire *Portsmouth Journal*, after reporting the proceedings, labeled Paugus a "distinguished warrior." That the event came to be remembered as "Paugus Day," giving the Indian warrior billing higher than that of Captain John Lovewell, shows the changed thinking among some New Englanders.[51]

Henry Wadsworth Longfellow's poem, *Commemoration Ode*, followed Daveis's speech at the centennial gala. Lovewell's Fight shattered the "warrior's spear / and our father bled / The Indians' power had been broken, / death had claimed them / and others would go to the setting sun." A melancholy air pervaded the brief poem; yet the Pigwacket battle story "Shall not pass from earth away"; in fact, "And free hearts the record keep, of this jubilee."[52]

Follow-up toasts were drunk in the Oxford House, Fryeburg's plushest inn, capping the festivities in a spirit of good fellowship. Liquid salutes enabled participants to craft messages in response to the earlier speeches. Although the *Portland Argus* could not identify the toastmasters, by printing their declarations the newspaper symbolically extended Fryeburg's centennial audience beyond the town's borders. Raised tankards honored the Pigwacket, Captain John Lovewell and his men, Chaplain Jonathan Frye, Seth Wyman, and even John Chamberlain. In toast number seven a speaker intoned: "The remnant of the Pequawket tribe; although expelled from these plains, where civilization has erected her standard, may they in happier climes experience the fostering hands of the American republic." Toast number ten touted the "Progress of Improvement," which stilled both tomahawk and scalping knife.

The next toast hinted at American and Indian unity, as seen by the "The days of Pocahontas and the New England Pilgrims, a glorious era in the history of man." Why Pocahontas, an inhabitant of Virginia, and not Massasoit the Pilgrim benefactor was left unsaid.[53]

What Fryeburg residents hoped to accomplish—namely, to incorporate a suitable historical memory into their town's identity—was duly reported by New England newspapers. Later town residents would label it as "one of Fryeburg's greatest days." Nevertheless, the newly founded *Worcester Magazine and Historical Journal* sounded a warning in its October 1825 issue, concerned by people's ignorance of Lovewell. To journal editors, the lack of a battlefield memorial at Pigwacket underscored this situation:

> A hundred years have gone by, and no enduring monuments have been reared by the gratitude of posterity to perpetuate the memory of the spot, and identify the locality of the combat. The names carved upon the bark have been obliterated; the scars of the bullets have become suspicious; the trees themselves have yielded to storms; the memories of men grow indistinct as the mist of age come over them—and no marks will remain to distinguish the graves of the slain who fell in the desperate fray, and to warn us that we do not profane with our footsteps the earth of their lowly beds.[54]

The editors raised some curious points: Were the battle of Pigwacket and the memory of Captain John Lovewell liable to fade in the absence of a memorial? Was sepulture undermined, as they implied, when people trampled on unmarked graves? At first glance, these worries appear exaggerated, as literary journals and poets had continued to keep Lovewell before the public. When Nathaniel Hawthorne later wrote "Roger Malvin's Burial," an 1832 short story about the moral consequences of the battle's aftermath, he referred just briefly to the fight, because "History and tradition are unusually minute in their memorials of this affair." However, this did not prevent him from pondering the moral consequences of abandoning comrades—the guilt felt by his main character, Reuben Bourne, for having left the gravely injured Roger Malvin behind, and failing to return as pledged to bury him, resulted in the later, accidental sacrifice of Bourne's own son at the same site. But these names were not Farwell, Frye, Davis, or Jones.

Town histories from Dunstable, Woburn, and Groton covered the battle as well—village fathers had fought and died alongside Lovewell. By the 1860s,

Nathaniel Bouton and Frederic Kidder had enlarged upon Symmes's effort, offering footnotes and editorial commentary in their respective treatments. How could New Englanders possibly forget Lovewell and the 1725 battle?[55]

However essential as a building block, printed official memory had its limits, trumped by popular memory and dependent on people's reading of historical tomes as it was. The *Worcester Magazine*'s editor had bemoaned the veil of ignorance that covered Lovewell. Worcester's location in western Massachusetts, removed from eastern New Hampshire and Maine, may have explained this: Lovewell did not qualify as a local boy. Time, too, removed the event from popular knowledge. Frederic Kidder's 1865 account of the Pigwacket fight acknowledged that it was only the elderly who continued to talk about the battle, leaving Lovewell "to be heard of on the pages of history."[56] The young had other heroes to enliven their conversations.

Proper sepulture, as the *Worcester Magazine* suggested, might elevate Lovewell by supplying a monument to mark the battle site. The first New England cemeteries had rarely drawn visitors once funerals had taken place and were haphazardly arranged, with the bones of the departed occasionally protruding from the ground. Fallen provincial soldiers received no monuments except in exceptional circumstances, and even then only prominent commanders merited stones or reinterments elsewhere. Unmarked Revolutionary battlefields were more often the norm than the exception. Yet by the early nineteenth century the dead had become sentimentalized figures, as evidenced by Upham and Longfellow's poetry; tombstones and burial plots grew increasingly elaborate in comparison to their colonial predecessors. The rural cemetery movement introduced verdant, gardenlike settings that encouraged visits to the resting places of departed loved ones. In turn, properly marked graves in such surroundings inspired reflection. Even the wartime dead had benefited from such renewed consideration. The *Jersey*, a dismasted British prison hulk, was one of several ships in Wallabout Bay, Brooklyn, home to American POWs in the Revolution; in 1808 thousands of these patriot prisoners, who had been carelessly buried in the sand, were given a gala procession and reinterment in a proper burial vault. In 1818 New Yorkers relocated Revolutionary general Richard Montgomery from his Quebec grave to St. Paul's Chapel in Manhattan. Memorials may not have guaranteed large numbers of visitors, but they could distinguish the final resting site.[57]

The *Worcester Magazine's* assertions dovetailed with a growing national interest in military sepulture and proper graves. Without monuments, the dead languished unseen and unhonored; over time, changes in the natural landscape led memories to fade. Lovewell's fort at Ossipee was already a ruin. The carved initials and bullet holes in the trees at Pigwacket were disappearing. William Williamson's 1832 *History of Maine* noted that bullets "have been cut out of the trees within a few years." Were these memento hunters inadvertently erasing Lovewell's memory by purloining the lead? The historically minded who trooped to the site would see little except trees and brush—nature restored, with an assist from musket-ball scavengers. Now that cemeteries were more elaborate and battle dead respectfully memorialized, should not the Pigwacket dead receive their due in stone?[58]

Ironically, Fryeburg bequeathed neither monument nor town history to remember the Lovewell expedition. With the 1825 centennial properly commemorated, residents returned to their axes and plows, managed their farms and mills, attended church, and sent favored sons to the academy. Regional gazetteers praised Fryeburg's bustling main street; local industries that included tanneries, sawmills, a wheel factory, and a pail manufacturer hummed with activity. Yet Fryeburg's history struggled to be preserved in the midst of development. During the 1850s and 1860s the Reverend Samuel Southers and James Osgood failed to compile a town chronicle, and funds voted by the town in 1881 to compile historic material achieved little.[59]

John Stuart Barrow, who authored a twentieth-century town history, pondered this historical apathy of early Fryeburg. Perplexed, he surmised: "It seems unaccountable that in a town like Fryeburg, with the amount of historical matter originally available, no interest was taken to conserve it, and to collect historical articles; but as those who know the most history often care the least about preserving the current of their times, and as generation succeeds generation, the happenings of the time become forgotten and lost."[60] Historical preservation seemingly aroused scant curiosity among Fryeburg residents.

For town visitors, Fryeburg's location and terrain signified more than Captain John Lovewell's historic battle site. The nearby White Mountains offered striking promontories and impressive vistas for passersby to sample. Indeed, rocky terrain and wooded ascents inappropriate for farms furnished the subjects for artists' sketches and watercolors, especially among those who appreciated nature in the rough. A belief in travel's healthful benefits further fueled visits: people physically or emotionally exhausted, it was thought, could rejuvenate themselves by exposure to northern New England air. Hiking, paddling, swimming, and bathing, topped off by hearty country fare, furnished the means to this end. Middle-class and well-to-do individuals, many of them city dwellers, could temporarily check notions of gentility at rural inns and farmhouse doors to enjoy a taste of authentic rustic living in Fryeburg and other White Mountain towns.[61]

One tourist, Caroline Barrett White, who left a diary account of an 1854 visit to Fryeburg (and other New England locales) attested to the town's charm. White had traveled from Boston by steamer to Portland before reaching Fryeburg to join her husband Frank, who was recovering from an illness. On August 12, the couple walked to the top of Jockey Cap—an immense boulder in Caroline's opinion—to obtain a fine prospect of the Saco river valley and the nearby peaks. Below was Lovewell's Pond, described by her as the "scene of Lovell's Fight." Descending, the Whites reached the pond by a beach, waded in the water, and paddled a canoe without bothering to explore the battlefield. Nevertheless, White later amended her original entry in a footnote, adding, "I find the true name of this is Lovewell's Fight." That her outing resulted in her catching cold barely lessened her pleasure and activities. In the following days she climbed mountains, observed a distant forest fire, and visited Colonel Joseph Frye's gravesite. After several weeks in the town she concluded, "the longer I stay in Fryeburg, the better I like this place. I love the mountains."[62]

Caroline White's response to Fryeburg reveals a tourist's perspective. For her, the mountain peaks looming above the town were its main attraction, offering scenery and exercise. White was not unmindful of history—as can be seen in her corrected spelling of Lovewell, most likely the result of a subsequent unrecorded conversation with a resident. Yet Lovewell's Pond eclipsed the historic battlefield, with wading and paddling in it the memorable activities that she saw fit to record in her diary. Colonel Joseph Frye, the town's founder, rated a graveside visit by White, but Captain Lovewell and his men did not. After all, what was there to attract her attention to the site other than trees and brush?[63]

Other travelers displayed similar ambivalence about the locale. The 1881 *Gazetteer of Maine* directed summer visitors to Fryeburg's "pleasant hotels and boarding houses," beyond which the White Mountains soared, while citing Captain John Lovewell's 1725 fight. Yet the poet John Greenleaf Whittier, who sojourned in Fryeburg during the summer of 1881, felt the allure of the peaks more strongly than he did that of the colonial battleground, as is evident in the title of the resulting poem he penned, "Apostrophe to a Mountain." But there was more to applaud in Fryeburg than mountain scenery—the town also touted its connection to Daniel Webster, the antebellum statesman and orator, whose brief teaching career in the community proved sufficient connection to celebrate. Given the recent memory of the Civil War, Webster's strong unionist principles struck a chord. Caroline Dana Howe, an expatriate daughter of the town, during a return visit in 1882 wrote a poem, "Memories," commissioned for a book devoted to Daniel Webster, in which mountains, cottages, church spires, the academy, and Webster of course, figured to the almost complete exclusion of Lovewell's Pond and Captain Lovewell. H. Bernard Carpenter, a Maine cleric, did refer to Lovewell in the Webster book, but he emphasized Chamberlain and Webster as the town's true heroes.[64]

A monument to Lovewell might have alerted people to the historic site and altered the dynamic of memory here. At the very least, writers and poets would have had a physical reminder to contrast Lovewell's exploits with the accomplishments of the oft-praised Daniel Webster. When people inquired about Webster, Fryeburg residents pointed to the academy or the house where he had boarded. Some went to look at the deeds that bore Webster's signature when he moonlighted from his teaching job. Lovewell's Pond provided recreational and scenic opportunities, to be sure, whereas the battlefield was hidden by forest. Although George Bancroft and Francis Parkman had both immortalized Lovewell in their majestic late nineteenth-century histories, the town was content to forgo such tributes to a local colonial notable.[65]

Sentiment toward Lovewell—particularly his action against the Pigwackets—had also shifted against him in some quarters. The Reverend Coffin's eighteenth-century qualms about Lovewell's men outnumbering and scalping a single Indian had been privately voiced. Later speakers such as Daveis had portrayed Paugus as a man of character. Henry David Thoreau had ironically wondered why Lovewell troopers received pensions with no thought for the Abenakis. That Lovewell had led roughly forty men against ten Indians during his successful second expedition also bothered Thoreau: he saw scant glory in surprising an outnumbered quarry. If nothing else, Thoreau symbolized the New England antebellum moral conscience, eager to challenge convention and champion the underdog. Other New Englanders seconded Thoreau: G. H. Holister, in his 1858 *History of Connecticut*, after acknowledging his state's refusal to provide aid during Dummer's War, chastised "the shameful maraud of John Lovell, desecrating the banks of the Penobscot and the shores of the Winnepesiuk in quest of scalps." Abraham E. Brown, author of an 1891 Bedford, Massachusetts, town history, denounced scalp hunting as barbaric, writing that Lovewell and company "must be condemned." The eighteenth-century land grants to Lovewell veterans led one 1907 Maine writer to denounce the awards for "such a murderous undertaking attempted chiefly for mercenary purposes upon a peaceful settlement of a disappearing race of men." Similar murmurings against scalping in the mid-1890s had induced James P. Baxter, Maine's preeminent historian, to urge that Lovewell's troop be judged in the context of their times instead of by present standards. Little wonder that Daniel Webster was seen as a safer, more comfortable figure for Fryeburg residents to embrace.[66]

Concern about Maine's overall reputation in the nation's chronicle lurked in the background of these historical squabbles over Lovewell and company. Put bluntly—what did Gilded Age Americans think of Maine? The nation's centennial observances had left the state's residents feeling shortchanged, and Joshua Chamberlain, a renowned Civil War general and former Maine governor, complained that outsiders considered Maine a "neighbor to the western savage." Elevating Lovewell, a scalp hunter, would hardly help matters, only reinforcing the image of a backward locale with barbarous sensibilities. As for the state's history, Chamberlain lamented that Massachusetts, and especially Plymouth as a result of Daniel Webster's 1820 speech, had reduced Maine's past "to absolute zero."

Chamberlain's remarks delivered before the state legislature underscored the gravity of the situation: Maine wanted to be seen as something more than a rustic venue. That some Maine residents felt themselves to be historical outliers may explain why Enoch Knight, another Maine champion, harped on the state's economic potential in an 1876 publication, appropriately entitled *The New Story of the State of Maine*. For Knight, Maine held unsurpassed advantages: "We have, I believe, more natural capacity, with our already disclosed natural and industrial wealth, to have in and of ourselves than any community in this broad and beautiful country." The underlying message seemed to be: if only the real Maine, past and present, could be recognized, justice would be done to the Pine Tree State.[67]

Properly restoring Maine's past and publicizing its present potential was a tall order to fulfill. In Fryeburg, past and future joined together symbolically in 1887 in the form of a three-mile horse-drawn street railway—the rails hinted at a steam- or electric-powered future; the horse power honored traditional locomotion. That Fryeburg was the only Maine town to have a street railway indicates a willingness to take chances and embrace the future. Whether a street railway could halt the town's economic decline was less certain: many late nineteenth-century northern New England towns experienced stagnant or decreasing populations. Western competition had undercut farmers' profit margins; sons could no longer count on the family farm to provide them a decent livelihood. In Fryeburg, the 1880 population of 1,633 had dropped to 1,418 by 1890 and 1,376 by 1900. Only tourism appeared steady.[68]

The Maine Historical Society did its duty by emphasizing Fryeburg's rich past. The society mustered members for an 1895 Fryeburg Field Day Excursion. Members looked at Daniel Webster's signature on town deeds, toured Governor Dana's restored mansion, and dined at the Oxford Hotel. But this time it was Lovewell, not Webster, who occupied pride of place in the proceedings. A battlefield tour was followed by visits to the Congregational church to hear James P. Baxter, leading Historical Society mover and shaker, deliver an address, "John Lovewell and the Peqwacket." For Baxter, Lovewell and company symbolized bravery and patriotism, not scalping and bounties. Yet, sadly, Baxter had to acknowledge that the current reality of Lovewell's exploits "has but little influence upon the life of the present."[69]

Even here, Lovewell had to share space. At the meeting in the Congregational church where Baxter spoke George B. Barrows, a Fryeburg resident, had advocated erecting a granite memorial to the fallen soldiers, but he wanted Paugus and the Pigwackets to have their names carved on top of Mount Pleasant, "the nearest and highest summit, which in the adjoining town looks down upon the spot where they lived." Advocates for a more balanced historical perspective were giving the Abenakis their due.[70]

At first nothing came of these efforts. Memorials cost money and no one in Fryeburg volunteered to collect funds. In San Francisco, Henry Pierce, the great-grandson of John Stevens, one of Fryeburg's first settlers, did wax nostalgic about the town. However, the Maine-born Pierce honored his ancestor in 1902 by spending fifteen hundred dollars on a monument that a provided a watering trough for weary, thirsty horses and a tap for tired pedestrians. Interest in civic improvements that included fence removals, tree plantings, and other forms of town beautification, a growing turn-of-the-century movement, led some Fryeburg residents to consider creating a Lovewell battle-ground park for teaching history. Nature would be tamed in the service of the past. But the plan yielded only talk and no results.[71]

Any proposed monument to Lovewell had to confront another hurdle. Plymouth Rock notwithstanding, the Revolution and increasingly the Civil War occupied the historical memory in the 1880s and 1890s. These bloody wars had shaped the national experience, forging an identity that was later forcibly re-created after the South's attempt at secession failed. Independence Day celebrations gave both Americans of long standing and more recent immigrants the opportunity to display their patriotism. Revolutionary monuments sprouted and mushroomed in a Gilded Age orgy of excess that even managed to include a British spy, Major John André, along with a number of patriotic worthies. Civil War veterans held reunions to hold fast to a personal past, inviting old comrades in arms to annual observances. The American Revolution had no surviving veterans, of course, but the Society of Cincinnati and the Sons of the Revolution supplied veterans' descendants with an organizational identity in which to solemnize the past.[72]

Attempts to stitch colonial battles into this commemorative tapestry admittedly faced challenges. Where could room be found in the evolving national canon to showcase such events, and for what purpose? Late nineteenth-century New Englanders answered that question by adopting the colonial past as the foundation stone of their regional cultural character. Increasing urban growth distinguished by growing numbers of Irish, Italian, Polish, and French Canadian immigrants had propelled old-stock New Englanders to tout their forebears as the only authentic Americans. The Society of Colonial Wars, founded, ironically enough, by several New York City businessmen in 1892, provided a useful organizational venue for New Englanders. The focus on the Revolution and subsequent wars, the society members believed, had improperly obscured the colonial past. Even worse, it banished their forebears to near oblivion. Remembering colonial battles would right the wrong. Massachusetts, Maine, and other eastern states modeled societies on the colonial wars theme. Like the Sons of the American Revolution, proper lineage provided the ticket of admission to membership.[73]

The Maine Society of Colonial Wars, organized in 1898, upheld ancestral bloodlines and sponsored historical theme talks. The largely Portland-based membership often convened in the city to hear speakers lecture on such topics as "Scarboro in Colonial Times" in 1902, "Sir Ferdinando Gorges" in

1903, and "Martin Pring" in 1904—all curiously peaceful-sounding subjects with nary a battle to their credit. Captain Lovewell escaped notice. Rather, the Massachusetts Society of Colonial Wars literally (and figuratively) stole a march on its Maine counterpart in 1904 with plans to honor Lovewell. The battlefield observances would unveil a stone memorial and bronze plaque dedicated to the men of the Lovewell expedition. Moreover, the date of the ceremony, June 17, the anniversary of the Battle of Bunker Hill, provided a symbolic link to a memorable Revolutionary event. The *Oxford Advertiser,* a nearby Norway, Maine, paper, announced the Field Day Excursion, complete with order of arrival, ceremony, and departure. Readers also learned that Fryeburg's mountain views and winding rivers offered pleasurable amenities, soothing travelers with "pure air, pure water, and beautiful scenery." What more could the historically minded want? They could pay homage to the past while enjoying the present healthful surroundings.[74]

The Massachusetts Society of Colonial Wars incorporated the Lovewell's Fight Memorial Association on May 8, 1904, the popular, albeit inaccurate, accepted date for the Pigwacket battle. The Association, headed by one Dr. Orin Warren of West Newbury, Massachusetts, proposed to obtain land parcels related to Lovewell's fatal Indian battle. Properly inscribed monuments devoted to Lovewell's fatal expedition would follow and dot various sites. And, naturally, the Massachusetts Society wished to include Lovewell's men, ensuring them their niche in colonial history. One dollar plus a signature entitled a person to join regardless of ancestry.[75]

The ceremony got off to a rousing start on a beautiful late spring day with highs in the mid-seventies. Both Massachusetts and Maine symbolically joined hands, as A. J. C. Sowdon, governor of the Massachusetts Society of Colonial Wars, and Dr. Warren shared space with James P. Baxter, now Portland's mayor and president of the New England Historical and Genealogical Society. Emerson Leland Adams, the principal of Fryeburg Academy, provided local representation on the official program along with several other Fryeburg citizens. Sowdon uttered brief remarks at the monument's unveiling. The stone listed May 8 as the date of the battle, mentioned Paugus as the slain leader of the Pigwackets, and cited the English dead by name and town, including those wounded who had died along the way. Seth Wyman received a line of credit for having led the survivors. John Chamberlain, sometimes credited with killing Paugus, went unmentioned.[76]

The subsequent meeting at the Congregational church belonged to Baxter, who contrasted the past and present while offering up some verse. William Gordon, a local official, noted the luminaries and ceremonies in his diary, a change from his usual description of weather, crops, and business. (Henry Eugene Walters, another local albeit less prominent Fryeburg citizen, seemed oblivious to the goings-on in his diary—it was just another day to him, bereft of significance.) The attendees, at least the visiting Massachusetts men, repaired to the Oxford Hotel for a hearty meal of soup (two kinds), fish, beef, lamb, and chicken entrees, various side dishes, and desserts sufficient to satisfy any palate. Sated Massachusetts Society members then went forth to tour other parts of northern New England the following day, their work memorializing Lovewell done.[77]

Captain John Lovewell and company had at last been commemorated and inscribed in bronze. The dead were now marked and sepulture complete. Lovewell's entry into the colonial pantheon of worthies appeared assured, and the *Worcester Magazine*'s long ago voiced concerns about unmarked graves more or less satisfied; at least people knew the battle site's precise location alongside Lovewell's Pond. It had been a long journey to reach this destination. Lovewell's Fight—the actual battle, not just the song—had evolved into a treasured northern New England story, in which outnumbered ambushed troops outlasted their attackers. Despite much praised Revolutionary heroes and battles, a few New Englanders had always kept Lovewell and his troop in mind. Side issues regarding who had been the killer of Paugus constituted ancillary concerns that rarely detracted from the overall heroic narrative.

Moral responsibility toward the unburied dead and abandoned wounded barely surfaced in the extended memory narrative. That men had been left behind was noted; that they might have been saved was conveniently cloaked. Lovewell contemporaries acknowledged these issues, but later generations generally steered cleared of them. Nathaniel Hawthorne, in "Roger Malvin's Burial," pondered the moral and emotional consequences of abandoning still living comrades. But he changed names and modified circumstances, not mentioning any deserter or negligent rear guard.[78]

As for the Abenakis, they played a subordinate role in the popular New England memory. A few individuals included them in the narrative; some even suggested that they were heroic too, or at least more than simple savages. That the 1904 monument to Lovewell and his men mentioned Paugus at all represented an achievement of sorts. In effect, the Massachusetts Society of Colonial Wars had acknowledged the original owners of the land as worthy of enshrinement by means of a modest backhanded compliment.

But no matter how remembered or contested, the memory of Lovewell's Fight could not be guaranteed by a monument and tablet. A physical identity in stone, a bit of delayed sepulture if you will, identified the trees, brush, and plains alongside Lovewell's Pond as historically significant. But would people remember to visit the now marked site? Would they know the history behind the stone in the years to come?

It fell to C. F. Whitman, a writer for the *Lewiston Evening Journal,* when visiting Fryeburg in 1908, to describe the memorial's shortcomings. Whitman acknowledged the town's rich historic tradition and overall picturesque quality. But Captain John Lovewell more specifically interested him. Whitman's guide, Seth Wyman Fife, a descendant of the famed Seth Wyman, provided a nice historical touch to the visit, yet the monument itself inspired barbed commentary: "It is to be regretted that the place shows marks of neglect and that bushes are thickly growing about the locality, which will in a few years hide the stone from the view of passersby on the highway. We were informed that the owners of the land now refuse to dispose of it to the association, formed for the purpose of preserving the ground as a public park, which is to be deplored."[79] Monuments sometimes failed to illuminate the past as intended by eager sponsors. A new age of automobiles promised visitors easier access to the battlefield, yet if nature triumphed and covered the stone, Americans would drive past to other destinations.

Whitman's remarks proved eerily prophetic in describing the ever-changing currents of public memory. Whatever the monument's subsequent state of repair, Fryeburg skipped a bicentennial observance in 1925, and hence a chance to showcase Captain John Lovewell. Perhaps the present outweighed interest in the past; or maybe the monument itself discouraged further commemoration. A sesquicentennial celebration of Fryeburg's founding in 1927 drew five thousand people including the governor of Maine, as local schoolboys re-created the battle. Still, a visiting journalist that year huffed that Fryeburg's tourists knew little about Maine's history. In 1928, another journalist regarded the monument coolly, judging Captain Lovewell neither a hero nor a martyr, and adding, "Whenever the water in the pond is very quiet, people tell me that the shadow of an Indian arrow can be plainly seen on the surface." When the Federal Writers Project of the WPA for the state of Maine issued a 1937 guidebook, *Maine: A Guide Down East,* Lovewell and the monument were nowhere to be found. Fryeburg, the guide reported, was a "prosperous summer resort" with well-maintained homes canopied by leafy trees nestled on a former Indian settlement site. A possible segue to Lovewell was missed here. Instead, the book proudly announced that Daniel Webster had taught at the Fryeburg Academy.[80]

Conclusion

Our journey featuring Captain John Lovewell and his troop has traversed northern New England. As we have seen, Lovewell started the trek by leading expeditions in retaliation for an Abenaki raid on Dunstable, his hometown. His death in Pigwacket, Maine, at the hands of Abenakis, should have ended the tale and the captain been a brief footnote to Dummer's War. However, the encounter assumed greater significance for its contemporaries than might be thought merited by the modest number of combatants involved. In Boston, Lovewell's Fight became part of the ongoing war narrative that included deaths and burials on and off the battlefield. Beyond Boston, Massachusetts and New Hampshire residents appreciated the drama of the celebrated slain scalp hunter John Lovewell, whose troopers held their ground under the command of Seth Wyman. The men who were left behind waiting for help from a never materializing rear guard added a certain moral poignancy to the tale. Thomas Symmes and Samuel Penhallow, in their written reconstructions of Lovewell's Fight, supplied broad-brush narratives, underscoring New England military courage and cowardice.

Yet what exactly did the episode mean to New Englanders? Lovewell's Fight, as scripted and recalled, demonstrated their insistence that men in arms retain Christian values, if only to distinguish them from their Native American foes. New England soldiers might fight like Indians, master woods lore, scout for enemies and scalp them without losing their own character, provided they maintained courage and discipline. As John Ferling noted in a seminal article several decades ago, courage and discipline constituted the sine qua non of the early New England soldier and were traits espoused by commanders and clerics alike.[1] And John Lovewell emerged as the standard bearer in the pages of his respective Boswells, Thomas Symmes and Samuel Penhallow. Lovewell had ventured twice into the woods, taken scalps, and returned his troops home safely. His fatal third expedition only enhanced his aura by turning him into a heroic sacrificial victim—in short, the model New England soldier/commander, whose courage should be honored and emulated.

Yet John Lovewell's story gained traction because other New England borderland soldiers did not always live up to the captain's standard. True, in the end, Lovewell's men did survive against a larger force, but their courage sometimes faltered. For example, when nearing Pigwacket, his troopers had feared being "dog'd by the enemy," hardly the reaction of brave soldiers, and were further unnerved when the watch reported hearing Indians by the camp—episodes the Reverend Thomas Symmes revealed.[2] (Neither Symmes nor Penhallow suggested that Lovewell displayed fear—the untested volunteers were the ones who trembled.) On sighting the solitary Indian from a distance, Lovewell had urged caution, as he was concerned about the possibility of Abenakis lurking nearby; his men responded in a chorus extolling manhood and resolve. They wanted to secure a scalp. How brave was it to gang up on a single Pigwacket just in order to gain a bounty? Perhaps not very. But when two Abenaki war parties assailed the unsuspecting troopers in the climatic ten-hour battle, the question seemingly became moot. Seth Wyman took over for the slain Lovewell, and only Benjamin Hassell ran off, leaving his comrades to their fate.

The Reverend Symmes's emphasis on valor also hints at the fears—apparent and coded—that concerned New Englanders about citizens turned soldiers. Some berated troopers who had failed in their duty. For instance, Lieutenant Governor Dummer blasted the rear guard who had refused to search for comrades—none of these men subsequently received service payouts. Both Symmes and Samuel Penhallow turned Hassell into a latter-day Cain. Identity concealed but actions branded, he was marked as the unnamed coward. Hassell's disgrace concealed the moral shortcomings of others: one coward per troop served sufficiently for a sermonic warning or a historical chronicle; two or more might suggest that New England's moral fabric had become too frayed to patch. Hence Solomon Kies's departure from the battle drew scant attention. More problematic were the four seriously wounded men—Josiah

Farwell, Jonathan Frye, Eleazer Davis, and Josiah Jones—left behind by their comrades. As the four had allegedly given their free consent to this, honor was satisfied—until Hassell's actions dashed any hopes of fast rescue. Josiah Jones, who subsequently left Farwell, Frye, and Davis, nonetheless escaped censure. The troopers who failed to return were "wounded, and lost by the way," in Symmes's words.[3]

Rescuing survivors and interring the dead assumed high priority. And here again some New Englanders proved undone: New Hampshire men were too scared to rendezvous with Massachusetts troops to search for survivors or bury the dead. Symmes had stressed the importance of burial. To leave the dead above ground would be unchristian, if not cowardly, and betokened a symbolic victory for the Abenakis. That one of the rescue parties faltered only underscored Symmes's point.

Samuel Penhallow kept certain judgments about cowardice to himself. True, he left Hassell unnamed, following the lead of the Reverend Symmes, but privately he considered the New Hampshire troops' role disgraceful: they had failed in their duty as men and soldiers. He also wondered more openly about Solomon Kies's approved departure from the fighting. But with the nameless Hassell there to absorb the shame, Penhallow saw little need to berate Kies; besides, his *History* was intended to be a paean of praise to New England military character, not a jeremiad of despair. So he touted New England soldiers and officials, creating a patriotic ode for regional readers to read and applaud. New England had come of age as a worthy junior partner in the British Empire. Like Symmes, Penhallow had composed the master narrative of Lovewell's Fight, leaving certain unpleasant facts in the manuscript hidden from public view or aired only obliquely in the published version, perhaps assisted by the Reverend Benjamin Colman's editing.

The government of Massachusetts reaffirmed Lovewell's courage by rewarding his men. Lieutenant Governor Dummer instructed the legislature to be generous; moreover, if compensation for loved ones killed or wounded was forthcoming, it would inspire others to bravery. Was there an unstated fear that to do otherwise would reduce the number of New England recruits in future wars? In any event, the ten-man rear guard never received these payouts, being judged equal to Hassell in the short run. Later, both the rear guard and Hassell did receive grants of land: claiming service under the slain Captain Lovewell entitled the previously disdained troopers to be rewarded, placing them on a par with the ambushed troopers in terms of real estate.

What we see here is a New England military culture, transcribed by Symmes and Penhallow, that applauded valor and condemned cowardice. This is hardly surprising: even today valorous soldiers receive applause or medals; deserters may be court-martialed, imprisoned, or in extreme cases shot. However, eighteenth-century New Englanders, though imbued with a Reformed Christian faith, also understood human limitations—people were bound to stray from the path of righteousness. In forging a heroic master narrative, Symmes and Penhallow did not fail to include faltering individuals. Perhaps most surprisingly, it was New Englanders themselves, not the Abenakis, who provided the culprits in the tale.

Consider, for instance, that when Lovewell's Fight is juxtaposed with the story of the Alamo—particularly its remembered, constructed quality—the differences are obvious. Early Anglo shapers of the Alamo lauded the mission's defenders, although not all had died fighting to the last man; that some, including Davy Crockett, had been executed was carefully omitted from the story until decades later. Nor was there room in it for the Tejanos who fought and died alongside Jim Bowie and William B. Travis; that would have disrupted what Richard R. Flores has called the emerging "Texas Modernity," a cultural trope developed from 1880 to 1920 that reinforced the changed social and economic environment. The Mexicans and the Tejanos were the "others"—that is, the alien primitives confined to a foggy zone of second-class citizenship, when not dispossessed and disenfranchised in an emerging, modern turn-of-the-century San Antonio. It was the constructed memory of the Alamo as much as the altered public space around the structure that served to legitimate Anglo cultural ascendancy in twentieth-century Texas.[4]

But were not the Abenakis or Pigwackets the cultural "others," in Lovewell's Fight, with Paugus serving as a symbol of Native cruelty? Yes, of course, the Abenakis fulfilled that role, and Paugus's death could be celebrated; but at least a few New Englanders had questioned and pondered both Dummer's War and Lovewell's Fight. For instance, when war was first declared, some legislators had wondered if alcohol-dispensing merchants were not to blame for Abenaki hostilities. Later, Thomas Hutchinson considered both Lovewell troopers and Pigwacket fighters courageous. Charles S. Daveis, in 1825, blamed the French rather than the Abenakis for the ascending violence, giving Paugus partial vindication. And Henry David Thoreau mused about pensionless Indians. As Native Americans in Maine became fewer and marginalized, however, the brave commander Lovewell became the main focus. Nineteenth-century New

Englanders had no Indian enemy or citizenry at their doors to subdue—that had already been accomplished. And scalping was part of a past that many New Englanders felt embarrassed to recall.

Saluting Lovewell consequently required touching only lightly on his bounty-hunting activities. Nathaniel Hawthorne identified Lovewell's men as scouts, not scalp hunters per se, sidestepping the moral quagmire of bounty hunting in Lovewell's Fight. Hawthorne's introduction to "Roger Malvin's Burial" proclaimed, "[the] open bravery displayed by both parties was in accordance with civilized ideas of valor; and chivalry itself might not blush to record the deeds of one or two individuals."[5] This was easy enough for Hawthorne to do. After all, the 1725 Lovewell ballad had lauded soldiers' valor, ignoring scalping, deserters, and abandoned men. Local citizens of Fryeburg, Maine, utilized Lovewell's Fight as a vehicle for praising past New England glories and encouraging present hopes. When Revolutionary and Civil War battles threatened to elbow aside Lovewell's Fight, the Society of Colonial Wars responded with a monument and site dedication in 1904. The descendants of early New England settlers wanted their niche in the national war narrative preserved.

What Thomas Symmes and Samuel Penhallow built was a historical model subject to reinterpretation. The narrative about Lovewell's Fight they created, while obviously a solid and enduring foundation, nonetheless allowed subsequent writers and orators to expand and alter the framework in line with changing tastes and sensibilities. The occupants of the narrative house— Lovewell, his troopers, Paugus, and the Pigwackets—remained constant tenants; however, their positions in the edifice varied. Sometimes they were closeted; at other times they occupied the main living space. Bravery may have been the ticket of admission, but by the nineteenth century Native Americans, first considered savages, could win a place as courageous adversaries. Wasn't Paugus mentioned on the 1904 memorial? The same could not be said for all of Lovewell's men. What might be called the New England moral conscience intruded to question who should be justly enshrined. And what it had meant to be a soldier in eighteenth-century New England, a region still fighting wars inside its borders, was very different from what it meant to be a soldier in the minds of early twentieth-century New England civilians.

Perhaps the ultimate irony about New England's cultural embracing of Lovewell and his men can be seen in the monument at Lovewell's Pond. The lavish ceremonies held there never seem to have attracted hoards of visitors, unlike the Alamo in Texas. Occasionally a ceremony would take place, as happened in 1927, but more often the site went unadvertised. Fryeburg residents knew about Lovewell. They also knew about Daniel Webster. It doesn't take much to ascertain which of the two men is more remembered today.

Perhaps I should add a codicil here. Historians often treat their topics with a certain professional detachment, easily enough assumed for people barely recalled and long dead. But monuments invite Clio's students to look at what others who lived before them felt was important. The stone with a metal plaque still stands in Fryeburg by the pond that bears Lovewell's name. The fence surrounding the small property has some rails down and is in need of repair; the trees shading the monument, set back several yards from the road, obscure the site from the road: it is easy to pass by in a car without spotting it. Parking is off-road, but posted signs warn trespassers to steer clear of the private lakeside homes. There is room for only a few cars at most to park by the monument anyway, suggesting that Lovewell and company have been effectively bypassed. My stopping there at the wrong time of year in early September 2011 resulted in my being descended upon by a swarm of flying bugs. I beat a hurried retreat back to my car almost as fast as Hassell's departure three centuries earlier. There was nothing more to see anyway.

Still, Captain John Lovewell's death had once had considerable resonance among his contemporaries; his burial gave them a necessary bit of closure and satisfied Christian tradition; and his memory long survived as a piece of northern New England folklore. That it did so for over a century illustrates the power of memory and the type of recollections about themselves that New Englanders wished to cherish. At least we can ponder their meaning to construct a narrative about Lovewell and company that, while seemingly finished for now, may in the future yet again prompt people to think about early American history and what it was in it their predecessors chose to remember and to forget.

Notes

Introduction

1. Gail H. Bickford, "Lovewell's Fight, 1725–1958," *American Quarterly* 10.3 (Autumn 1958): 358–66; Samuel Penhallow, *The History of the Wars of New England with the Eastern Indians* (1726), ed. Edward Wheelock (1924; repr., Freeport, New York: Books for Libraries, 1971), 112–14; Francis Parkman, *France and England in North America,* ed. David Levin, 2 vols. (New York: Library Classics, 1983), 2:511–13. A recent, popular work on the subject is Alfred E. Kayworth and Raymond G. Potvin, *The Scalphunters: Abenaki Ambush at Lovewell's Pond, 1725* (Boston: Branden Books, 2002).
2. Although the Pigwacket encounter occurred during Dummer's War, named for the Massachusetts governor, people called it Lovewell's Fight, seemingly convinced that the captain's actions had defined the conflict.
3. Jeremy Belknap, *History of New Hampshire,* vol. 2 (Boston: Thomas and Andrews, 1791), 66–67; Bickford, "Lovewell's Fight," 359. Various sources interpret the number of dead and wounded differently, distinguishing between those immediately dead and those who apparently died after the fighting; but twelve bodies of English were found by rescue parties at the battle site.
4. Parkman, *France and England,* 2:510, 513; Frederic Kidder, *Expeditions of Captain John Lovewell* (Boston: Bartlett and Halliday, 1865), 75–80, 83–84; Belknap, *History of New Hampshire,* 66–68; Nathaniel Bouton, ed., *Capt. John Lovewell's Great Fight with the Indians at Pequawket, 1725,* by the Reverend Thomas Symmes (Concord, NH: P. B. Cogswell, 1861); Samuel A. Green, *Groton during the Indian Wars* (Groton, MA: Town of Groton, 1882), 146–47; Charles J. Fox, *History of the Old Township of Dunstable* (Nashua, NH: Charles T. Gill, 1846), 123.
5. Kidder, *Expeditions of Captain John Lovewell,* 103; Bouton, *Capt. John Lovewell's Great*

Fight, 32n; Green, *Groton during the Indian War,* 146; William Wells Newell, "Early American Ballads," *Journal of American Folklore* 12.47 (October–December 1899): 253–54; Robert Stafford Ward, "Longfellow's Roots in Yankee Soil," *New England Quarterly* 41.2 (June 1968): 180–92; Frederic Kidder, "The Adventures of Capt. Lovewell," *New England Historical and Genealogical Register* 7.1 (January 1853): 68; David S. Lovejoy, "Lovewell's Fight and Hawthorne's Roger Malvins's Burial," *New England Quarterly* 27.4 (December 1954): 527–31; Simon Schama, *Landscape and Memory* (New York: Knopf, 1995).

6. See Michael Kammen, *Mystic Chords of Memory: The Transformation of Tradition in American Culture* (New York: Knopf, 1991), 8–9; Paul Cortledge, *Thermopylae: The Battle That Changed the World* (Woodstock, NY: Overlook, 2006); William Chester Jordon, *Europe in the High Middle Ages* (New York: Viking, 2003), 130–31; James E. Crisp, *Sleuthing the Alamo: Davy Crockett's Last Stand and Other Mysteries of the Texas Revolution* (New York: Oxford University Press, 2005); Richard R. Flores, *Remembering the Alamo: Memory, Modernity, and the Master Symbol* (Austin: University of Texas Press, 2002); Michael A. Elliott, *Custerology: The Enduring Legacy of the Indian Wars and George Armstrong Custer* (Chicago: University of Chicago, 2007), 2–6; Nathaniel Philbrick, *Custer, Sitting Bull, and the Battle of the Little Big Horn* (New York: Viking, 2011); Edward T. Linenthal, *Sacred Ground: Americans and Their Battlefields* (Urbana: University of Illinois Press, 1991), 55–58, 62–67, 72–73, 131–33.

7. Crisp, *Sleuthing the Alamo,* 145.

8. Nathaniel Hawthorne, "Roger Malvin's Burial," in *The Complete Short Stories of Nathaniel Hawthorne* (Garden City, NY: Doubleday, 1959), 376; Thomas Kidd, "The Devil and Father Rallee: The Narration of Father Rale's War in Provincial Massachusetts," *Historical Journal of Massachusetts* 30.2 (Summer 2002): 159–80; Carleton Sprague Smith, "Broadsides and Their Music in Colonial America," in *Music in Colonial Massachusetts, 1630–1820,* ed. Barbara Lambert (Boston: Colonial Society of Massachusetts, 1980), 181, 192, 197.

9. John Demos, *The Unredeemed Captive: A Family Story from Early America* (New York: Knopf, 1994); Evan Haefeli and Kevin Sweeney, *Captors and Captives: The 1704 French and Indian Raid of Deerfield* (Amherst: University of Massachusetts Press, 2003); Jill Lapore, *The Name of War: King Philip's War and the Origins of American Identity* (New York: Knopf, 1998); Thomas Hutchinson, *History of the Colony and Province of Massachusetts Bay,* 2 vols., ed. Lawrence Mayo, 2 vols. (Cambridge: Harvard University Press, 1936), 2:239; Parkman, *France and England in North America,* 502–16; George Bancroft, *History of the United States,* 6 vols. (1885; repr., Port Washington, NY: Kennikat Press, 1967), 2:220; Herbert L. Osgood, *The American Colonies of the Eighteenth Century,* 4 vols. (1924–1925; repr., Gloucester, MA: Peter Smith, 1958), 3:170.

10. "Letter Eleazer Tyng to Lt. Gov. Dummer, May 12, 1725," in *Documentary History of the State of Maine, Containing the Baxter Manuscripts,* ed. James Phinney Baxter, vol. 10 (Portland: Maine Historical Society, 1907), 269–70; Thomas Symmes, *Lovewell*

Lamented, or a Sermon Occasion'd by the Fall of the Brave Capt. John Lovewell and several of his Valiant Company in the late Heroic Action at Piggwackett (Boston: S. Gerrish, 1725), ix; Henry David Thoreau, *A Week on the Concord and Merrimack Rivers* (Boston: Houghton Mifflin, 1961), 124–26; Fannie Hardy Eckstorm, "Pigwacket and Parson Symmes," *New England Quarterly* 9.3 (September 1936): 378–402. Preston Tuckerman Shea, "Rhetoric of Authority in the *New England Courant*" (PhD diss., University of New Hampshire, 1992), chap. 4, suggests that the Reverend Symmes was more concerned with avoiding mention of the deserter, Hassell, than in protecting Frye's reputation.

11. Peter Silver, *Our Savage Neighbors: How Indian War Transformed Early America* (New York: W. W. Norton, 2008); Richard White, *The Middle Ground: Indians, Empires, and Republics in the Great Lakes Regions, 1650–1815* (New York: Cambridge University Press, 1991); James H. Merrell, *Indians' New World: Catawbas and Their Neighbors from European Contact through the Era of Removal* (Chapel Hill: University of North Carolina Press, 1989); Francis Jennings, *The Invasion of America: Indians, Colonialism and the Cant of Conquest* (Chapel Hill: University of North Carolina Press, 1975), 166–68; Douglas E. Leach, *Northern Colonial Frontier* (New York: Holt, Rinehart, and Winston, 1966), 133; Haefeli and Sweeney, *Captors and Captives*, 92, 192; One significant exception in treating Lovewell is David Jaffee, *People of the Wachusett: Greater New England and Memory, 1630–1860* (Ithaca, NY: Cornell University Press, 1999), 95–99.

12. Symmes, *Lovewell Lamented*, 29–30; Penhallow, *History of the Wars of New England*, 116–17.

13. See Patrick M. Malone, *The Skulking Way of War; Technology and Tactics among New England Indians* (Latham, MD: Madison Books, 1991); Steven C. Eames, *Rustic Warriors: Warfare and the Provincial Soldier on the New England Frontier, 1689–1748* (New York: New York University Press, 2011); Guy Chet, *Conquering the American Wilderness: the Triumph of European Warfare in the Colonial Northeast* (Amherst: University of Massachusetts Press, 2003); Wayne E. Lee, "Mind and Matter—Cultural Analysis in American Military History: A Look at the State of the Field," *Journal of American History* 93.4 (March 2007): 1116–1142. On Dustin, see Kathryn Whitford, "Hannah Dustin: The Judgment of History," *Essex Institute Historical Collections* 108.4 (October 1972): 302–25.

14. Ezra Stearns, "Deposition of John Lovewell, Sr.," *Granite State Magazine* 5 (January to December 1908): 100–101.

15. See William Pencak, *War and Politics in Provincial Massachusetts* (Boston: Northeastern University Press, 1981), for the political situation. Also see David Stannard, *The Puritan Way of Death: A Study in Religion, Culture, and Social Change* (New York: Oxford University Press, 1977); Gloria L. Main, *Peoples of a Spacious Land: Families and Culture in Colonial New England* (Cambridge: Harvard University Press, 2001), 183–86; Nancy Isenberg and Andrew Burstein, eds., *Mortal Remains, Death in Early America* (Philadelphia: University of Pennsylvania Press, 2003); Robert V. Wells, *Facing the King of Terrors: Death and Society in an American Community, 1750–*

1990 (Cambridge: Harvard University Press, 2000); Linenthal, *Sacred Ground;* Drew Gilpin Faust, *The Republic of Suffering: Death and the American Civil War* (New York: Knopf, 2008), for treatments of death.

16. Lepore, *Name of War;* Penhallow, *History of the Wars of New England;* Symmes, *Lovewell Lamented.* Also see Ian K. Steele, *Warpaths: Invasions of North America* (New York: Oxford University Press, 1994), 161–62.

17. On public welfare, see Robert W. Kelso, *History of Poor Relief in Massachusetts, 1620–1920* (Boston: Houghton Mifflin, 1922). A more recent source is Louis J. Piccarello, "Poverty, the Poor, and Public Welfare in Massachusetts: A Comparative History of Four Towns, 1643–1855" (PhD diss., Brandeis University, 1991).

18. The literature on memory is huge, but a few relevant titles that have greatly helped include Alfred F. Young, *The Shoemaker and the Tea Party* (Boston: Beacon Press, 1999); Thomas A. Chambers, *Memories of War: Visiting Battlegrounds and Bonefields in the Early American Republic* (Ithaca, NY: Cornell University Press, 2012); Michael Kammen, *Mystic Chords of Memory;* John Bodnar, *Remaking America: Public Memory, Commemoration and Patriotism in the Twentieth Century* (Princeton: Princeton University Press, 1992). On the Indian memory of Lovewell's Fight, see Kayworth and Potvin, *Scalphunters,* 157–58.

Chapter 1. Captain John Lovewell's Fatal Expedition

1. Gail H. Bickford, "Lovewell's Fight, 1725–1958," *American Quarterly* 10.3 (Autumn 1958): 358–59; Nathaniel Bouton, ed., *Capt. John Lovewell's Great Fight with the Indians at Piguawket, 1725,* by the Reverend Thomas Symmes (Concord, NH: P. B. Cogswell, 1861), 26–27n; "Letter Eleazer Tyng to Lt. Gov. Dummer, May, 12, 1725," in *Documentary History of the State of Maine, Containing the Baxter Manuscripts,* ed. James Phinney Baxter, vol. 10 (Portland: Maine Historical Society, 1907), 10:268–69; Thomas Symmes, *Lovewell Lamented, or A Sermon Occasion'd by the Fall of the Brave Capt. John Lovewell and several of the Valient Company in the late Heroic Action at Piggwackett* (Boston: S. Gerrish, 1725).

2. *Boston News Letter,* May 13, 1725; Francis Parkman, *France and England in North America,* ed. David Levin, 2 vols. (New York: Library Classics, 1983), 2:502–16; Fannie Hardy Eckstorm, "Pigwacket and Parson Symmes," *New England Quarterly* 9.3 (September 1936): 380–81nn3–4.

3. Parkman, *France and England in North America,* 2:511–14; Samuel Penhallow, *The History of the Wars of New England with the Eastern Indians* (1726), ed. Edward Wheelock (1924; repr., Freeport, NY: Books for Libraries, 1971), 113–15; Symmes, *Lovewell Lamented,* vii–x.

4. Increase Mather, *Discourse concerning the Grace of Courage* (Boston: B. Green, 1710), 5; Benjamin Wadsworth, *True Piety the Best Policy in Wars* (Boston: B. Green, 1722), 10; William Hubbard, *History of the Indian Wars in New England,* ed. Samuel Gardner Drake, 2 vols. (1865; repr., New York: Kraus Reprints, 1969), 2:120–21. Also see John Ferling, "The New England Soldier: A Study in Changing Perceptions," *American Quarterly* 33.1 (Spring 1981): 26–45.

5. Jeremy Black, *Natural and Necessary Enemies: Anglo-French Relations in the Eighteenth Century* (Athens: University of Georgia Press, 1986), 3–19, passim.

6. Dale Miquelon, *New France, 1701–1744: A Supplement to Europe* (Toronto: McClelland and Stewart, 1987), 102–7; Yves F. Zoltvany, *Philippe de Rigand de Vandreuil: Governor of New France* (Ottawa: McClelland and Stewart, 1974), 138–39, 150, 179–83. See Andrew Miller, "Abenakis and Colonists in Northern New England, 1675–1725" (PhD diss., Johns Hopkins University, 2005), 205–7, 217–18, 261–62.

7. John Farmer and Jacob B. Moore, eds., *Collections, Topographical, Historical and Biographical, Relating Principally to New Hampshire*, vol. 1 (1822; repr., Concord, NH: M. E and J. W. Moore, 1831), 25–26; Symmes, *Lovewell Lamented*, 24; Penhallow, *History of the Wars of New England*, 110; Bouton, *Lovewell's Great Fight*, 8–9.

8. George P. Hadley, *History of Goffstown, New Hampshire, 1733–1920*, 2 vols. (Goffstown, NH: Published by the Town, 1922), 1:51–52; Steven C. Eames, *Rustic Warriors: Warfare and the Provincial Soldier on the New England Frontier, 1689–1748* (New York: New York University Press, 2011), chap. 4.

9. Nathan Bowen, *The New England Diary, or Almanack for the Year 1724* (Boston: Green, 1724), n.p.; Nathaniel Whittenmore, *The Farmer's Almanack for the Year of our Lord, 1724* (Boston: Green, 1724), n.p.

10. Frederic Kidder, *Expeditions of Capt. John Lovewell* (Boston: Bartlett and Halliday, 1865), 14–15; Henry S. Nourse, *Early Records of Lancaster, Massachusetts, 1643–1725* (Lancaster, MA: Clinton, 1884), 216–17; *Laws and Statutes of Massachusetts, 1724, Following Resolve* (Boston: Green, 1724).

11. George H. Evans, *Pigwacket* (Conway, NH: Conway Historical Society, 1939), 57; William Cronon, *Changes in the Land: Indians, Colonists, and the Ecology of New England* (New York: Hill and Wang, 1983), 26–27; Bruce J. Bourque, *Twelve Thousand Years: American Indians in Maine* (Lincoln: University of Nebraska Press, 2001), 269–70; Peter N. Carroll, *Puritans and the Wilderness: The Intellectual Significance of the New England Frontier, 1629–1700* (New York: Columbia University Press, 1969).

12. Samuel Penhallow, "History of the Wars of New England with the Eastern Indians," manuscript, Library of Congress, Washington, DC., Reel, 55:119–20; Eames, *Rustic Warriors*, 76, 86; Kidder, *Expeditions of Capt. John Lovewell*, 14; *Boston News Letter*, January 7, 1724; Peter Silver, *Our Savage Neighbors: How Indian War Transformed Early America* (New York: W. W. Norton, 2008), 75–79. The body of the Indian male was still there, undisturbed, weeks later when Lovewell passed that route on his second expedition, suggesting that the anticipated Abenaki troop had not arrived at the site. *Boston News Letter*, March 4, 1725.

13. Penhallow, "History of Wars of New England," 120; Bouton, *Lovewell's Great Fight*, 9; Jeremiah Belknap, *History of New Hampshire* (Boston: Thomas and Andrews, 1791), 2:54, 57–59.

14. *Boston News Letter*, January 7, 1725.

15. Samuel Sewall, *Diary of Samuel Sewall, 1674–1729*, ed. M. Halsey Thomas, 2 vols. (New York: Farrar, Straus and Giroux, 1973), 2:1021, cites Johnson Harmon's expedition but does not mention Lovewell until later. "Diary of Jeremiah Bumstead," *New*

England Historical and Genealogical Register 15.3 (July 1861): 193–204, was also silent on Lovewell until later.

16. Penhallow, *History of the Wars of New England,* 107.

17. Penhallow, "History of the Wars of New England," 122; Parkman, *France and England in North America,* 2:508; Frederic Kidder, "The Adventures of Capt. Lovewell," *New England Historical and Genealogical Register* 7.1 (January 1853): 61; *Letters of Colonel Thomas Westbrook and others relative to Indian Affairs in Maine, 1722–1726* ed. William Blake Trask (Boston: George E. Littlefield, 1901), shows just several companies with more men than Lovewell's scouting party. Nathaniel Whittenmore, *An Almanack for the Year of our Lord 1725* (Boston: For the Bookseller, 1725), n.p.; Nathan Bowen, *New England Diary or Almanack 1725* (Boston: Green, 1725) also promised cold, unsettled weather.

18. Kidder, "Adventures of Capt. Lovewell," 62; Parkman, *France and England in North America,* 508.

19. Eames, *Rustic Warriors,* provides the best overview of scouting expeditions.

20. Ibid., 152–53; Kidder, "Adventures of Captain Lovewell," 62; Belknap, *History of New Hampshire,* 2:62. New Englanders typically viewed military enlistment as a covenant agreement of sorts—the enlisted agreed to serve for a set term and no longer. See Fred Anderson, *A People's Army: Soldiers and Society in the Seven Years' War* (Chapel Hill: University of North Carolina Press, 1984).

21. Kidder, "Adventures of Captain Lovewell," 63;

22. Ibid.; Penhallow, "History of the Wars of New England," 122; Belknap, *History of New Hampshire,* 2:62; Herbert M. Sylvester, *Indian Wars of New England,* 3 vols. (Boston: W. B. Clarke, 1910), 3:244–45; *Boston News Letter,* March 11, 1725.

23. Justin Winsor, ed., *Narrative and Critical History of America,* 8 vols. (Boston: Houghton Mifflin, 1884–89), 5:109; "Diary of Jeremy Bumstead," 204; "Samuel Sewall to Rev. Timothy Woodbridge, February 24, 1725," in *Letter Book of Samuel Sewall,* 2 vols., *Collections of the Massachusetts Historical Society,* 6th ser. (Boston: Massachusetts Historical Society, 1886–88), 2:182–83; Penhallow, *History of the Wars of New England,* 110; *Boston News Letter,* March 11, 1725.

24. Belknap, *History of New Hampshire,* 2:63.

25. Penhallow, *History of the Wars of New England,* 112; Farmer and Moore, *Collections, Topographical, Historical and Biographical,* 125; Samuel Green, *Groton during the Indian Wars* (Groton, MA: Town of Groton, 1882), 135.

26. Bouton, *Capt. John Lovewell's Great Fight,* 10.

27. David L. Ghere, "Abenaki Factionalism, Emigrants, and Social Continuity: Indian Society in Northern New England, 1725–1765" (PhD diss., University of Maine, 1988), 53–58; Bunny McBride and Harold E. L. Prins, "Walking the Medicine Line: Moly Ocket, A Pigwacket Doctor," in *Northeastern Indian Lives, 1632–1816,* ed. Robert S. Grumet (Amherst: University of Massachusetts Press, 1996), 321–25.

28. John Farmer, *Catechism of the History of New Hampshire,* 2nd ed. (Concord, NH: Hoag and Atwood, 1830), 47; Eliphalet Merrill and Phineas Merrill, *Gazetteer of the State of New Hampshire* (Exeter, NH: C. Norris, 1817), 60–61; Capt. John Lovewell to

Lt. Governor, April 15, 1725, vol. 52., Massachusetts Archives, Boston, 141; William Little, "Capt. Eleazer Tyng's Scout Journal," *Granite Monthly* 15.6 (June 1893): 184–85.

29. David Jaffe, *People of the Wachusett: Greater New England in History and Memory, 1630–1860* (Ithaca, NY: Cornell University Press, 1999), 95; John Grenier, *The First Way of War: American War Making on the Frontier* (New York: Cambridge University Press, 2005), 51; data drawn from Ezra Stearns, "Lovewell Men," *New England Historical and Genealogical Register* 63.3 (July 1909): 289–93; Bouton, *Capt. John Lovewell's Great Fight*, 20; Alfred E. Kayworth and Raymond G. Potvin, *The Scalphunters: Abenaki Ambush at Lovewell's Pond, 1725* (Boston: Branden Press, 2002), 133.

30. Green, *Groton during the Indian Wars*, 98–101. Eames, *Rustic Warriors*, 187–88, provided the source of this information.

31. Charles J. Fox, *History of the Old Township of Dunstable* (Nashua, NH: C. T. Gill, 1846), 115; *Boston News Letter*, April 15, 1725.

32. Penhallow, *History of the Wars of New England*, 112; Symmes, *Lovewell Lamented*, iii.

33. Symmes, *Lovewell Lamented*, iii; Bouton, *Capt. John Lovewell's Great Fight*, 18n3.

34. Symmes, *Lovewell Lamented*, iii, v; Merrill and Merrill, *Gazetteer of the State of New Hampshire*, 119, and William Williamson, *History of the State of Maine*, 2 vols. (Hallowell, ME: Glazier, Masters, and Smith, 1839), 2:135, cite the distance between the stockade and Pigwacket as twenty-two miles. "Letter Eleazer Tyng to Lt. Gov. Dummer, May 12, 1725," *Documentary History of the State of Maine*, 10:269. On fear of Indians, see Silver, *Our Savage Neighbors*, 40–71.

35. Symmes, *Lovewell Lamented*, v; Penhallow, *History of the Wars of New England*, 112; Sewall, *Diary of Samuel Sewall*, 2:1030; Fannie Hardy Eckstrom, "Pigwacket and Parson Symmes," *New England Quarterly* 9.3 (September 1936): 378–402; "Letter Corp. Benj. Hassell to Lt. Gov. Dummer, May 11, 1725," *Documentary History of the State of Maine*, 10:268. Preston Tuckerman Shea, "Rhetoric of Authority in the *New England Courant*" (PhD diss., University of New Hampshire, 1992), 202, suggests that such speeches were unlikely except as rhetorical devises similar to those employed in classical history.

36. Paul Coffin, *Memoirs and Journals of the Reverend Paul Coffin*, ed. Cyrus Woodman (Portland, ME: B. Thurston, 1855), 68; Grenier, *First Way of War*, 51.

37. Symmes, *Lovewell Lamented*, v–vi.

38. "Letter Eleazer Tyng to Lt. Gov. Dummer, May 12, 1725," 268–69; Penhallow, *History of the Wars of New England*, 112–13; Symmes, *Lovewell Lamented*, vi–vii; Belknap, *History of New Hampshire*, 2:65–67.

39. "Letter Eleazer Tyng to Lt. Gov. Dummer, May 12, 1725," 268–69; Symmes, *Lovewell Lamented*, ix; Eames, *Rustic Warriors*, 161–62; *Boston News Letter*, May 20, 1725; William Howard Brown, *Colonel John Goffe: Eighteenth Century New Hampshire* (Manchester, NH: L. A. Cummings, 1950), 42, argued that Hassell "could do nothing to aid his comrades," since it would reveal his position to the Indians, hence retreat proved the only option.

40. Symmes, *Lovewell Lamented*, vii.

41. Ibid., vii; Penhallow, *History of the Wars of New England*, 114; Ezra S. Stearns, "Lovewell's Men," 292, gives Wyman's age; Eames, *Rustic Warriors*, 152, 201.

42. Symmes, *Lovewell Lamented*, ix; Penhallow, *History of the Wars of New England*, 115–16; Shea, "Rhetoric of Authority in the *New England Courant*," 191, 204–5.

43. Symmes, *Lovewell Lamented*, vii; *Boston News Letter*, May 20, 1725; Penhallow, *History of the Wars of New England*, 114–17; "Letter Eleazer Tyng to Lt. Gov. William Dummer, May 14, 1725," *Documentary History of the State of Maine*, 10:271–72.

44. Symmes, *Lovewell Lamented*, vi–vii; Belknap, *History of New Hampshire*, 2:70, noted the bullet holes during his 1784 visit to the site.

45. Symmes, *Lovewell Lamented*, vii–viii; Penhallow, *History of the Wars of New England*, 116.

46. Stearns, "Lovewell's Men," 288–89; Symmes, *Lovewell Lamented*, viii; Penhallow, *History of the Wars of New England*, 115; Eleazer Melvin Account, May 8, 1725, Photostats Collections, Massachusetts Historical Society, Boston, Massachusetts. Although Penhallow considered the tale of Robbins's gun remarkable, suggesting disbelief, Melvin, an eyewitness, confirms that Robbins did indeed ask for a loaded gun. I am grateful to the society for sending a photostat copy of Melvin's deposition.

47. Stearns, "Lovewell's Men," 290; Sylvester, *Indian Wars of New England*, 3:240–42.

48. Symmes, *Lovewell Lamented*, vii.

49. Ibid., viii. "Lovewell Fight," *The Worcester Magazine and Historical Journal*, vol. 1.1 (October 1825): 24.

50. Paul Schneider, *Brutal Journal: Cabeza de Vaca and the Epic First Crossing of North America* (New York: Henry Holt, 2006), 214–16, 228–30; Andres Resendez, *A Land So Strange: Epic Journey of Cabeza de Vaca* (New York: Basic Books, 2007), 148–52.

51. Belknap, *History of New Hampshire*, 2:68; Penhallow, *History of the Wars of New England*, 113–16; Symmes, *Lovewell Lamented*, ix; Shea, "Rhetoric of Authority," 204–5.

52. Symmes, *Lovewell Lamented*, ix.

53. Ibid., ix.

54. Penhallow, *History of the Wars of New England*, 114; Symmes, *Lovewell Lamented*, iv.

55. Penhallow, *History of the Wars of New England*, 114–15; Symmes, *Lovewell Lamented*, x.

56. Penhallow, *History of the Wars of New England*, 114–115; Symmes, *Lovewell Lamented*, ix; "Letter Lt. Gov. J. Wentworth to ?" *Documentary History of the State of Maine*, 10:284. Berwick was an outpost community at the time of Dummer's War, see George J. Varney, *Gazetteer of the State of Maine* (Boston: B. B. Russell, 1881), 111.

57. *Boston News Letter*, May 27, 1725; *New England Courant*, May 31, 1725; Farmer and Moore, *Collections, Topographical, Historical and Biographical*, 33.

58. "Letter Corp. Benj. Hassell to Lt. Gov. Dummer May 11, 1725," "Letter Eleazer Tyng to Lt. Governor Dummer, May 12, 1725," "Letter Lt. Gov. Dummer to Col. Eleazer Tyng, May 13, 1725," *Documentary History of the State of Maine*, 10:268–70.

59. Sewall, *Diary of Samuel Sewall*, 2:1030; *Diary of the Honorable Theodore Atkinson*, ed. George Augustus Gordon (Society of Colonial Wars, NH: 1907), 53; *Boston News Letter*, May 20, 1725; *New England Courant*, May 31, 1725.

60. "Letter Lt. Gov. to Colonel Eleazer Tyng May 13, 1725," "Letter Lt. Gov. to Colonel Eleazer Tyng, May 14, 1725," *Documentary History of the State of Maine*, 10:271, 273; Symmes, *Lovewell Lamented*, 29.

61. George H. Evans, *Pigwacket* (Conway, NH: Conway Historical Society, 1939), 67; "Letter Eleazer Tyng to Lt. Gov. Dummer, May 14, 1725," "Letter Lt. Gov. J. Wentworth to Lt. Gov. Dummer May 23, 1725," "Letter Lt. Gov., J. Wentworth to Lt. Gov. Dummer, May 28, 1725," *Documentary History of the State of Maine*, 10:272, 278–79, 283.

62. Belknap, *History of New Hampshire*, 2:67; Grenier, *First Way of War*, 53; Kayworth and Potvin, *Scalphunters*, 164–65; Richard Slotkin, *Regeneration through Violence: The Mythology of the American Frontier, 1600–1860* (Middletown, CT: Wesleyan University Press, 1973), 181–82; David Stewart-Smith, "The Pennacook Indians and the New England Frontier, circa 1604–1733" (PhD diss., Union Institute, Cincinnati, 1988), 282.

63. Penhallow, *History of the Wars of New England*, 116; Miller, "Abenakis and Colonists in Northern New England, 1675–1725," 30.

64. "Col. T. Westbrook to Lt. Gov. William Dummer, June 22, 1725," *Documentary History of the State of Maine*, 10:289; John B. Hill, *Bi-Centennial of Old Dunstable* (Nashua, NH: E. H. Spalding, 1878), 53, 116.

65. *New England Courant*, May 31, September 4, 1725; *Boston News Letter*, September 9, 1725.

66. "Conference with the Eastern Indians at the Ratification of the Peace, Falmouth, Casco Bay, July and August, 1726," "Subsequent Treaty, July 1727, Falmouth, Casco Bay," in *Collections of the Maine Historical Society*, 1st ser., vol. 3 (Portland: Maine Historical Society, 1853), 377–405, 407–47.

67. Oliver Peabody, *A Sermon Preached before the Honorable Artillery Company, 1732* (Boston: Fleet, 1732), 12–18, passim.

68. Ibid., 29–30.

Chapter 2. War and Survival in Dunstable, Massachusetts, 1673–1725

1. Timothy Dwight, *Travels in New England and New York*, ed. Barbara M. Solomon, 4 vols. (1822; repr. Cambridge: Harvard University Press, 1969) 2:170–71.

2. Ibid., 171, lists that Dunstable had over one thousand inhabitants by 1810. Edward E. Parker, *History of the City of Nashua, New Hampshire* (Nashua, NH: Telegraph Publishing, 1897), 22.

3. David Jaffee, *People of the Wachusett: Greater New England in History and Memory, 1630–1860* (Ithaca, NY: Cornell University Press, 1999); Daniel Melvoin, *New England Outpost: War and Society in Colonial Deerfield* (New York: W. W. Norton, 1989); Neal Salisbury, *Manitou and Providence: Indians, Europeans, and the Making of New England, 1500–1643* (New York: Oxford University Press, 1982), are among a growing list of scholarly works to chart the interaction of Indians and Europeans in New England.

4. Kenneth M. Morrison, *The Embattled Northeast* (Berkeley: University of California Press, 1984), 15–17, 89; Jere R. Daniell, *Colonial New Hampshire: A History* (Milkwood, NY: KTO Press, 1981), 4–5.

5. Daniell, *Colonial New Hampshire*, 9–10; Jaffee, *People of Wachusett*, 35–40.

6. Charles J. Fox, *History of the Old Township of Dunstable* (Nashua, NH: Charles T. Gill, 1846), 18; Elias Nason, *History of the Town of Dunstable* (Boston: Alfred Mudge and Son, 1877), 15.

7. Daniell, *Colonial New Hampshire*, 5–11; Fox, *History of the Old Township*, 19–20; Colin G. Calloway, "Wannalancet and Kancagamus: Indian Strategy and Leadership on the New Hampshire Frontier," *Historic New Hampshire* 43.4 (Winter 1988): 266–72.

8. Quoted in Nason, *History of the Town of Dunstable*, 21; Calloway, "Wannalancet and Kancagamus," 272–77; Daniell, *Colonial New Hampshire*, 11, 16; Mary Josephine Hodgdon, *Historic Nashua: A Few Notes from Local History* (Nashua, NH: Telegraph Publishing, 1902), 10.

9. *Vital Records of Dunstable, Massachusetts, to the end of the Year, 1849* (Salem, MA: Essex Institute, 1913), 4; Kenneth Lockridge, *A New England Town: The First Hundred Years* (New York: W. W. Norton, 1970), popularized the phrase about closed communities; Michael Zuckerman, *Peaceable Kingdoms: New England Towns in the Eighteenth Century* (New York: Knopf, 1970), did likewise for peaceable kingdoms.

10. George A. Gordon, *The Early Grants of Land in the Wildernesse North of Merrimack* (Lowell, MA: Morning Mail, 1891), 26–29; Parker, *History of the City of Nashua*, 12, 21–22; John Fredrick Martin, *Profits in the Wilderness: Entrepreneurship and the Founding of New England Towns in the Seventeenth Century* (Chapel Hill: University of North Carolina Press, 1991), 20–22.

11. Gordon, *Early Grants of Land*, 26–29, Fox, *History of the Old Township of Dunstable*, 60. Daniel Vickers, "Competency and Competition: Economic Culture in Early America," *William & Mary Quarterly* 47.1 (January 1990): 3–29.

12. Benjamin Church, *Diary of King Philip's War, 1675*, ed. Alan and Mary Simpson (Tiverton, RI: Lockwood, 1975), 77–78.

13. See Robert E. Cray Jr., "'Weltering in their own Blood': Puritan Casualties in King Philip's War," *Historical Journal of Massachusetts* 37.2 (Fall 2009): 115–16.

14. Samuel Gardiner Drake, Introduction to *History of King Philip's War by the Reverend Increase Mather, also a History of the Same War by the Reverend Cotton Mather* (1862; repr., Bowie, MD: Heritage 1990), 255–59; quoted in George Sheldon, *History of Deerfield, Massachusetts*, 2 vols. (Deerfield, 1895), 1:162, 165–66; William Hubbard, *History of the Indian Wars in New England*, ed. Samuel Gardner Drake, 2 vols. (1865; repr., New York: Kraus Reprints, 1969), 1:120–22.

15. Hubbard, *History of the Indian Wars*, 2:120; Drake, *History of King Philip's War*, 66–67, 85; Douglas Leach, *Flintlock and Tomahawk: New England in King Philip's War* (New York: Macmillan, 1958); Russell Bourne, *The Red King's Rebellion: Racial Politics in New England* (New York: Oxford 1991), 158–59; Denton R. Bedford, "The Great Swamp Fight," *The Indian Historian* 4.2 (Summer 1971): 40.

16. Hubbard, *History of the Indian Wars*, 1:110–11; Drake, *History of King Philip's War*, 81; Leach, *Flintlock and Tomahawk*, 87; Eric B. Schultz and Michael J. Tougias, *King Philip's War: The History and Legacy of America's Forgotten Conflict* (Woodstock, VT: Countryman 1999), 163–68; Jill Lepore, *The Name of War: King Philip's War and the*

Origins of American Identity (New York: Knopf, 1998), 105, 286n31; Josiah H. Tempe, *History of the Town of Northfield, Massachusetts* (Albany, NY: Munsell, 1875), 75n3, 78–79.

17. See Daniel R. Mandell, *King Philip's War: Colonial Expansion, Native Resistance, and the End of Indian Sovereignty* (Baltimore: Johns Hopkins University Press, 2010), 134–37; Sherburn Cook, "Interracial Warfare and Population Decline among the New England Indians," *Ethnohistory* 20 (1973): 20–21, for various estimates of casualties.

18. Calloway, "Wannalancet and Kancagamus," 273–75, Fox, *History of the Old Township of Dunstable*, 21–22, Nason, *History of the Town of Dunstable*, 22.

19. Mandell, *King Philip's War: Colonial Expansion*, 52, 82. Fox, *History of the Old Township of Dunstable*, 35–36; Nason, *History of the Town of Dunstable*, 23–24; Stephen Winship, *A Testing Time: Crisis and Revival in Nashua, New Hampshire* (Nashua, NH: Nashua–New Hampshire Foundation, 1989), 4–5; Ezra S. Stearns, *Early Generations of the Founders of Old Dunstable: Thirty Families* (Boston: G. E Littlefield, 1911), 83; Leach, *Flintlock and Tomahawk*; James D. Drake, *King Philip's War: Civil War in New England* (Amherst: University of Massachusetts Press, 1999).

20. *Nashua Experience: History in the Making, 1673–1978* (Nashua, NH: Phoenix Publishing, 1978), 18–19; Parker, *History of the City of Nashua*, 17.

21. *Genealogical and Family History of the State of New Hampshire*, ed. Ezra Stearns (New York: Lewis Publishing, 1908), 3:635; Fox, *History of the Old Township of Dunstable*, 42–48.

22. David D. Hall, *The Faithful Shepherd: A History of the New England Ministry in the Seventeenth Century* (Chapel Hill: University of North Carolina Press, 1972), 183n16; Clifford Shipton, *Sibley's Harvard Graduates*, 17 vols. (Boston: Massachusetts Historical Society, 1933–75), 2:388–90.

23. Hall, *Faithful Shepherd*, 176–96, passim, for second-generation ministers. Shipton, *Sibley's Harvard Graduates*, 2:389; Fox, *History of the Old Township of Dunstable*, 42–46; John Wesley Churchill, *History of the First Church in Dunstable–Nashua* (Boston: Fort Hill Press, 1918), 14–15.

24. Quoted in Parker, *History of the City of Nashua*, 25.

25. Colin Calloway, "Wannalancet and Kancagamus," 264–90n19, for quote.

26. Evan Haefeli and Kevin Sweeney, *Captors and Captives: The 1704 French and Indian Raid on Deerfield* (Amherst: University of Massachusetts Press, 2003), 83–84; Calloway, "Wannalancet and Kancagamus," 282–86. On King William's War in general, see Francis Parkman, *France and England in North America*, ed. David Levin, 2 vols. (New York: Library Classics, 1983), 1:209–314.

27. Benjamin Church, *History of the Eastern Expedition, 1689, 90, 92, 96, 1704* (Boston: Wiggin and Lunt, 1867), 55–59; Calloway, "Wannalancet and Kancagamus," 284–86; John Grenier, *The First Way of War: American War Making on the Frontier* (New York: Cambridge University Press, 2005), 36–38.

28. Fox, *History of the Old Township of Dunstable*, 62–63; *Vital Records of Dunstable, Massachusetts*, 218, 225; Winship, *A Testing Time*, 6–7.

29. *Acts and Resolves, Public and Private, of the Province of Massachusetts*, 21 vols.

(Boston: Wright and Potter, 1869–1922), 7:575–76; Fox, *History of the Old Township of Dunstable*, 62–64; Winship, *Testing Time*, 7; Parker, *History of the City of Nashua*, 27, 37; Shipton, *Sibley's Harvard Graduates*, 5:124.

30. Melvoin, *New England Outpost*, 124; Mary Beth Norton, *In the Devil's Snare: The Salem Witchcraft Crisis of 1692* (New York: Knopf, 2002); *Acts and Resolves*, 7:575–76; Parker, *History of the City*, 28.

31. James Axtell, *Natives and Newcomers: The Culture Origins of Native Americans* (New York: Oxford University Press, 2001), 268; Grenier, *First Way of War*, 39.

32. Grenier, *First Way of War*, 40–41; Laura Thacher Ulrich, *Good Wives: Image and Reality in the Lives of Women in Northern New England, 1650–1750* (New York: Knopf, 1982), 167; Kathryn Whitford, "Hannah Dustin: The Judgement of History," *Essex Institute Historical Collections* 108.4 (October 1972): 302–25; Joyce E. Chaplin, *Subject Matter: Technology, the Body, and the Science of the Anglo-American Frontier* (Cambridge: Harvard University Press, 2001), 267.

33. Ulrich, *Good Wives*, 167–68; Whitford, "Hannah Dustin," 309; Leverett Saltonstall, "An Historic Sketch of Haverhill in the County of Essex," *Collections of the Massachusetts Historical Society*, vol. 4 (Boston: Massachusetts Historical Society, 1846), 128–29.

34. A historic sign in Nashua, New Hampshire, originally Dunstable, Massachusetts, alleges that Hannah Dustin lodged in Lovewell's home after her escape on March 30, 1697. This has become part of town folklore. See www.nashuahistory.com.

35. *Acts and Resolves*, 7:702; Fox, *History of the Old Township of Dunstable*, 71.

36. Nason, *History of the Town of Dunstable*, 33–34; Fox, *History of the Old Township of Dunstable*, 77.

37. Samuel Penhallow, *History of the Wars of New England with the Eastern Indians (1726)*, ed. Edward Wheelock (1924; repr., Freeport, NY: Books for Libraries, 1971), 9–11; "Journal of the Reverend John Pike," *Massachusetts Historical Society Proceedings*, ser. 1, vol. 14 (1875–76), 14:136; Haefelli and Sweeney, *Captors and Captives*, 92.

38. "Journal of the Reverend John Pike," 142; Fox, *History of the Old Township of Dunstable*, 180–85; Nason, *History of the Town of Dunstable*, 36; Winship, *Testing Time*, 7.

39. *Nashua Experience*, 39–40; Stearns, *Genealogical and Family History*, 3:635.

40. Penhallow, *History of the Wars of New England*, 36; Fox, *History of the Old Township of Dunstable*, 86–88; "Journal of the Reverend John Pike," 142–43.

41. John Williams, *The Redeemed Captive*, ed. Edward W. Clark (Amherst: University of Massachusetts Press, 1976), 49–50.

42. Parker, *History of the City*, 32.

43. Colin G. Calloway, *The Western Abenaki of Vermont, 1600–1800: War, Migration, and the Survival of an Indian People* (Norman: University of Oklahoma Press, 1990), 105–8; Penhallow, *History of the Wars of New England*, 48–49. See Steven C. Eames, *Rustic Warriors: Warfare and the Provincial Soldier on the New England Frontier, 1689–1748* (New York: New York University Press, 2011), chap. 4.

44. Ezra S. Stearns, *Early Generations of the Founders of Old Dunstable: Thirty Families* (Boston: G. E. Littlefield, 1911), 38, 85–86.

45. Parker, *History of the City*, 30–34, quote is on 32. Shipton, *Sibley's Harvard Graduates*,

5:326–27; Winship, *Testing Time*, 7; Larry Gragg, *A Quest for Security: Life of Samuel Parris, 1653–1720* (Westport, CT: Greenwood Press, 1990), 179–82.

46. Fox, *History of the Old Township of Dunstable*, 89–90.

47. *Boston Gazette*, January 27, 1724; Shipton, *Sibley's Harvard's Graduates*, 5:651.

48. See Virginia DeJohn Anderson, *New England Generation: The Great Migration and the Formation of a Society and Culture in the Seventeenth Century* (Cambridge: Harvard University Press, 1991).

49. See Ian Roy, "England Turned German: The Aftermath of the English Civil War in Its European Context," *Transactions of the Royal Historical Society* 28 (December 1978): 127–44.

50. See Nathaniel Bouton, ed., *Captain John Lovewell's Great Fight with the Indians of Pequawket, 1725*, by the Reverend Thomas Symmes (Concord, NH: P. B. Cogswell, 1861), v. On Cromwell, see Malcolm Atkin, *Cromwell's Crowning Mercy: The Battle of Worcester, 1651* (Thrupp, Stroud, Gloucestershire, UK: Sutton, 1998).

51. Bouton, *Captain John Lovewell's Great Fight*, 7.

52. *Nashua Experience*, 28; Janice Webster Brown, Family Trees of Merrimack, NH, www.nh.searchroots.com, 2–3; Stearns, *Early Generations*, 34–35

53. "Town Records of Dunstable, Vol. 1, 1729–1816," Town Hall, Nashua, New Hampshire, 37; *American National Biography*, s.v. John Lovewell, by Charles E. Clark; *Nashua Experience*, 28; "Family Trees of Merrimack," 1–2.

54. Parker, *History of the City*, 29–30; Stearns, *Early Generations*, 36; John B. Hill, "Reminiscences of Old Dunstable," in *Bi-Centennial of Old Dunstable* (Nashua, NH: E. H. Spaulding, 1878), 52–54.

55. Parker, *History of the City*, 37–38; Nason, *History of the Town of Dunstable*, 50; *Nashua Experience*, 28.

56. David Freeman Hawke, *Everyday Life in Early America* (New York: Harper Collins, 1989), 143–46; Jackson T. Main, *The Social Structure of Revolutionary America* (Princeton: Princeton University Press, 1965), 82–83. Of interest is Laura T. Ulrich, *A Midwife's Tale: Martha Ballard in Her Diary, 1785–1812* (New York: Knopf, 1990), 19–20.

57. Hodgdon, *Historical Nashua*, 6; Parker, *History of the City*, 49; Jaffee, *People of the Wachusett*, 95.

58. Stearns, *Early Generations*, 36–38; Nason, *History of the Town of Dunstable*, 37; *Nashua Experience*, 39.

59. *Nashua Experience*, 39–40; Ezra Stearns, "Deposition of John Lovewell, Sr.," *Granite State Magazine* 5 (January–December 1908): 100–101.

60. Stearns, *Early Generations*, 37–38; *American National Biography*, s.v. Lovewell. See Gloria L. Main, *Peoples of a Spacious Land: Families and Cultures in Colonial New England* (Cambridge: Harvard University Press, 2001), on birthrates.

61. *American National Biography*, s.v. Lovewell.

62. Parker, *History of the City*, 38; Fox, *History of the Old Township of Dunstable*, 99.

63. Jaffe, *People of the Wachusett*, 92; William Pencak, *War, Politics, and Revolution in Provincial Massachusetts* (Boston: Northeastern University Press, 1981), 71; Calloway, *Western Abenaki*, 108, 113–14.

64. Thomas S. Kidd, "The Devil and Father Rallee: The Narration of Father Rale's War in Provincial Massachusetts," *Historical Journal of Massachusetts* 30.2 (Summer 2002): 158–80.

65. Captain John Cagon's Journal, vol. 38A, p. 19, Massachusetts Archives, Boston. Also see Steven C. Eames, *Rustic Warriors*, 78.

66. Quoted in Herbert M. Sylvester, *Indian Wars of New England*, 3 vols. (Boston: W. B. Clarke 1910), 3:240–42n; *Nashua Experience*, 40; Hodgdon, *Historical Nashua*, 12–13.

67. *Nashua Experience*, 40; *Boston News Letter*, September 10–17, 1724.

68. J. Farmer and J. B. Moore, eds., *Collections, Topographical, Historical, and Biographical, Relating Principally to New Hampshire*, vol. 1 (1822; repr., Concord, NH: M. E. and J. W. Moore, 1831), 25; Eames, *Rustic Warriors*, 172–73.

69. Quoted in Frederic Kidder, "The Adventures of Captain Lovewell," *New England Historical and Genealogical Register* 7.1 (1853): 61–62; Kidder, *Expeditions of Captain John Lovewell* (Boston: Bartlett and Halliday, 1865), 12–13; Parkman, *France and England in North America*, 2:507.

Chapter 3. Deaths and Burials in Dummer's War, 1722–1725

1. Samuel Penhallow, *The History of the Wars of New England with the Eastern Indians* (1726), ed. Edward Wheelock (1924; repr., Freeport, NY: Books for Libraries, 1971), 89; Bruce J. Bourque, *Twelve Thousand Years: American Indians in Maine* (Lincoln: University of Nebraska Press, 2001), 185–87; Francis Parkman, *A Half Century of Conflict: England and France in North America*, 2 vols., ed. David Levin (New York: Library Classics, 1983), 2:477–516, passim, provides a useful descriptive account of the war.

2. William Williamson, *History of the State of Maine* (1832; repr., Berwyn Heights, MD: Heritage Books, 1991), 2:151; *Boston News Letter*, July 23, 1722.

3. See Jill Lepore, *The Name of War: King Philip's War and the Origins of American Identity* (New York: Knopf, 1998).

4. Gary Nash, *Urban Crucible: Social Origins, Political Consciousness, and the Origins of the American Revolution* (Cambridge: Harvard University Press, 1979), 103; John Duffy, *Epidemics in Colonial America* (Baton Rouge: Louisiana State University Press, 1953), 50–51; Thomas Hutchinson, *History of the Colony and Province of Massachusetts Bay*, ed. Lawrence Shaw Mayo, 2 vols. (Cambridge: Harvard University Press, 1936), 2:205–8; David E. Stannard, *The Puritan Way of Death: A Study in Religion, Culture, and Social Change* (New York: Oxford University Press, 1977), 114–15, 122.

5. Jeremy Black, *Natural and Necessary Enemies: Anglo French Relations in the Eighteenth Century* (Athens: University of Georgia Press, 1986).

6. Thomas S. Kidd, "The Devil and Father Rallee: The Narrative of Father Rale's War in Provincial Massachusetts," *Historical Journal of Massachusetts* 30.2 (Summer 2002): 161–67; David L. Ghere, "Diplomacy and War on the Maine Frontier, 1678–1759," in *Maine: The Pine Tree State from Prehistory to the Present*, ed. Richard W. Judd, Edwin A. Churchill, and Joel Eastman (Orono: University of Maine Press, 1995),

120–42. Also see Andrew Miller, "Abenakis and Colonists in Northern New England, 1675–1725" (PhD diss., Johns Hopkins University, 2004).

7. Max Savelle, *The Origins of American Diplomacy: International History of Anglo America, 1492–1763* (New York: Macmillan, 1967), 243.

8. Parkman, *Half Century of Conflict,* 2:482; Hutchinson, *History of the Colony and Province of Massachusetts Bay,* 2:198–99; T. J. Campbell, S.J., *Pioneer Priests of North America, 1642–1710,* 3 vols. (New York: American Press, 1910–13), 3:280–82; Colin G. Calloway, *New Worlds for All: Indians, Europeans and the Making of Early America* (Baltimore: Johns Hopkins University Press, 1997), 88.

9. James Axtell, *The Invasion Within: The Contest of Cultures in Colonial North America* (New York: Oxford University Press, 1985), 50–51; Reuben Gold Thwaites, ed., *The Jesuit Relations and Allied Documents: Travels and Explorations of the Jesuit Missionaries in New France,* 73 vols. (New York: Pageant, 1959), 67:91–99; Mary R. Calvert, *Black Robe on the Kennebec* (Monmouth, ME: Monmouth Press 1991), 155–56, 171–72.

10. Axtell, *Invasion Within,* 251–53; Kenneth Silverman, ed., *Selected Letters of Cotton Mather* (Baton Rouge: Louisiana State University Press, 1971), 275. Also consult Thomas J. Lappas, "A Victim of His Own Love: Sebastien Rale, Native Americans, and Religious Politics in Eighteenth-Century New France" (PhD diss., Indiana University, 2003), 155–60.

11. Lappas, "Victim of His Own Love," 145–46; Calvert, *Black Robe on the Kennebec,* 170–73; David D. Hall, *Worlds of Wonder, Days of Judgment: Popular Religious Belief in Early New England* (New York: Oxford University Press, 1989), 236.

12. Lappas, "Victim of His Own Love," 166, 169, Penhallow, *History of the Wars of New England,* 85–86; *Boston News Letter,* March 12, 1722; Parkman, *Half Century of Conflict,* 494.

13. Penhallow, *History of the Wars of New England,* 87–88; Parkman, *Half Century of Conflict,* 2:494; Williamson, *History of the State of Maine,* 2:116–17. George A. Wheeler and Henry W. Wheeler, *History of Brunswick, Topsfield, and Harpswell, Maine* (Boston: Higginson, 1878), 54–55. On the dynamic behind Indian hating and the anti-Indian sublime in the middle colonies, see Peter Silver, *Our Savage Neighbors: How Indian War Transformed Early America* (New York: W. W. Norton, 2008); for New England, see Lepore, *Name of War.*

14. Hutchinson, *History of the Colony and Province of Massachusetts Bay,* 2:209.

15. Colin G. Calloway, *The Western Abenakis of Vermont, 1600–1800: War, Migration, and the Survival of an Indian People* (Norman: Oklahoma University Press, 1990), 114–25. J. H. Temple and George Sheldon, *History of the Town of Northfield, Massachusetts* (Albany, NY: J. Munsell, 1875), 189; G. H. Hollister, *History of Connecticut* (Hartford, CT: L. Stebbins, 1855), 386–87.

16. *Boston Gazette,* July 30, 1722; *Boston News Letter,* July 30, 1722; "Diary of Jeremiah Bumstead, 1722–1727," *New England Historical and Genealogical Register,* 15.3 (July 1861): 195–96; Hutchinson, *History of Massachusetts Bay,* 2:211, 222; Bourque, *Twelve Thousand Years,* 193–94.

17. John Demos, *The Unredeemed Captive: A Family Story from Early America* (New York: Knopf, 1994), 170–71; *New England Courant,* September 2, September 16, September 23, and October 14, 1723; Penhallow, *History of the Wars of New England,* 98; Nathaniel B. Shurtleft, *A Topographical and Historical Description of Boston* (Boston; City Council, 1871), 492–93.

18. *New England Courant,* October 22, 1722; Hutchinson, *History of Massachusetts Bay,* 2:211–12; "Diary of Jeremy Bumstead," 196; Samuel Sewall, *Diary of Samuel Sewall, 1674–1729,* ed. M. Halsey Thomas, 2 vols. (New York, 1973), 2:997.

19. Stannard, *Puritan Way of Death,* 129–33; Cotton Mather, *A Christian Funeral* (Boston: Timothy Green, 1713), 1.

20. Charles E. Clark, *The Public Prints: The Newspaper in Anglo-American Culture, 1665–1740* (New York: Oxford University Press, 1994), 92–93, 106, 120–24; T. H. Breen, *The Character of a Good Ruler: A Study of Puritan Political Ideas in New England* (New Haven: Yale University Press, 1970), 261–62; *New England Courant,* September 3, 1722. On the *Courant* and its role, see Preston Tuckerman Shea, "Rhetoric of Authority in the *New England Courant*" (PhD diss., University of New Hampshire, 1992).

21. *Boston Gazette,* July 23, 1722; Silver, *Our Savage Neighbors,* 75–78.

22. William R. Cutter, *Genealogical and Personal Memories: Relating to the Families of Boston and Eastern Massachusetts,* 4 vols. (New York: Lewis Historical Publishing, 1908), 4:1954–55; Wheeler and Wheeler, *History of Brunswick, Topsfield and Harpswell,* 55.

23. *Boston Gazette,* July 23, 1722; Wheeler and Wheeler, *History of Brunswick,* 55; Andrew Lipman, "'A Meanes to Knitt Them Togeather': The Exchange of Body Parts in the Pequot War," *William & Mary Quarterly* 65 (2008): 3–28. Moses Eaton was also listed in the muster roll of Captain Johnson Harmon's company between February 28, 1722, and November 20, 1722, as "killed." *Letters of Colonel Thomas Westbrook and others Relative to Indian Affairs in Maine, 1722–1726,* ed. William Blake Trask (Boston: Littlefield, 1901), 161.

24. Wheeler and Wheeler, *History of Brunswick,* 339; *Boston Gazette,* July 23, 1722.

25. *Boston Gazette,* July 23, 1722.

26. Wheeler and Wheeler, *History of Brunswick,* 55.

27. "Letter John Gyles to Lt. Gov. Dummer, April 15, 1725," in *Documentary History of the State of Maine, Containing the Baxter Manuscripts,* ed. James Phinney Baxter, vol. 10 (Portland: Maine Historical Society, 1907), 246–47; *Boston News Letter,* April 29, 1725.

28. On the rhetoric of fear, see Silver, *Our Savage Neighbors.*

29. *New England Courant,* May 20, 1723; *Boston News Letter,* September 5, 1723; Jeremy Belknap, *History of New Hampshire,* vol. 2 (Boston: Thomas and Andrews, 1791), 55n.

30. Nathaniel B. Shurtleft, *A Topographical and Historical Description of Boston* (Boston, 1871), 182, 186–89, 197–99; Justin Winsor, ed., *Memorial History of Boston,* 4 vols. (Boston, 1880–81), 2:469, 470, 474; *Acts and Laws of His Majesty's Province of Massachusetts Bay in New England* (Boston: B. Green, 1726), 309; Standard, *Puritan Way of Death,* 115.

31. Samuel Gardiner Drake, *The History and Antiquities of Boston* (Boston: Luther Stevens, 1856), 561–63; Nash, *Urban Crucible,* 103; Hutchinson, *History of the Colony*

and Province of Massachusetts Bay, 206–8; G. B. Warden, *Boston, 1689–1776* (Boston: Little Brown, 1970), 86–87; Sewall, *Diary of Samuel Sewall,* 2:982–84.

32. Benjamin Wadsworth, *True Piety the Best Policy in War* (Boston: B. Green, 1722), 22–23; Kidd, "The Devil and Father Ralle," 168–70.

33. Cotton Mather, *Advice from Taberah* (Boston: B. Green, 1711), 32.

34. Carl Bridenbaugh, *Cities in the Wilderness: The First Century of Urban Life in America, 1625–1742,* 2nd ed. (New York: Oxford University Press, 1938), 211–12. Warren, *Boston, 1698–1776,* 67–68; "Diary of Jeremiah Bumstead," 197–98; Sewall, *Diary of Samuel Sewall,* 2:1007.

35. William D. Piersen, *Black Yankees: The Development of an Afro-American Subculture in Eighteenth-Century New England* (Amherst: University of Massachusetts Press, 1988), 21, 77–78; Neil Caplan, ed., "Some Unpublished Letters of Benjamin Colman, 1717–1725," *Proceedings of the Massachusetts Historical Society,* vol. 77 (Boston: Massachusetts Historical Society, 1965): 131; Lorenzo J. Greene, *The Negro in Colonial New England,* preface by Benjamin Quarles (1942; repr., New York: Athenaeum, 1971), 115, 284–85. Also see Robert E. Destrochers Jr., "Slaves for Sale Advertisements and Slavery in Massachusetts, 1704–1781," *William & Mary Quarterly* 59.3 (July 2002): 623–64.

36. Caplan, "Some Unpublished Letters of Benjamin Colman," 131; Bridenbaugh, *Cities in the Wilderness,* 384–85; "Diary of Jeremiah Bumstead," 197–98; *New England Courant,* April 1, April 8, April 15, and April 22, 1723, *Boston News Letter,* April 18, 1723. Quote about the Reverend Sewell's discourse in Joshua Coffin, *An Account of Some of the Principal Slave Insurrections* (New York: American Anti-Slavery Society, 1860), 12–13.

37. *New England Courant,* April 15, April 29, May 6, and May 20, 1723.

38. *Boston Gazette,* May 13, 1723; *Boston New Letter,* July 11, 1723; *New England Courant,* June 17, July 10, 1723; "Diary of Jeremiah Bumstead," 198.

39. "Diary of Jeremiah Bumstead," 197–98.

40. Marcus Rediker, *Between the Devil and the Deep Blue Sea: Merchant Seamen, Pirates and the Anglo-American Marine World, 1700–1750* (Cambridge: Cambridge University Press, 1987), 256; *New England Courant,* June 24, 1723; *Boston News Letter,* April 16, 1724; William Weeden, *Economic and Social History of New England, 1620–1789,* 2 vols. (Boston: Houghton Mifflin, 1899), 2:561–64, passim; Winsor, *Memorial History of Boston,* 447–48; Daniel E. Williams, "Puritans and Pirates: A Confrontation between Cotton Mather and William Fly in 1726," *Early American Literature* 22.3 (Winter 1987): 234–35.

41. Quoted in Weeden, *Economic and Social History of New England,* 561; *New England Courant,* May 20, June 3, June 24, and July 29, 1723.

42. Cotton Mather, *Useful Remarks: An Essay upon Remarkables in the Way of Wicked Men* (New London, CT: T. Green, 1723), 16; Drake, *History and Antiquities of Boston,* 570; "Diary of Jeremiah Bumstead," 199, 201; *New England Courant,* June 8, 1724; Williams, "Puritans and Pirates," 236–37.

43. Kenneth B. Murdock, *Increase Mather, the Foremost American Puritan* (1925; repr., New York: Russell and Russell, 1966), 389–90; Michael G. Hall, *Last American Puritan, Life of Increase Mather* (Middletown, CT: Wesleyan University Press, 1988); "Diary of Jeremiah Bumstead," 199; Sewall, *Diary of Samuel Sewall,* 2:1008.

44. Louise Parkman Thomas, ed., *Journal of the Reverend Israel Loring (1682–1772) of Sudbury, Massachusetts* (Columbus, GA: L. P. Thomas, 1983), 104; Sewall, *Diary of Samuel Sewall,* 2:1011–13; *Boston Gazette,* February 10, 1724; Increase Mather, *A Call to the Tempted* (Boston: Green for Gerrish, 1724); "Diary of Jeremiah Bumstead," 200.

45. Thomas, ed., *Diary of Samuel Sewall,* 2:1012–15; "Diary of Jeremiah Bumstead," 201; Mather, *A Call to the Tempted;* Peter Laslett, *The World We Have Lost* (1965; repr., New York: Scribner's, 1971), 145–46; Georges Minois, *History of Suicide: Voluntary Death in Western Culture,* trans. Lydia G. Cochrane (Baltimore: Johns Hopkins University Press, 1999), 25–28, 72–75, 191–92.

46. Patrick M. Malone, *The Skulking Way of War: Technology and Tactics among New England Indians* (Latham, MD: Madison, 1991); Penhallow, *History of the Wars of New England,* 95, lists four to five hundred Canadian and Cape Sable Indians who fell upon Arrowsic, Maine—the largest number cited in the text for the war. That the English were less careful about burying their dead seems to have been the case by the Seven Years' War; see Erik R. Seeman, *Death in the New World, Cross Cultural Encounters* (Philadelphia: University of Pennsylvania Press, 2010), 266.

47. *Boston Gazette,* July 23, 1722; *Boston News Letter,* September 10, 17, 1724; *New England Courant,* October 14, November 25, 1723; Herbert M. Sylvester, *Indian Wars of New England,* 3 vols. (Boston: W. B. Clarke, 1910), 3:205.

48. *Letters of Colonel Thomas Westbrook,* 103, 105–6.

49. Ibid., 14–15; Sewall, *Diary of Samuel Sewall,* 2:944n.

50. "Letter Captain John Penhallow to Lt. Gov. Dummer, May 16, 1724," in *Documentary History of the State of Maine,* 199–200.

51. Sewall, *Diary of Samuel Sewall,* 2:981n; John Gorham Palfrey, *History of New England* (Boston: Little Brown, 1875), 4:436.

52. Sewall, *Diary of Samuel Sewall,* 2:981n.

53. "Letter Col. Thomas Westbrook to Lt. Gov. Dummer, April 6, 1723," in *Documentary History of the State of Maine,* 162; Palfrey, *History of New England,* 4:436.

54. Williamson, *History of the State of Maine,* 2:126–27.

55. Sylvester, *Indians Wars of New England,* 3:221–22; Hutchinson, *History of Massachusetts Bay,* 2:233.

56. Cotton Mather, *Edulcorator, Brief Essay on the Waters of Marah Sweetened* (Boston: Green, 1725), 27–34, passim.

57. *Letters of Colonel Thomas Westbrook,* 62–63; Penhallow, *History of the Wars of New England,* 100.

58. Quoted in David Shields, *Oracles of Empire: Poetry, Politics, and Commerce in British North America, 1690–1750* (Chicago: University of Chicago Press, 1990), 204–5; Mather, *Edulcorator,* 27, 34.

59. Mather, *Edulcorator,* 34.

60. John Adams, *Poems on Several Occasions* (Boston: D. Gookin, 1745), 72–77.

61. Cyrus R. Eaton, *Annals of the Town of Warren* (Hallowell, ME: Masters and Smith, 1851), 37–38.

62. James Axtell and William G. Sturtevant, "The Unkindest Cut or Who Invented Scalping," *William & Mary Quarterly* 37.3 (July 1980): 451–72.

63. Hutchinson, *History of Massachusetts Bay,* 2:231–33; J. H. Temple and George Sheldon, *History of the Town of Northfield, Massachusetts* (Albany, NY: Munsell, 1875), 194–95, 204; Penhallow, *History of the Wars of New England,* 99–104; *Boston News Letter,* July 23, July 30, 1724; *Boston Gazette,* March 2, March 11, June 15, 1724.

64. Hutchinson, *History of Massachusetts Bay,* 2:234. Whether Massachusetts expected Rale's capture to speed the war's end has never been directly stated.

65. Sylvester, *Indian Wars of New England,* 3:231–32; Mary R. Calvert, *Black Robe on the Kennebec,* 197–98; Williamson, *History of the State of Maine,* 2:129; Penhallow, *History of the Wars of New England,* 104–5.

66. Williamson, *History of the State of Maine,* 2:130–31; Penhallow, *Indian Wars,* 105; Calvert, *Black Robe on the Kennebec,* 197–98; Hutchinson, *History of Massachusetts Bay,* 236.

67. Penhallow, *History of the Wars of New England,* 105; Lappas, "Victim of His Own Love," 190–91; Hutchinson, *History of Massachusetts Bay,* 2:236–37.

68. Hutchinson, *History of Massachusetts Bay,* 234–35.

69. Williamson, *History of the State of Maine,* 2:132; Hutchinson, *History of Massachusetts Bay,* 2:235–37; Reverend T. J. Campbell, S.J., *Pioneer Priests of North America, 1642–1710,* 3 vols. (New York: American Press, 1911–1914), 3:306–7.

70. Mather, *Edulcorator,* 27; Colman quoted in Campbell, *Pioneer Priests,* 2:303; Kidd, "The Devil and Father Rale," passim; Penhallow, *History of the Wars of New England,* 106.

71. Williamson, *History of the State of Maine,* 2:132; Sewall, *Diary of Samuel Sewall,* 2:1021: Hutchinson, *History of Massachusetts Bay,* 2:203, 238.

72. *Journals of the House of Representatives of Massachusetts,* 52 vols. (Boston: Massachusetts Historical Society, 1919–1986), 6:87–88.

73. *The Rebels Drowned, Or English Courage Displayed at Norridgewock* (Boston: J. Franklin, 1724); Ann M. Little, *Abraham in Arms: War and Gender in Colonial New England* (Philadelphia: University of Pennsylvania Press, 2007), 189.

74. Steven C. Eames, *Rustic Warriors: Warfare and the Provincial Soldier on the New England Frontier, 1689–1748* (New York: New York University Press, 2011), 86; *Boston News Letter,* September 3, 17, 24, 1724; Sewall, *Diary of Samuel Sewall,* 2:1023; Penhallow, *History of the Wars of New England,* 113–17; By the Honorable William Dummer, Esq., *Proclamation for a General Thanksgiving* (Boston: B. Green, 1724)

Chapter 4. Scripting the Fight

1. Clifford K. Shipton, *Sibley's Harvard Graduates,* 17 vols. (Boston: Massachusetts Historical Society, 1933–75), 4:411–17; John Adams Vinton, *The Symmes Memorial: A Biographical Sketch of the Reverend Zecharius Symmes, Minister of Charlestown, 1634–1671* (Boston: David Clap and Son, 1873); Michael Warner, *The Letters of the Republic: Publication and the Public Sphere in Eighteenth Century America* (Cambridge: Harvard University Press, 1990), 22–23.

2. Samuel A. Green, *Remarks on some early editions of the Reverend Thomas Symmes's Sermon at Bradford, Massachusetts, May 16, 1725* (Boston: Massachusetts Historical Society, 1896); Thomas Symmes, *Lovewell Lamented, or a Sermon Occasion'd by the Fall of the Brave Capt. John Lovewell and Several of the Brave Company in the heroic action at Piggwackett* (Boston: S. Gerrish, 1725).

3. *American National Biography*, s.v. Samuel Penhallow, by David E. Van Deventer; Nathaniel Adams, "Memoir of the Honorable Samuel Penhallow," Collections of the New Hampshire Historical Society, 1 vol. (1824; repr., Concord, NH: McFarlane and Jenks, 1871), 9–11; Samuel Penhallow, *History of the Wars of New England with the Eastern Indians (1726)*, ed. Edward Wheelock (1924; repr., Freeport, NY: Books for Libraries, 1971).

4. See Richard D. Brown, *Knowledge Is Power: Diffusion of Information in Early America, 1700–1865* (New York: Oxford University Press, 1989), 27–28, 33–34; Penhallow, *History of the Wars of New England*, vi–vii, 115.

5. On disaster and enshrinement, see Michael Kammen, *Mystic Chords of Memory: The Transformation of Tradition in American Culture* (New York: Knopf, 1991), 8–9. On the Alamo and the Little Big Horn, see James E. Crisp, *Sleuthing the Alamo: Davy Crockett's Last Stand and the Other Mysteries of the Texas Revolution* (New York: Oxford University Press, 2005); Richard R. Flores, *Remembering the Alamo: Memory, Modernity and the Master Symbol* (Austin: University of Texas Press, 2002); Michael A. Elliott, *Custerlogy: The Enduring Legacy of the Indian Wars and George Armstrong Custer* (Chicago: University of Chicago Press, 2007).

6. Vinson, *Symmes Memorial*, 26, 37–38; Samuel Sewall, *Diary of Samuel Sewall, 1674–1729*, ed. M. Halsey Thomas (New York, 1973), 1:591–92.

7. Vinson, *Symmes Memorial*, 37; J. D. Kingsbury, *Memorial History of Bradford, Massachusetts* (Haverhill, MA: C. C. Morse and Son, 1883), 72–73. John Brown, *Divine Help Implored: A Funeral Sermon preached at Bradford, October 31, 1725* (Boston: T. Fleet, 1726), 15, for quote.

8. Sidney Perley, *History of Boxford, Essex County, Massachusetts* (Boxford, MA: Author, 1880), 142–43; Kingsbury, *Memorial History of Bradford*, 16, 23; Brown, *Divine Help Implored*; Gardner B. Perry, *History of Bradford, Massachusetts* (1821 reprint, Haverhill, MA: C. C. Morse and Son, 1873), 40–41.

9. Kingsbury, *Memorial History of Bradford*, 19, 41, 71.

10. Perry, *History of Bradford*, 39; John Brown, *A Particular Plain and Brief Memorable Account of the Reverend Thomas Symmes* (Boston: Fleet, 1726), 4–5, 22, 42–43.

11. Brown, *Particular Plain and Brief Memorable Account*, 2–5, 7, 25; Perry, *History of Bradford*, 39–40; Kingsbury, *Memorial History of Bradford*, 74, 79–81.

12. Perry, *History of Bradford*, 39; Brown, *Particular Plain and Brief Memorable Account*, 19–20. Wise quoted in Shipton, *Sibley's Harvard Graduates*, 2:437; George A. Selement, "Publications of Puritan Ministers," *William & Mary Quarterly* 37.2 (April 1980): 219–41.

13. Oliver Ayer Roberts, *History of the Militia Company of the Massachusetts now called the Ancient and Honorable Artillery Company of Massachusetts, 1637–1888* (Boston: A. Mudge and Son, 1895), 408–9.

14. Thomas Symmes, *Good Soldiers Described and Animated* (Boston: Kneeland, 1720), 2, 4–5, 7, 12–18, 29–31; Sewall, *Diary of Samuel Sewall*, 1: xxvii, 2:951; *American National Biography*, s.v. Benjamin Colman, by Rick Kennedy.

15. Penhallow, *American National Biography*; Sewall, *Diary of Samuel Sewall*, 1:156, 325, 525; *Diary of Cotton Mather*, 2 vols. (New York: Ungar, 1957), 2:34–35, 37, 170–71, 174–76; "Memoir of the Honorable Samuel Penhallow," 9–11; Thomas Goddard Wright, *Literary Culture in Early New England, 1620–1730* (New Haven: Yale University Press, 1920), 100.

16. Joseph A. Conforti, *Saints and Strangers: New England in British North America* (Baltimore: Johns Hopkins University Press, 2006), 82–86; "Memoir of the Honorable Samuel Penhallow," 11–12; Samuel Penhallow, *American National Biography*.

17. "Memoir of the Honorable Samuel Penhallow," 11–12; Samuel Penhallow, *American National Biography*; David E. Van Deventer, *Emergence of Provincial New Hampshire, 1623–1741* (Baltimore: Johns Hopkins University Press, 1976), 217.

18. "Mission of Penhallow and Atkinson in 1703 to the Penobscot Indians," *New England Historical and Genealogical Register* 34.1 (January 1880): 91–93; Andrew Miller, "Abenakis and Colonists in Northern New England, 1675–1725" (PhD diss., Johns Hopkins University, 2005), 217–18.

19. Penhallow, *History of the Wars of New England*, 80–81, 83–84; "Treaty of 1717, Georgetown," in *Collections of the New Hampshire Historical Society*, 2 vols. (Concord, NH: Jacob B. Morse, 1827), 2:242–56.

20. Sewall, *Diary of Samuel Sewall*, 1:712.

21. Penhallow, *History of the Wars of New England*, introduction, unpaginated.

22. Fannie Hardy Eckstorm, "Pigwacket and Parson Symmes," *New England Quarterly* 9.3 (September 1936): 385–87; Symmes, *Lovewell Lamented*, ix; Preston Tuckerman Shea, "Rhetoric of Authority in the *New England Courant*" (PhD diss., University of New Hampshire, 1992), 191–92. Chandler E. Potter, *The Military History of the State of New Hampshire, 1623–1861* (1869; repr., Baltimore: Genealogical Publishing, 1972), 50.

23. Selement, "Publications of Puritan Ministers," 219–39. Symmes once started composing a sermon at Thursday noon and finished by noon the following Friday (238–39), so he could have written the Lovewell sermon in the time allotted.

24. Thomas S. Kidd, "The Devil and Father Rallee: The Narration of Father Rale's War in Provincial Massachusetts," *Historical Journal of Massachusetts* 30.2 (Summer 2002): 159–80.

25. Ibid., 159–80; Thomas S. Kidd, *The Protestant Interest: New England after Protestantism* (New Haven: Yale University Press, 2004), 91–114.

26. Symmes, *Lovewell Lamented*, 2–14, passim, quotes on pages 6 and 9.

27. Ibid., 24–25; Kidd, *Protestant Interest*, 110–12.

28. Symmes, *Lovewell Lamented*, 25–29.

29. Ibid., 29–30; Slotkin, *Regeneration through Violence: The Mythology of the American Frontier, 1630–1860* (Middletown, CT: Wesleyan University Press, 1973), 182–83.

30. Symmes, *Lovewell Lamented*, 31–32.

31. *Boston News Letter*, June 10, 1725; Shea, "Rhetoric of Authority in the *New England Courant*," 188.

32. David D. Hall, "The Use of Literacy in New England, 1600–1850," in *Printing and Society in Early America*, ed. William Joyce, David D. Hall, Richard B. Brown, and John B. Hench (Worcester, MA: American Antiquarian Society, 1983), 1–47; Isaiah Thomas, *History of Printing in America*, 2 vols. (1874; repr., New York: Burt Franklin, n.d.), 2:216; Lawrence C. Wroth, *Colonial Printer* (1938; repr., Charlottesville: University Press of Virginia, 1969), 19–20, 62–63; Symmes, *Lovewell Lamented*, ii–iv; Shea, "Rhetoric and Authority in the *New England Courant*," 193.

33. Symmes, *Lovewell Lamented*, xii; *Boston News Letter*, July 1, 1725.

34. Symmes, *Lovewell Lamented*, ix; Shea, "Rhetoric of Authority in the *New England Courant*," 195–97; Eckstorm, "Pigwacket and Parson Symmes, 384, claims that Symmes thrust a prepared text before the men, part of her larger argument that Symmes deliberately falsified the date of the battle.

35. Penhallow, *History of the Wars of New England*, vii–viii.

36. *New England Chronicle*, May 31, 1725; David S. Shields, ed., *American Poetry; The Seventeenth and Eighteenth Centuries* (New York: Library of America, 2007), 280–83, 860; *Diary of Cotton Mather*, 2:241; Carleton Sprague Smith, "Broadsides and Their Music in Colonial America," in *Music in Colonial Massachusetts, 1630–1820*, ed. Barbara Lambert (Boston: Colonial Society of Massachusetts, 1980), 157–58, 170–71, 192–97.

37. *Boston News Letter*, July 1, 1725; *New England Courant*, July 10, 1725.

38. *New England Courant*, July 10, 1725; *Boston News Letter*, July 15, 1725; Thomas Symmes, *Historical Memoirs of the Late Fight at Piggwacket* (Boston: Green, 1725); Slotkin, *Regeneration through Violence*, 181–83; Samuel A. Green, *Remarks on Some Early Editions*, 4.

39. Slotkin, *Regeneration through Violence*, 182, cites the ballad's popularity, which created an alternative script from the elegy Symmes first crafted.

40. Symmes, *Lovewell Lamented*, i–ii.

41. Ibid., ii–viii; *Boston News Letter*, May 27, 1725. Also see John Ferling, "The New England Soldier: A Study in Changing Perceptions," *American Quarterly* 33.1 (Spring 1981): 38–40, on bravery and Lovewell's troop.

42. Robert E. Cray, " 'Weltering in Their Own Blood': Puritan Casualties in King Philip's War," *Historical Journal of Massachusetts* 37.2 (Fall 2009): 106–23; Symmes, *Lovewell Lamented*, viii–ix.

43. Symmes, *Lovewell Lamented*, ix–xii.

44. Symmes, *Historical Memoirs*, 2n.

45. Ibid., 2n.

46. *Boston News Letter*, October 14, 1725; Brown, *A Particular Plain and Brief Memorable Account of the Reverend Thomas Symmes*, advertisement, not paginated.

47. Penhallow, *History of the Wars of New England*, vii, 105.

48. Ibid., viii–ix.

49. Ibid.

50. Ibid., x.

51. Ibid., xi.

52. Ibid., 2, 67, 69, 75, 77, 79–80, 83, 85, 91, 96, 123, 130–32, 134; William Pencak, *War, Politics, and Revolution in Provincial Massachusetts* (Boston: Northeastern University Press, 1981), 71, 76–77.

53. Penhallow, *History of the Wars of New England*, 16, 21–23, 84–85, 95, 101.

54. Ibid., 105–6n31.

55. Ibid., iv.

56. Ibid., 107, 110.

57. Ibid., 115–16.

58. Ibid., 112–14.

59. Ibid., Notes, p. 37, line 21.

60. Ibid., 116, cites the "immortal honour of the men of Jabeth Gilead . . . that they prepared a decent burial for their bodies."

61. Ibid., 11n38.

62. Ibid., 116–17.

63. Ibid., ii.

64. Ibid., xii–xiii.

Chapter 5. Social Welfare and Lovewell's Men

1. *Journals of the House of Representatives of Massachusetts,* 52 vols. (Boston: Massachusetts Historical Society, 1919–1986), 6:220, 237–38; *Acts and Resolves, Public and Private, of the Province of Massachusetts,* 21 vols. (Boston: Wright and Potter, 1869–1922), 10:587.

2. Ezra S. Stearns, *Genealogical and Family History of the State of New Hampshire,* 4 vols. (New York: Lewis Publishing, 1908), 3:1029; Stearns, *Early Genealogies of the Founders of Old Dunstable: Thirty Families* (Boston: Heritage Books, 1911), 39; *Journals of the House of Representatives,* 7:21, 33–34; *Acts and Resolves,* 10:612; 11:17–18.

3. Samuel Sewall, *History of Woburn* (Boston: Wiggin and Lunt, 1868), 194.

4. There has been relatively little on colonial veterans' pensions, but a start was made by Jack S. Radabaugh, "The Military System of Colonial Massachusetts, 1690–1740" (PhD diss., University of Southern California, 1965), 494–501.

5. Homer, *The Odyssey,* trans. Edward McCrorie (Baltimore: Johns Hopkins University Press, 2004).

6. Benjamin Church, *Diary of King Philip's War,* ed. Alan and Mary Simpson (Tiverton, RI: Lockwood, 1975); John Ferling, "The New England Soldier: A Study in Changing Perceptions," *American Quarterly* 33.1 (Spring 1981): 37.

7. See William Pencak, *War, Politics, and Revolutions in Provincial Massachusetts* (Boston: Northeastern University Press, 1981), 71, 77–78; *Journals of the House of Representatives,* 6:viii, 334–35, 436–38; *American National Biography,* s.v. William Dummer, by Jonathan M. Chu.

8. *New England Courant,* June 7, 1725.

9. Radabaugh, "Military System of Colonial Massachusetts," 498–501.

10. *Journals of the House of Representatives,* 5:152–53, 160; 6:200; John A. Schultz,

Legislators of the General Court, 1691–1780: A Biographical Dictionary (Boston: Northeastern University Press, 1997), 50–51.

11. Jonathan Edwards, *A Strong Rod Broken and Withered* (Boston: Rogers and Fowle, 1748); James Russell Trumbull, *History of Northampton, Massachusetts, from its First Settlement in 1654*, 2 vols. (Northampton, MA: Northampton Town, 1898–1902), 2:20–21, 35–36.

12. *Journals of the House of Representatives*, 6: vii; Schultz, *Legislators of the General Court*, 69; Gregory H. Nobles, *Divisions throughout the Whole: Politics and Society in Hampshire County, Massachusetts, 1740–1775* (Cambridge: Cambridge University Press, 1983), 7, 28–30.

13. *Journals of House of Representatives*, 6:238.

14. William F. Ricketson, "To be Young, Poor, and Alone, 1675–1676," *New England Quarterly* 64.1 (March 1991): 113–27.

15. Alexander Keyssar, "Widowhood in Eighteenth Century Massachusetts: A Problem in the History of the Family," *Perspectives in American History* 8 (1974): 83–119. For a broad-brush perspective on colonial widows, see Vivian Bruce Conger, *The Widows' Might: Widowhood and Gender in Early British America* (New York: New York University Press, 2009).

16. Cotton Mather, *Marah Spoken To* (Boston: T. Crump, 1718); Mather, *Widow of Nain* (Boston: n.p., 1728); Stephen Foster, *Their Solitary Way: The Puritan Social Ethic in the First Colony of Settlement in New England* (New Haven: Yale University Press, 1971), 149.

17. Foster, *Their Solitary Way*, 134–43; G. B. Warden, *Boston, 1689–1776* (New York: Little Brown, 1970), 80–86; Christine Heyrman, "A Model of Christian Charity: The Rich and the Poor in New England, 1630–1730" (PhD diss., Yale University, 1977); Gary Nash, *Urban Crucible: Social Change, Political Consciousness, and the Origins of the American Revolution* (Cambridge: Harvard University Press, 1979), charts the course of expanding and contracting Atlantic economies in colonial seaports.

18. *Journals of the House of Representatives*, 6:261–62.

19. Ibid., 6:278–79; *Acts and Resolves*, 10:612.

20. *Journals of the House of Representatives*, 6:312–13, 328.

21. Ibid., 7:27; Radabaugh, "Military System of Colonial Massachusetts," 503; Trumbull, *History of Northampton*, 2:35–37, shows that Northampton had its share of political disunity. Clifford Shipton, *Sibley's Harvard Graduates*, 17 vols. (Boston: Massachusetts Historical Society, 1933–75), 4:245–48.

22. *Journals of the House of Representatives*, 7:33–34.

23. Ibid., 6:4, 94, 216, 268, 278, 384; 7:33–34.

24. Ezra S. Stearns, "Lovewell Men," *New England Historical and Genealogical Register* 63.3 (July 1909): 288; Reverend Nathan F. Carter and T. L. Fowler, *History of Pembroke, New Hampshire*, 2 vols. (Concord, NH: Republican Press, 1895), 1:15; John Grenier, *The First Way of War: American War Making on the Frontier* (Cambridge: Cambridge University Press, 2005), 38; Francis Parkman, *France and England in North America*, 2 vols., ed. David Levin (New York: Library Classics, 1983), 2:507.

25. *Journals of the House of Representatives*, 7:175–76.
26. Ibid., 7:175–76; *Acts and Resolves*, 9 96; Stearns, "Lovewell Men," 290.
27. Samuel Penhallow, *The History of the Indian Wars of New England with the Eastern Indians (1726)*, ed. Eleazer Wheelock (1924; repr., Freeport, NY: Books for Libraries, 1971), 117; Stearns, "Lovewell Men," 293; Louis J. Piccarello, "Poverty, the Poor, and Public Welfare in Massachusetts: A Comparative History of Four Towns, 1643–1855" (PhD diss., Brandeis University, 1991), 145–46.
28. Stearns, "Lovewell Men," 288–90; Alfred E. Kayworth and Raymond G. Potvin, *The Scalphunters: Abenaki Ambush at Lovewell's Pond, 1725* (Boston: Branden Books, 2002), 133; *Acts and Resolves*, 11:102; *Journals of the House of Representatives*, 7:178–79.
29. Penhallow, *History of the Indian Wars*, 117; *Journals of the House of Representatives*, 8:69–70; *Acts and Resolves*, 11:245–46.
30. *Journals of the House of Representatives*, 8:70–71; *Acts and Resolves*, 11:245–46; Henry S. Nourse, *Early Records of Lancaster, Massachusetts, 1643–1725* (Lancaster, MA: W. J. Coulter, 1884), 227; David Jaffee, *People of the Wachusett: Greater New England in History and Memory, 1630–1860* (Ithaca, NY: Cornell University Press, 1999), 93.
31. *Journals of the House of Representatives*, 8:255, 262; Stearns, "Lovewell Men," 288.
32. Laura T. Ulrich, *Good Wives: Image and Reality in the Lives of Women in Northern New England* (New York: Knopf, 1982); Radabaugh, "Military System of Colonial Massachusetts," 503.
33. Gary B. Samuel, *Enduring Roots: Encounters with Trees, History and the American Landscape* (New Brunswick, NJ: Rutgers University Press, 1999), 24–26.
34. *Journals of the House of Representatives*, 6:421, 426; Radabaugh, "Military System of Colonial Massachusetts," 109–10.
35. Samuels, *Enduring Roots*, 24–26; George H. Evans, *Pigwacket* (Conway, NH: Conway, 1939), 94–97; Clifford K. Shipton, *New England Life in the Eighteenth Century* (Cambridge: Belknap Press of Harvard University Press, 1963), 213–15.
36. *Journals of the House of Representatives*, 5:142; 6:330.
37. Ibid., 5:166; 6:256.
38. Ibid., 6:248; "Letter Lt. Gov. Dummer to Col. Eleazer Tyng, May 13, 1725," in *Documentary History of the State of Maine, Containing the Baxter Manuscripts*, ed. James Phinney Baxter, vol. 10 (Portland: Maine Historical Society, 1907), 10:268–70.
39. Ibid., 6:248.
40. George W. Chase, *History of Haverhill, Massachusetts, From its First Settlement in 1640 to the Year 1860* (Haverhill, MA: Author, 1861), 312–14, 328; *Acts and Resolves*, 10:606; *Journals of the House of Representatives*, 6:256–57.
41. *Journals of the House of Representatives*, 6:334–35, 344, 352.
42. Ibid., 6:334–35, 436–37.
43. Ibid., 6:326–27, 330, 332; *Acts and Resolves*, 10:656–57, 659, 700; Stearns, "Lovewell Men," 290; Radabaugh, "Military System of Colonial Massachusetts," 198.
44. Nourse, *Early Records of Lancaster*, 224–25; Radabaugh, "Military System of Colonial Massachusetts," 492–94, table 13, 495.
45. *Journals of the House of Representatives*, 6:326, 421, 426; *Acts and Resolves*, 10:720.

46. *Journals of the House of Representatives,* 6:321, 326; *Acts and Resolves,* 10:654–55.

47. *Journals of the House of Representatives,* 6:421, 426, *Acts and Resolves,* 11:93.

48. *Journals of the House of Representatives,* 6:325, 328–29; *Acts and Resolves,* 10:656.

49. *Journals of the House of Representatives,* 7:41, 46, 55, 65.

50. Ibid., 7:134–35, 175, 180, 248, 252; *Acts and Resolves,* 10:174, 179; 13 247, 367; Charles J. Fox, *History of the Old Township of Dunstable* (Nashua, NH: C. T. Gill, 1846), 123.

51. William Henry Glasson, *History of Military Pension Legislature in the United States* (New York: Columbia University Press, 1900), 12–14.

52. Ezra S. Stearns, *History of Plymouth, New Hampshire,* 2 vols. (Cambridge, MA: University Press, 1906), 2:371–72; Carter and Fowler, *History of Pembroke, New Hampshire,* 1:25–26, 32–38; Stearns, "Lovewell Men," 290.

53. Stearns, *History of Plymouth,* 2:372–73; Nathaniel Bouton, ed., *Captain John Lovewell's Great Fight with the Indians of Pequawket* by the Reverend Thomas Symmes (Concord, NH: P. B. Cogswell, 1861), 24n.

54. Lemuel Shattuck, *History of the Town of Concord* (Boston: Russell, Odiorne and Company, 1835), 218; *Acts and Resolves,* 12:245, 577; 13:92–93; Stearns, "Lovewell Men," 292.

55. Stearns, "Lovewell Men," 291–92; Henry S. Nourse, *History of the Town of Harvard, Massachusetts, 1733–1893* (Harvard, MA: Higginson, 1894), 52, 95–96, 113, 420–21, 433–34, 543.

56. Thomas Symmes, *Lovewell Lamented, or a Sermon Occasion'd by the Fall of the Brave Capt. John Lovewell and several of the Valiant company in the late Heroic Action at Piggwackett* (Boston: S. Gerrish, 1725), iii, 15, 25; Penhallow, *History of the Wars of New England,* 113–14.

57. Frederic Kidder, *Expeditions of Capt. John Lovewell* (Boston: Bartlett and Halliday, 1865), 105–6; Ezra S. Stearns, *Early Generations of the Founders of Old Dunstable: Thirty Families* (Boston: Heritage, 1911), 30; William H. Brown, *Colonel John Goffe: Eighteenth Century New Hampshire* (Manchester, NH: L. A. Cummings, 1950), 142–43.

58. George W. Chamberlain, *John Chamberlain: The Indian Fighter at Pigwacket* (Weymouth, MA: Waymouth and Braintree, 1898).

59. Samuel A. Green, *Groton during the War* (Groton, MA: J. Wilson, 1882), 145.

60. Caleb Butler, *History of the Town of Groton* (Boston: T. R. Malvin, 1848), 102–4, 105–6n, 107n.

61. Grenier, *First Way of War,* 38; Stearns, "Lovewell Men," 292–93, 295; Douglas Edward Leach, *Roots of Conflict: British Armed Forces and Colonial Americas, 1677–1763* (Chapel Hill: University of North Carolina Press, 1986), 64–75.

62. See John Frederick Martin, *Profits in the Wilderness: Entrepreneurship and the Founding of New England Towns in the Seventeenth Century* (Chapel Hill: University of North Carolina Press, 1991), for a fine perspective on town formation and land acquisition.

63. *Journals of the House of Representatives,* 7:305; Carter and Fowler, *History of Pembroke, New Hampshire,* 1:15.

64. Carter and Fowler, *History of Pembroke*, 16.

65. Ibid., 16–20, 2–23; *Journals of the House of Representatives*, 9:31–32; Jaffe, *People of the Wachusetts*, 129–32, shows the dynamics behind veterans and land promises dating back to King Philip's War. Farmers desiring a competency pushed the government to award them land for wartime services.

66. Carter and Fowler, *History of Pembroke*, 1:25–30, Stearns, "Lovewell Men," 296.

67. Robert C. Williams, *Lovewell's Town: Lovewell, Maine: From Howling Wilderness to Vacationland in Trust* (Topsham, ME: Just Write Books, 2007), 27–29.

68. Ibid., 31–32.

69. Penhallow, *History of the Wars of New England*, 116–17.

Chapter 6. Remembering Lovewell through the Centuries

1. *New England Courant*, May 31, 1725; David S. Shields, ed., *American Poetry: The Seventeenth and Eighteenth Century, Library of America* (New York: Library of America, 2007), 280–83. Other Lovewell ballads can be found in George H. Evans, *Pigwacket* (Conway, NH: Conway Historical Society, 1939), 87–93. Although originally titled the "Volunteer's March," the ballad was more typically referred to as "Lovewell's Fight."

2. Henry David Thoreau, *A Week on the Concord and Merrimack Rivers* (Boston: Houghton Mifflin, 1961), 123–26.

3. Ibid., 124. Linck C. Johnson, *Thoreau's Complex Weave: The Writing of a Week on the Concord and Merrimack Rivers* (Charlottesville: University Press of Virginia, 1986), 143–44.

4. Shields, *Oracles of Empire*, 204–6; Shields, *American Poetry*, 839, 846; John Adams, *Poems on Several Occasions* (Boston: D. Gookin, 1745), 72–75; David D. Hall, *Cultures of Print: Essays in the History of the Book* (Amherst: University of Massachusetts Press, 1996), 79–96.

5. Phillips Barry, "Songs of the Pigwacket Fight," *Bulletin of the Folk-Song Society of the Northeast* 4 (1932): 3–5; David S. Shields, *Oracles of Empire: Poetry, Politics and Commerce in British North America, 1690–1750* (Chicago: University of Chicago Press, 1990), 206–8; Shields, *American Poetry*, 860.

6. George Lyman Kitteridge, "The Ballad of Lovewell's Fight," in *Bibliographical Essays: Tribute to Wilberforce Eames*, ed. Bruce Rogers (Cambridge: Harvard University Press, 1924), 101–2.

7. Samuel Penhallow, *History of the Wars of New England with the Eastern Indians (1726)*, ed. Edward Wheelock (1924; repr., Freeport, NY: Books for Libraries, 1971), 116–17.

8. Barry, "Songs of the Pigwacket Fight," 8–9; Kitteridge, "Ballads of Lovewell's Fight," 104–5, suggests these two ballads were published in 1725. It is just as likely they were printed in 1736, the original date of the contract.

9. Kitteridge, "Ballads of Lovewell's Fight," 104–5.

10. Joseph Stow, "The Brave Capt. Lovell of Dunstable," n.p. (173?), Houghton Library, Harvard University, Cambridge, MA, Hollis number 007119129. The card catalogue

for this entry draws upon the manuscript inscription that says it "came forth January, 1739–40," which I have used as a possible publication date. George Tolman, *Concord, Massachusetts, Births, Marriages, and Deaths, 1635–1850* (Boston: Beacon Press, 1894), 121; Lemuel Shattuck, *History of the Town of Concord* (Boston: Russell and Odiorne, 1835), 384.

11. Ibid.; Elijah Russell, *The History of the Fight of the Intrepid Captain John Lovewell* (Fryeburg, ME: Author, 1799), 23–24.

12. Stow, "Brave Capt. Lovell of Dunstable."

13. Quoted in Samuel Briggs, ed., *The Essays, Humor, and Poems of Nathaniel Ames, Father and Son, of Dedham, Massachusetts, from the Almanacs* (Cleveland, OH: Short and Forman 1891), 185–86.

14. Timothy Dwight, *Travels in New England*, ed. Barbara Miller Solomon, 4 vols. (Cambridge: Harvard University Press, 1969), 2:170–71.

15. Frederic Kidder, *Expeditions of Capt. John Lovewell* (Boston: Bartlett and Halliday, 1865), v; John Fitzmeir, *New England Moral Legislator: Timothy Dwight, 1752–1817* (Bloomington: Indiana University Press, 1998). Timothy Dwight, *American National Biography*, s.v. William Dowling.

16. Simon Schama, *Landscape and Memory* (New York: Knopf, 1995). See Thomas A. Chambers, *Memories of War: Visiting Battlegrounds and Bonefields in the Early American Republic* (Ithaca, NY: Cornell University Press, 2012), 18–27; and Thomas P. Slaughter, *The Whiskey Rebellion: Frontier Epilogue to the American Revolution* (New York: Oxford University Press, 1988), 62, on the exposed bones from the Braddock expedition. The situation bothered visitors but not the settlers, whose children played among them.

17. John Gyles, "Statement of the Number of Indians in each Tribe in 1726," in *Collections of the Maine Historical Society*, vol. 3 (Portland: Maine Historical Society, 1853), 357–58. "Samuel Willard's Journal," in Henry S. Nourse, *Early Records of Lancaster, Massachusetts, 1643–1725* (Lancaster, MA: W. J. Coulter 1884), 239–42; Evans, *Pigwacket*, 74–75; "Walter Bryent's Agreement and Journal, 1740/1741," in *Documents and Records Relating to New Hampshire, 1623–1800*, ed. Nathaniel Bouton (Concord, Manchester, Nashua, and Bristol, NH: John B. Clark, 1891), 19:507–8. On the Abenakis' persistence, contrary to older accounts emphasizing their decline, see David L. Ghere, "Myths and Methods in Abenaki Demography: Abenaki Population Recovery, 1725–1750," *Ethnohistory* 44.3 (Summer 1997): 511–34.

18. "Walter Bryent Agreement and Journal," 508–9.

19. John Farmer and Jacob B. Moore, *Collections, Topographical, Historical and Biographical Relating Principally to New Hampshire*, 1 (1822; repr., Concord, NH: M. E. Hill and J. W. Moore, 1831), 29–30n. David E. Stannard, *The Puritan Way of Death: A Study in Religion, Culture, and Social Change* (New York: Oxford University Press, 1977), 116–22, 156–61.

20. Fred Anderson, *The War That Made America: A Short History of the French and Indian War* (New York: Penguin, 2006); Stephen Brumwell, *White Devil: A True Story of War, Savagery, and Vengeance in Colonial America* (New York: De Capo, 2005).

21. John Stuart Barrows, *Fryeburg, Maine: An Historical Sketch* (Fryeburg, ME: Pequawket Press, 1938), 28–36; John Mack Faragher, *A Great and Noble Scheme: The Tragic Story of the Expulsion of the French Acadians from their American Homeland* (New York: W. W. Norton, 2005), 350–51, 402, 412; Ian K. Steele, *Betrayals: Fort William Henry and the Massacre* (New York: Oxford University Press, 1990), 166–67.

22. Barrow, *Fryeburg*, 32–33, 38–43. On speculators and town builders, see Bernard Bailyn, *The Peopling of British North America: An Introduction* (New York: Knopf, 1986), 65–85; Alan Taylor, *William Cooper's Town: Power and Persuasion on the Frontier of the Early American Republic* (New York: Knopf, 1996).

23. "An Accurate Map of His Majesty's Province of New Hampshire in New England, 1761," New Hampshire State Library, Concord, New Hampshire; I am grateful to the State Library for transmitting a copy of the map via e-mail. Also see Robert C. Williams, *Lovewell's Town: Lovewell, Maine: From Howling Wilderness to Vacationland in Trust* (Topsham, ME: Just Write Books, 2007), 15.

24. Russell M. Lawson, *Passconway's Realm: Captain John Evans and the Exploration of Mount Washington* (Hanover, NH: University Press of New England, 2002), 28–36, 52–55; David L. Ghere, "The Disappearance of the Abenakis in Western Maine: Political Organization and Ethnocentric Assumptions," *American Indian Quarterly* 17.2 (Spring 1993): 193–207, esp. 199–202; H. E. Mitchell, B. V. Davis, and F. E. Daggett, comps., *The Town Register of Fryeburg, Lovell, Sweden, Stow, and Chatham* (Brunswick, ME: H. E. Mitchell, 1907), 30–31.

25. Paul Coffin, *The Memoirs and Journals of the Reverend Paul Coffin*, ed. Cyrus Woodman (Portland, ME: B. Thurston, 1855), 53–54, 56–57.

26. Coffin, "Memoirs and Journals of the Reverend Paul Coffin", 60–64, 66–67.

27. Ibid., 67–68.

28. Alfred E. Kayworth and Raymond G. Potvin, *The Scalphunters: Abenaki Ambush at Lovewell's Pond, 1725* (Boston: Branden Press, 2002), 157–58.

29. On Molly Ocket I have drawn from the following: Laurel T. Ulrich, *The Age of Homespun: Objects and Stories in the Creation of the American Myth* (New York: Knopf, 2001), 251–54; Henry Tufts, *Autobiography of a Criminal*, ed. Neal Keating (Port Washington, NY: Breakout Productions, 1993), 53–55; Kathryn Whitford, "Hannah Dustin: The Judgment of History," *Essex Institute Historical Collections* 108.4 (October 1972): 302–25; Catherine S. C. Newell, *Molly Ockett* (Bethel, ME: Bethel Historical Society, 1981); N. T. True, "Last of the Pigwacket," *Oxford Democrat*, January 2, 1863. I am grateful to the Bethel Historical Society, for sending me a copy of the newspaper article. Bunny McBride and Harold E. L. Prins, "Walking the Medicine Line: Molly Ocket, A Pigwacket Doctor," in *Northeastern Indian Lives, 1632–1816*, ed. Robert Grumet (Amherst: University of Massachusetts Press, 1996), 324–25. Also see Williams, *Lovewell's Town*, 21.

30. See chapter 4 for treatments of Hassell by Symmes and Penhallow.

31. See *Social Memory and History: Anthropological Perspectives*, ed. Jacob Climo and Maria Cattell (Walnut Creek, CA: Altamira Press 2002), 1–36, on the elasticity of memory and un-remembering. Kidder, *Expeditions of Capt. John Lovewell*, v; William

Willis, *History of Portland* (Portland, ME: Bailey and Noyes, 1865), 519–24. On the memory of a Boston shoemaker, see Alfred Young, *The Shoemaker and the Tea Party: Memory and the American Revolution* (Boston: Beacon Press, 1999).

32. "Tour of the White Mountains, July 29, 1784, Jeremy Belknap Papers," in *Collections of the Massachusetts Historical Society,* 5th ser., vol. 2 (Boston: Massachusetts Historical Society, 1877), 397–98; Louis Leonard Tucker, *Clio's Consort: Jeremy Belknap and the Founding of the Massachusetts Historical Society* (Boston: Massachusetts Historical Society, 1990), 48–50; Russell M. Lawson, *The American Plutarch: Jeremy Belknap and the Historian's Dialogue with the Past* (Westport, CT: Praeger, 1998), 7, 69–77, 89–95.

33. Jeremy Belknap, *History of New Hampshire,* vol. 2 (Boston: Thomas and Andrews, 1792), 61–65, 65–66n, 70n; Tucker, *Clio's Consort,* 37–38. See Bernard Bailyn, *The Ordeal of Thomas Hutchinson* (Cambridge: Harvard University Press, 1974).

34. *History of the Press of Maine,* ed. Joseph Griffin (Brunswick, ME: Author, 1872), 118; William Nelson, *Notes toward a History of the American Newspaper* (New York: C. F. Heartmann, 1918), 166–68.

35. Russell, *The History of the Fight of the Intrepid Captain John Lovewell,* iii–viii.

36. Ibid., 23–24. See George W. Chamberlain, *John Chamberlain: The Indian Fighter at Pigwacket* (Weymouth, MA: Weymouth and Braintree, 1898), which touts Chamberlain as the slayer of Paugus.

37. David Waldstreicher, *In the Midst of Perpetual Fetes: The Making of American Nationalism* (Chapel Hill: University of North Carolina Press, 1997); John Bodnar, *Remaking America: Public Memory, Commemoration and Patriotism in the Twentieth Century* (Princeton: Princeton University Press, 1992), 24–25, 34–35; James Riker, *Evacuation Day, Its Many Stirring Events . . .* (New York: Author, 1883); Young, *Shoemaker and the Boston Tea Party.*

38. Williams, *Lovewell's Town; A Brief History of the Battle which was fought on the 8th of May, 1725 Between Capt. John Lovell and his Associates and a Body of Indians under the Command of Paugus* (Portland, ME: A. J. Shirley, 1818), 5–6; Thomas Symmes, *Historical Memoir of the Late Fight at Pigwacket* (Boston: N. Coverly, 1819), no pagination.

39. Quoted in Evans, *Pigwacket,* 102–3. Thomas C. Upham, *American National Biography,* s.v. Alfred H. Fuchs. The possibility that Upham was the anonymous wordsmith comes from Farmer and Moore, *Collections, Topographical, Historical, and Biographical,* 35–36.

40. Thomas C. Upham, *American Sketches* (New York: D. Longworth, 1819), 110–11.

41. Ibid., 57–58; Evans, *Pigwacket,* 98–99.

42. Henry W. Longfellow, *American National Biography,* s.v. Edward Wagenknecht; Donald Sears, "Folk Poetry in Longfellow's Boyhood," *New England Quarterly* 45.1 (March 1972): 96–105.

43. Edwin M. Bacon, *Literary Pilgrimages in New England* (New York: Silver, Burdett and Company, 1902), 138; See Robert Stafford Ward, "Longfellow's Roots in Yankee Soil," *New England Quarterly* 41.2 (June 1968): 180–92, quoted on 183.

44. Ward, "Longfellow's Roots in Yankee Soil," 183; quoted in Evans, *Pigwacket,* 104–5.

45. Farmer and Moore, *Collections, Historical and Miscellaneous*, 25–35; John Farmer and Jacob B. Moore, *Collections, Topographical, Historical, and Miscellaneous, and Monthly Literary Journal*, vol. 3 (Concord, NH: B. Moore, 1824), 64–66; John Farmer and Jacob B. Moore, *A Gazetteer of the State of New Hampshire* (Concord, NH: Hill and Moore, 1823), 122.

46. *North American Review*, n.s., 9 (Boston, 1824): 35.

47. John Seelye, *Memory's Nation: The Place of Plymouth Rock* (Chapel Hill: University of North Carolina Press, 1998); Joseph A. Conforti, *Imagining New England: Explorations of Regional Identity from the Pilgrims to the Mid-Twentieth Century* (Chapel Hill: University of North Carolina Press, 2001), 183–85; David Jaffee, *People of the Wachusett: Greater New England in History and Memory, 1630–1860* (Ithaca, NY: Cornell University Press, 1999), 239–41.

48. Charles S. Daveis, *An Address Delivered on the Commemoration at Fryeburg* (Portland, ME: J. Adams, Jr., 1825). I am grateful to the Fryeburg Historical Society for sending me a copy of this pamphlet. See *Sprague's Journal of Maine History* 8 (1920): 56, for information on Daveis. *Portsmouth Journal*, May 14, 1825. On Webster declining the invitation, see *Fryeburg's Webster Centennial* (Fryeburg, ME: A. F. Lewis, 1902), 23. Fryeburg Historical Society, Fryeburg, Maine.

49. Daveis, *An Address*, 10.

50. Luigi Castiglioni, *Viaggio: Travels in the United States of North America, 1785–1787,* trans. and ed. Antonio Pace (Syracuse, NY: Syracuse University Press, 1983), 29–37; Edward Augustus Kendall, *Travels Through the Northern Parts of the United States in the Years 1807 and 1808*, 3 vols. (New York: I. Riley, 1809), 3:73; William Tudor, *Letters on the Eastern States* (New York: Kirk and Mercein, 1820), 236–43. Also see Micah Abell Pawling, "Petitions and the Reconfiguration of Homeland: Persistence and Tradition among Wabanaki Peoples in the Nineteenth Century" (PhD diss., University of Maine, 2010), 508–35, for Indians and public welfare needs.

51. Daveis, *An Address*, 13–14, 29, 31; *Portsmouth Journal*, May 25, 1815; Mitchell, Davis, and Daggett, *The Town Register of Fryeburg, Lowell, Sweden, Stow, and Chatham*, 16. The Reverend Samuel Souther, *Centennial Celebration at the Settlement of Fryeburg, Maine* (Worcester, MA: Tyler and Seagrave, 1864), 9, cites the 1825 celebration as "Paugus Day." See Jill Lepore, *The Name of War: King Philip's War and the Origins of American Identity* (New York: Knopf, 1998), 191–226, on shifting cultural portrayals of Indians, in this instance King Philip; Jaffee, *People of the Wachusett*, 245–46.

52. Quoted in Evans, *Pigwacket*, 115–17.

53. Barrows, *Fryeburg, Maine*, 24–26. On toasts and nationalism, see Waldstreicher, *In the Midst of Perpetual Fetes*.

54. *Portsmouth Journal*, May 25, 1825; Souther, *Centennial Celebration of the Settlement of Fryeburg, Maine*, 39. "Lovewell's Fight," *Worcester Magazine and Historical Journal* 1.1 (October 1825): 26.

55. Nathaniel Hawthorne, "Roger Malvin's Burial," in *The Complete Short Stories of Nathaniel Hawthorne* (Garden City, NY: Doubleday, 1959), 376; David S. Lovejoy, "Lovewell's Fight and Hawthorne's Roger Malvin's Burial," *New England Quarterly*

27.4 (December 1954): 527–31; Charles J. Fox, *History of the Old Township of Dunstable* (Nashua, NH: C. T. Gill, 1846), 122–23; Caleb Butler, *History of the Town of Groton* (Boston: T. R. Marvin, 1848), 102–5; Samuel Sewell, *History of Woburn, Massachusetts* (Boston: Wiggin and Lunt, 1868), 194–206; Kidder, *Expeditions of Captain John Lovewell*; Nathaniel Bouton, ed., *Capt. John Lovewell's Great Fight with the Indians at Pequawket, 1725*, by the Rev. Thomas Symmes (Concord, NH: P. B. Cogswell, 1861).

56. "Lovewell's Fight," *Worcester Magazine*, 26; Kidder, *Expeditions of Captain John Lovewell*, vi.

57. David E. Stannard, *The Puritan Way of Death*, 157–60, 171–84; Chambers, *Memories of War*, 87–95; John F. Sears, *Sacred Places: American Tourist Attractions in the Nineteenth Century* (New York: Oxford, 1989), 97–115, passim. On Richard Montgomery, see Charles Royster, *A Revolutionary People at War: The Continental Army and American Character, 1775–1783* (Chapel Hill: University of North Carolina Press, 1979), 120–26. On the 1808 reinterment of the prison-ship dead, see Robert E. Cray Jr., "Commemorating the Prison Ship Dead: Revolutionary Memory and the Politics of Sepulture in the Early Republic, 1776–1808," *William & Mary Quarterly*, 3rd ser., 55.3 (July 1999): 565–90. On reburials in general, see Michael Kammen, *Digging up the Dead: A History of Notable American Reburials* (Chicago: University of Chicago Press, 2010).

58. William D. Williamson, *History of the State of Maine*, 2 vols. (Hallowell, ME: Glazier, Masters and Company, 1832), 2:141.

59. John Hayward, *The New England Gazetteer* (Boston: Author, 1841), 135–36; Barrows, *Fryeburg, Maine*, 210–11.

60. Barrows, *Fryeburg, Maine*, 210.

61. Ibid., 225; Sears, *Sacred Places*, 72–86. Dona Brown, *Inventing New England: Regional Tourism in the Nineteenth Century* (Washington, DC: Smithsonian Press, 1995), provides a useful perspective on tourism.

62. Brown, *Inventing New England*, 62–62, 226n56. Diary of Caroline Barrett White, American Antiquarian Society, vol. 5, August 11 to September 4, microfilm.

63. Diary of Caroline Barrett White, August 28, 1854, cited the visit to Colonel Frye's grave.

64. George J. Varney, *Gazetteer of the State of Maine* (Boston: B. B. Russell, 1881), 246–47; *The Illustrated Fryeburg Webster Memorial: Newly Discovered Fourth of July Oration of Daniel Webster* (Boston: A. F. and C. W. Lewis, 1882), 29, 32–40.

65. (Connecticut) *Meriden Daily Journal*, September 15, 1889, 3; *Boston Evening Transcript*, August 14, 1902, 12; Souther, *Centennial Celebration*, 67–68; "Field Day: Excursion to Fryeburg, September 12, 1895," in *Collections of the Maine Historical Society*, 2nd ser., vol. 7 (Portland: Maine Historical Society, 1896), 212. Francis Parkman, *France and England in North America*, ed. David Levin, 2 vols. (New York: Library Classics, 1983), 2:502–16; George Bancroft, *History of the United States*, 6 vols. (1885; repr., Port Washington, NY: Kennikat Press, 1967), 2:220.

66. Thoreau, *Week on the Concord and Merrimack Rivers*, 126; Johnson, *Thoreau's Complex Weave*, 141–42; Robert F. Sayres, *Thoreau and the American Indians* (Princeton:

Princeton University Press, 1977); G. H. Holister, *History of Connecticut* (Hartford, CT: L. Stebbins, 1858), 386–87; Abraham E. Brown, *History of the Town of Bedford, Middlesex County, Massachusetts* (Bedford, MA: Author, 1891), 21; *Town Register of Fryeburg,* 15; "Field Day: Excursion to Fryeburg, September 12, 1895," 217–18.

67. Joshua L. Chamberlain, *Maine: Her Place in History: Address delivered Philadelphia, November 4, 1876 and in Convention of the Legislature of Maine, February 6, 1877* (Augusta, ME: Sprague, Owen, and Nash, 1877), 10, 13–14, for quotations; Enoch Knight, *The New Story of the State of Maine* (Portland, ME: Dresser, McLellan and Company, 1876), 22.

68. *Town Register of Fryeburg,* 46; Hal S. Barron, *Those Who Stayed Behind: Rural Society in Nineteenth Century New England* (New York: Cambridge University Press, 1984), *McGraw Electric Railway Manual: Red Book of American Street* (New York: McGraw, 1906), 96, for the population figures.

69. "Field Day Excursion to Fryeburg, Maine," 213.

70. Ibid., 218–19.

71. Barrow, *Fryeburg, Maine,* 254; *North Conway Reporter,* March 6, 1902; *Lewiston Saturday Journal,* October 8, 1903, 7.

72. On Major John André's monument, see Robert E. Cray Jr., "The John André Monument: The Politics of Memory in Gilded Age New York," *New York History* 77.1 (January 1996): 5–32; On Civil War reunions, see Michael Kammen, *Mystic Chords of Memory: The Transformation of Tradition in American Culture* (New York: Knopf, 1991), 101–21, 218–19, 255–56.

73. Conforti, *Imagining New England,* 204–15; *Society of Colonial Wars, 1892–1992: The Centennial History* (Philadelphia: Society of Colonial Wars, 1992), 1–20, passim.

74. Charles J. Nichols, *History of the Society of Colonial Wars in the State of Maine* (Portland, ME: Society of Colonial Wars, 1947), ix, 3–16, 23–38, 45–46; *Oxford County Advertiser* (Norway, Maine), June 17, 1904, 7; *Boston Evening Transcript,* April 6, 1904, 22.

75. The Lovewell's Fight Memorial Association, Fryeburg Historical Society, Fryeburg, Maine.

76. Society of Colonial Wars, Exercises in the Congregation Church, June 17, 1904, Fryeburg Historical Society; *Portland Daily Press,* June ?, 1904, clipping, Fryeburg Historical Society, Fryeburg, Maine.

77. *Portland Daily Press,* June ?, 1904, clippings, Fryeburg Historical Society, Fryeburg, Maine; The Oxford Menu, Xerox, Portland Public Library, Portland, Maine; Diary of William Gordon, vol. 4, June 17, 1904; Diary of Henry Eugene Walters, 1903–1904, June 17, 1904, Fryeburg Historical Society, Fryeburg, Maine.

78. See David S. Lovejoy, "Lovewell's Fight," 527–31.

79. *Lewiston Evening Journal,* November 28, 1908.

80. (Maine) *Biddeford Weekly Journal,* August 12, 1927, August 3, 1928; Gail H. Bickford, "Lovewell's Fight, 1725–1958," *American Quarterly* 10.3 (Autumn 1958): 363–64; *Maine: A Guide Down East* (Boston: Houghton Mifflin, 1937), 368.

Conclusion

1. John Ferling, "The New England Soldier: A Study in Changing Perceptions," *American Quarterly* 33.1 (Spring 1981): 26–45.
2. Thomas Symmes, *Lovewell Lamented or, A Sermon Occasion'd by the Fall of the Brave Capt. John Lovewell and Several of his Valiant Company in the late Heroic Action at Piggwacket* (Boston: Gerrish, 1725), v.
3. Ibid., xii.
4. Richard Flores, *Remembering the Alamo: Memory, Modernity and Master Symbol* (Austin: University of Texas Press, 2002).
5. Nathaniel Hawthorne, "Roger Malvin's Burial," in *The Complete Short Stories of Nathaniel Hawthorne* (Garden City, NY: Doubleday, 1959), 376.

Index

Born in Mamaroneck, New York, Robert E. Cray received his undergraduate and graduate degrees from Stony Brook University. His first book, *Paupers and Poor Relief: New York City and Its Rural Environs, 1700–1830*, was published by Temple University Press in 1988. A 1997 article in the *Journal of the Early Republic*, "Memory Wars: Major John Andre and His Captors, 1780 to 1830," received the journal's Ralph D. Gray Best Article Award in 1998. Other articles have appeared in the *William & Mary Quarterly, Slavery & Abolition,* and *New York History.* Cray has taught at the University of Puget Sound and now teaches at Montclair State University. He currently resides in Berkeley Heights, New Jersey, with his wife, Cindy, and daughter, Pamela.